Edited by
Uma Narayan and
Julia J. Bartkowiak

Having and Raising Children

Unconventional Families, Hard Choices, and the Social Good

THE PENNSYLVANIA STATE UNIVERSITY PRESS
UNIVERSITY PARK, PENNSYLVANIA

Library of Congress Cataloging-in-Publication Data

Having and raising children : unconventional families,
    hard choices, and the social good / edited by
    Uma Narayan and Julia J. Bartkowiak.
        p.   cm.
        Includes bibliographical references and index.
        ISBN 0-271-01886-0 (cloth : alk. paper)
        ISBN 0-271-01887-9 (pbk. : alk. paper)
        1. Parenting—Social aspects. 2. Parents—
    Legal status, laws, etc. 3. Parent and child (Law)
    4. Children's rights. 5. Family.
    I. Narayan, Uma.   II. Bartkowiak, Julia J.
    HQ755.8.H335   1999
    649'.1—dc21   98-39336
                                                CIP

It is the policy of The Pennsylvania State University
Press to use acid-free paper for the first printing
of all clothbound books. Publications on uncoated
stock satisfy the minimum requirements of
American National Standard for Information
Sciences—Permanence of Paper for Printed Library
Materials, ANSI Z39.48–1992.

Contents

Introduction

UMA NARAYAN AND JULIA J. BARTKOWIAK

Familial relationships between parents and children are at the center of a number of important moral, social, and political controversies. The welfare of families and children often occupies a significant space in contemporary political rhetoric, cutting across the political spectrum. Conservative rhetoric about "family values" is echoed by liberal homilies about how "it takes a village to raise a child." Issues such as how family relationships should be normatively assessed, what types of family relationships should be regarded as valuable, who should count as parents and what rights they should have with respect to their children, and what sorts of protections should be accorded to children against their parents all surface in these debates as matters of ongoing social concern and political contestation. While both children and the institution of the family are often idealized in these debates, both the complexities of families as entities and the realities of the predicaments and problems faced by children as a group often tend to receive inadequate attention.

The idealization of families and children coexists in contemporary discourse with depictions of the family as "an institution in crisis" and on the verge of "breaking down." There is much divergence, however, in understandings of what exactly constitutes the "crisis" or the symptoms of "family breakdown." For some, the threat to the family is constituted by the high divorce rate, by premarital sex and abortion, by teenage pregnancy and women raising children on welfare, and by the increasing acceptance and legitimization of same-sex relationships and of various nontraditional families. For others, the crises confronting families have to do with lack of state funding for abortion and affordable child care, and with the inadequacy of public policy initiatives that would address the conflicts faced by working women and single mothers, ensure the protection of women and their children from violence within the home, and work to combat the prejudices and hostility that continue to confront single-parent, same-sex, or interracial families that deviate in various ways from the imagined "normal family."

The political persistence of these debates and the degree of moral interest and concern they elicit are not surprising. Issues pertaining to families and children continue to engage many of us since most of us live large portions of our lives within the institution of the family and since a great many of us have, or plan to have, children. Children under eighteen make up roughly a quarter of the U.S. population and are directly affected by issues and policies pertaining to their well-being. Parents directly impact, and are affected by, their children's well-being, and individual child-rearing practices may be regulated by public policies intended to protect the social good. In addition, since children represent a society's future, each citizen has some interest in the upbringing of children. Laws and public policy issues pertaining to children and to the fabric of family relationships are hence relevant to all of us and are likely to affect the shapes of our lives and choices.

Many contemporary issues pertaining to the having and raising of children pose genuinely hard choices for policy makers, for those who make and enforce the laws, and for those citizens who would like to engage in informed and critical democratic debate on these issues. The difficulty of the choices posed by these issues has to do with the fact that they often involve significant conflicts between the competing rights of adult parents, between the rights of parents and the interests of their children, as well as between individual rights and the social good. The essays in this volume all reflect on particular issues where these conflicts and tensions arise, clarifying the stakes and the potential trade-offs, and offering measured and reflective suggestions as to how these conflicts would best be resolved.

A number of common themes and concerns run through several of these essays. Some of the essays engage directly or indirectly with the hegemonic effect of the idealized "traditional family," calling attention to the problematic effects it has on legal, political, and public policy discourse. The "traditional family," consisting of two heterosexual parents and their genetic offspring, functions—often tacitly but sometimes explicitly—to delegitimize a variety of families that fail to conform to this norm in different ways. This ideal functions, for instance, to call into question the legitimacy and benefits of single-parent families, most of which are headed by single mothers, and is used to suggest that women's choices to be single parents are bad for their children, who will grow up in a "deficient" family structure. A number of these essays raise questions about the normative implications of this "traditional family," drawing our attention to the fact that even families that correspond to this norm are often not the havens of love and tranquillity they are depicted as being and that a great many families today fail to correspond to this norm but continue to provide both the benefits and the burdens of the family institution.

The normative picture of the "traditional family" also works to shape social and legal doctrines about the bases for parental status and for determining who stands in a parental relationship to a particular child. One effect of the dominant picture of the "traditional family" is that legal doctrines have traditionally favored the genetic connection as the basis for the recognition of parental rights. However, a number of difficult questions concerning parental status are increasingly posed by "unconventional" families—families that deviate in significant ways from the conventional assumptions that families consist of two heterosexual married partners and their biological children. The growth of practices such as sperm and egg donation, surrogacy, and adoption result in a number of families where one or more social parent may not be genetically related to the child and where one or more genetic parent may not be a social parent to the child. This confronts the law with many cases in which it has to adjudicate competing claims to custody of the child between genetic, gestatory, and social parents. Matters are additionally complicated in the case of gay and lesbian couples raising children since same-sex couples are legally denied the right to marry, creating complications with regard to legally establishing the parental rights of nonbiological gay and lesbian social parents.

A number of the essays in this volume show why it is important for law and public policy to develop a sensitive and comprehensive account of the bases for parental rights to children, one that takes into account the variety of ways in which adults may stand in valuable parental relationships to children. They suggest that laws and public policies need to resist succumbing unreflectively to the normative pressure of picturing parenthood modeled on the heterosexual patriarchal family. That such a narrow model has adverse effects can be seen in instances where the law has difficulty acknowledging the parental status of individuals who are neither genetically related to the child nor married to a biological parent of the child but who function as important caregivers and social parents to the child. Converse problems are created by laws that recognize the parental claims of genetic fathers who have in no way provided for the care and maintenance of the child, sometimes to the detriment of the interests of the mothers and these children.

Additionally, several essays reflect on the normative bases that ground individual choices to form or maintain familial relationships. Women who face unwanted pregnancies confront difficult choices with respect to whether to have the child and whether to maintain a parental relationship to the child. Paradoxically, many of those who criticize families comprised of single mothers raising children are also in favor of restricting women's rights and access to abortion, thus confronting unmarried pregnant women with a catch-22 situation in which they would end up doing the wrong thing whether they chose to have an abortion or to raise their child. The legal and constitutional bases for women's rights to have an abortion in the case of an unwanted pregnancy invite clarification and debate in a context where state initiatives to strengthen the family would ideally coexist with state protection of individual rights not to have a family or to add another child to it.

A different set of normative considerations are at stake in issues pertaining to the standing and say children should have with respect to decisions involving their relationships to their families—issues that are raised in situations where children may have preferences as to who should be their custodial parent or have reason to wish to legally terminate the parental rights of one or more of their parents. Such issues require a nuanced understanding of the nature of, and the limits to, children's autonomy, bearing in mind that the category *children* refers to infants as well as those verging on adulthood, encompassing individuals whose capacities for reflection and rational decision making vary widely.

A number of essays in this volume focus on the welfare and interests of the children that occupy center stage in a number of these ongoing debates concerning the institution of the family. Children often occupy complex locations in their relationships to their families, locations that often differ from each other as much as the families of which they are a part. Well-functioning families routinely provide children not only with what they require for material well-being and security, but also with the caregiving, emotional intimacy, and moral training they require in order to flourish as adults. Although many children continue to receive these forms of sustenance and protection from their families, we are increasingly aware of the many ways in which children are at risk of harm from family members. Many children suffer both physical and sexual abuse and other forms of neglect within the family. The very institution that best provides for their needs and interests when it functions well can also be a source of trauma and ill treatment. How to extend adequate protection to the rights and interests of children is a challenging task because of children's material and emotional dependence on the very family members who pose a threat to their well-being, their underdeveloped autonomy and lack of power compared to adults, and their inability and lack of standing to seek legal and social recourse.

Given that the institution of the family can both profoundly sustain and also harm the well-being of children in numerous ways, laws and public policies pertaining to children's relationships to their families must be sensitive to a variety of considerations. The dual nature of the family as a source of both protection and threat to children positions the state in a complicated and often unclear adjudicative relationship to children and their families. When families safeguard the interests of children reasonably well, the state has an obligation not to unduly interfere with parental decisions about having children or with the various ways in which families may decide to rear and socialize their children. Such noninterference is required both by the right of parents to raise their children in the various distinctive ways they see fit and by the need to restrict potentially dangerous state interference in the domain of intimate relationships.

However, when children are at risk of abuse, neglect, and other forms of rights-violations from family members, the state must guarantee children's rights to safety, physical integrity, and care even when it means seriously interfering with, restricting, or terminating parental rights. In other instances, states have to deal with children who are at risk, not because of harmful treatment from family members, but because, as dependents, they are adversely affected by the illness, unemployment, and life crises of adults. Some of the hardest of such issues arise in the context of parental rights to impose or withhold medical or psychiatric treatment for children in situations where the parents may act in what they perceive to be the interests of the child but where their choices nevertheless endanger the child's welfare. Other difficult questions are posed when parental desires to raise their child in accordance with narrow, rigid, or prejudiced views conflict with a liberal society's interest in encouraging tolerance and open-mindedness among its citizens. In many of these instances, determining whether risk of harm to children warrants intrusion into parental rights and what the nature and degree of the intrusion is are genuinely difficult questions.

Such interconnected questions as who warrants legal recognition as a child's parent, what is the scope of parental rights to determine the well-being and socialization of their children, what constitutes sufficient grounds for the state to interfere with these rights in order to ensure the well-being of children and the furtherance of social interests, and how much say children should have in determining relationships to particular adult members of their families all arise in a number of public policy domains. The essays in this volume seek to explore and answer these urgent and difficult questions, which provide rich material for ethical, political, and legal analyses. Such analyses can help us be more critically reflective about the competing interests at stake in these issues, revealing why these issues often constitute genuinely hard choices between competing goods. Difficult questions, such as whether the social good is better served by increasingly subjecting family relationships to state monitoring and surveillance or by curbing state interference and risking a failure to protect vulnerable individuals from mistreatment by others in the family, are virtually impossible to answer in the abstract. However, sustained reflection on concrete instances and issues where such tensions arise often enables us to more clearly register the competing interests and trade-offs that are at stake and to understand why some resolutions to these issues might be fairer or less harmful than others.

This volume opens with Iris Young's essay, "Mothers, Citizenship, and Independence: A Critique of Pure Family Values," which argues against views that regard the "intact two-parent heterosexual family" as the preferred family form, paying particular critical attention to claims that it is the family form that best ensures that children emerge as independent and contributing citizens. Young examines sociological studies and social data used to argue for the superiority of the two-parent family and argues that the data reveal little or no difference between the capacities and well-being of children raised in a two-parent family and those raised by single mothers. While Young agrees that children in single-mother families are economically disadvantaged, she strongly criticizes the view that marriage is the cure for childhood poverty and calls attention to the ways in which women's lower wages and the high cost of child care are major contributors to the poverty of single-mother households. Pointing out that "dependency work" done by women who take care of children, the old, the ill, and the disabled, either within the home or in the workforce, is socially devalued and badly paid, Young argues that a just society would provide better recognition and payment for dependency work. Examining the notions of "independence" that are deployed in these debates over "good families," Young concludes that while we have reason to value independence understood as autonomy, the idea of independence as self-sufficiency is not relevant in a world of complex economic interdependencies.

One important issue that arises in the context of families that fail to correspond to the norm of the "traditional family" is the vexed issue of the rights of unwed biological fathers. In the second essay, "Fathers' Rights, Mothers' Wrongs? Reflections on Unwed Fathers' Rights and Sex Equality," Mary L. Shanley focuses on the issue of fathers' rights in legal contexts where unwed biological fathers attempt to reverse the biological mother's decision to place the child for adoption. Shanley uses the details of a number of recent legal cases to support the argument that neither the "fathers' rights" perspective (which holds that a biological father's claims should automatically outweigh those of a potential adoptive parent) nor the "maternal autonomy" perspective (which argues that mothers alone should make decisions about adoption without interference by the biological father or the state) uniformly result in satisfactory outcomes. With respect to parental wishes over adoption, Shanley argues that it would not be unreasonable for the law to treat an unwed father who had been in a long-term relationship and had shared living expenses with the mother differently from someone who was a biological father because of casual or coercive sex. Shanley argues that the weight accorded to unwed fathers' rights ought to depend primarily on the degree to which the father acts to assume responsibility for the child. The claims of fathers who display interest and responsibility soon after they are aware of a woman's pregnancy would, on this analysis, outweigh those of a father who has shown no interest prior to asserting his rights in order to veto an adoption. Shanley also points to cases where a mother who wishes to place her child for adoption might have good reason to object to the biological father assuming custody, and she argues that the law and social policy should put the lived relationships between particular parents and children at the center when determining parental claims.

Nontraditional bases for claims to parental relationships also occur as a result of the practice of genetic or gestatory surrogacy. In the third article, "Family Ties: Rethinking Parental Claims in the Light of Surrogacy and Custody," Uma Narayan begins by examining a variety of criticisms leveled at the practice of commercial surrogacy—charges that it subjects women to coercive intrusions on their autonomy and privacy, that it involves the economic as well as the gender-role exploitation of women, and that it involves the commodification of children. Pointing out that these charges apply equally to many cases of gift surrogacy as well as to cases of "ordinary motherhood" in the context of heterosexual patriarchal families, Narayan cautions against assuming that market-mediated reproductive relationships are necessarily worse for women or radically discontinuous with noncommercial reproductive relationships. Criticizing and rejecting proposals to criminalize commercial surrogacy and to treat surrogacy arrangements as private adoptions, Narayan argues that conflicting parental claims to children who result from sur-rogacy arrangements would best be treated as custody disputes. Echoing Shanley's interests in securing an adequate normative basis for parental rights, Narayan proceeds to use conflicts resulting from custody arrange-ments to rethink the bases for granting adults parental claims to chil-dren. Arguing that genetic and gestational connections as well as the provision of social care to a child should be recognized as prima facie bases for parental rights, Narayan proposes that conflicts between com-peting parental rights be resolved in the light of the "best interests of the child." However, Narayan argues that the law needs to rethink its domi-nant "two parents of opposite sexes" model of parental rights that insists that a child cannot have more than two legal parents at any given time, or more than one parent of the same sex. Narayan explores the ways in which recognizing the parental rights of more than two parents at a time, and of more than one person of the same sex, would be in the best interests of many parents and children who live in a variety of nontradi-tional family relationships.

In the fourth essay, "A Parent(ly) Knot: Can Heather Have Two Mommies?" Shelley A. M. Gavigan explores the ramifications of "family ideology" with respect to the families of lesbian parents and legal responses to conflicts over parental rights in lesbian households. Gavi-gan pays particular attention to two different kinds of cases where "Heather and her two mommies meet the law," cases that both reveal the need for legal clarity in the matter of the rights of nonbiological lesbian mothers. The first sort of case pertains to instances when the nonbiolog-ical lesbian mother wishes to discontinue her relationship to the biolog-ical mother and seeks to evade financial and legal responsibilities for the child she co-parented by insisting that she is merely a "legal stranger" to the child. The second sort of case involves the biological mother insist-ing that her lesbian partner is merely a "legal stranger" to the child despite the partner's having functioned in multiple ways as the social co-parent of the child. Gavigan argues that both sorts of cases reveal how lesbian women can use discriminatory laws that prohibit same-sex marriages and the law's sex-specific definition of a spouse and its patriarchal definition of children to their own ends in attempts to abandon their own parental relationships to their partner's biological child or to deny their partner parental standing with respect to a child they co-parent. Gavigan concludes that all of us who parent children need to be clear as to the nature of the relationships we are in and not deny our responsibilities upon separation.

The fifth essay, Brenda Almond's "Family Relationships and Reproductive Technology," argues for a viewpoint that is in significant tension with the positions in all the essays that precede it. While the essays by Shanley, Narayan, and Gavigan give considerable import and weight to social parenting in their analyses, Almond argues for the view that it would be a mistake to assume that biological parenthood has no significance. Almond disagrees with positions that regard the new reproductive technologies positively for having brought us into an age of relationships by choice, and argues that these technologies cannot negate the essential naturalness of conception, pregnancy, and childbirth as well as the relationships they create. Almond draws on the work of anthropologists like Marilyn Strathern to point to the importance of biological ties of kinship and to the fact that these ties are embedded in expectations of understanding, sympathy, and closeness. Almond argues that the new reproductive technologies open up a frightening slippery slope where aborted fetuses can be harvested for eggs and where clinically dead women could be kept alive to gestate and deliver babies. She believes that we should not see these technologies as of purely medical significance but should focus on the fact that these technologies can result in the birth of "orphans" born in exile from the kinship network provided by biological bonds. Almond cautions against the view that regards gametes as detachable and the weight of genetic bonds as negligible, arguing that some unrecognized factual assumptions are being made about the quality of care that can be relied on where purely social connections are involved. Almond suggests that nonbiological, socially chosen families might result in children who are unwilling to engage in self-sacrificing care for their elders and in parents who might not wish to accept responsibility for a child's subsequent disability. Almond's analysis is also significantly different from that of Iris Young in that Almond argues that social provision for single mothers has eroded the need for partnership between the sexes.

An issue that might be regarded as the converse of issues relating to parental rights is the issue of deciding not to be a parent. The sixth essay, Anita Allen's "Privacy and Equal Protection as Bases for Abortion Law: Citizenship, Gender, and the Constitution," revisits the controversial territory of abortion rights—rights that are crucial to women having a say in whether and when to enter into a parental relationship to a child. Motivated by an interest in clarifying the links between abortion rights and the ideals of citizenship and gender equality, Allen examines the comparative merits of privacy-based and equal-protection-based grounding for abortion rights and responds critically to claims that equal protection is superior to privacy as a constitutional basis for abortion law. Allen argues that it is unlikely that current conflicts over abortion would be less vehement if women's equality rather than their privacy had been the justification for our abortion laws and points out that resting abortion rights on privacy grounds (with its connotations of state noninterference) does not imply that the state should not fund abortions. Underlining the fact that the burdens of sexuality, pregnancy, and child rearing fall disproportionately on women, Allen argues that legal restrictions on abortion function to underwrite a form of "second-class citizenship" for women, thus echoing Young's concern with women's status and citizenship. Examining the situation in both the United States and Germany, Allen draws concerned attention to the fact that many democratic nations have failed to recognize that full citizenship implies a range of legally guaranteed reproductive choices for women.

While Allen focuses on the legal bases for pregnant women's choices not to have a child by means of abortion, the next two essays focus on the normative basis for, and ramifications of, allowing children to exercise choices and to have a say in contexts of familial decisions regarding custody and the legal termination of parental relationships. In "Circumscribed Autonomy: Children, Care, and Custody," Hugh LaFollette distinguishes between questions of descriptive autonomy (questions about the intellectual and volitional abilities of children) and questions of normative autonomy (questions about how parents and legal institutions should relate to children's choices and desires). Taking issue with views that completely deny both descriptive and normative autonomy to children, LaFollette points out that there is not a hard-and-fast conceptual or empirical distinction between the capacities of adults and those of older children who are in fact more capable of judging and acting on their own than is typically assumed. Pointing out that autonomy should not be construed as all or nothing, and stressing the fact that children's autonomy and decision-making capacities develop only by being allowed to exercise them, LaFollette argues that children should be given circumscribed normative autonomy in matters such as the choice of custodial parent, in keeping with their age, understanding, and capabilities.

Laura Purdy also argues that, under certain circumstances, children should be provided with some choices concerning their own lives. In her essay "Boundaries of Authority: Should Children Be Able to Divorce Their Parents?" Purdy uses the Gregory K. case as a means of reviewing various current positions on children's rights, focusing in particular on children's right to "divorce" their parents. Rejecting these other positions, Purdy argues that her view, which would allow children to terminate parental rights only in those circumstances where there is no other good means of protecting the child's interests, is more flexible than these other approaches. She points out that the variety within actual relationships between parents and children is best accommodated with such flexibility. Finally, Purdy argues that, if we are going to adequately address the needs of all children, fundamental questions concerning social priorities must be answered. Her essay offers some suggestions regarding the role the state should play in raising children.

Being a parent requires one to make a number of significant choices with respect to the health, well-being, and upbringing of one's children. Each of the last three articles deals with different issues concerning the scope of parental rights to make choices with respect to their children in contexts where there are competing interests at stake. In "Regulating Sexuality: Gender Identity Disorder, Children's Rights, and the State," Ellen Feder examines the problematic bases for the psychiatric diagnosis of Gender Identity Disorder (GID), and reveals the troublesome ways in which it is used to "treat" the behavior of children whose only "problem" is that they violate social stereotypes of masculine and feminine behavior. Analyzing the proliferation of GID as a diagnosis and the increasing pathologization of the mothers of GID children, Feder draws attention to the historical and diagnostic continuities between the "psychiatric treatment" of children with GID and the "medical treatment" of gay and lesbian teenagers. While the therapeutic intrusions that lesbian and gay youth are subject to are more punitive than those imposed on children diagnosed with GID, Feder argues that treatment is being imposed in both cases for behavior that is perfectly harmless and perceived as problematic only because it violates dominant social norms about gender and sexuality. Feder insists that the state has an obligation to protect these children and youth from medical and psychiatric intrusion and from needless manipulation and surveillance as well as a duty to monitor diagnostic categories to ensure that they are not simply legitimizations of social prejudices. Feder draws attention to the ways in which the maintenance of disorders such as GID is located not only in the medical and legal establishments, but also dispersed among parents, teachers, and peers. She endorses state-funded programs that would educate parents, teachers, and others not to be threatened or rendered anxious by children's gender and sexual nonconformity.

While Feder's essay focuses on children who are needlessly subject to psychiatric and medical treatment, in "Protecting Faith Versus Protecting Futures: Religious Freedom and Parental Rights in Medical Decision Making for Children," Lynn Pasquerella focuses on the converse issue of children who are denied the medical treatment they need or forced to endure medically futile treatment against their will because of their parents' religious commitments. Arguing that strict limits need to be placed on parents' rights in the context of medical decisions, Pasquerella argues that the religiously motivated denial of medical care should be subsumed under child abuse and neglect statutes rather than be exceptions to them. Pasquerella points to legal cases where rights to religious freedom and parental rights over children were restricted in order to protect children's health and well-being and argues that such restrictions are justified on the grounds of both children's rights and the state's role in ensuring "open futures" for children. Pasquerella provides additional support for the restriction of parental rights by examining the doctrine of equal protection of the laws and the Establishment Clause of the First Amendment. Pasquerella also notes that the practice of denying children any decision-making role in their own medical treatment is a consequence of the "incapacity theory" of childhood. This theory mistakenly asserts that unlike adults, children have an impaired ability to reason. Pointing out that the parents' interests are not always the child's interests, Pasquerella argues that many children can and should participate in decisions regarding their own medical treatment. Pasquerella concludes by making a strong case for judicial reforms that would provide children with a voice in the courts with respect to medical decisions that affect their future and well-being.

The final essay, "Fear of God: Religious Education of Children and the Social Good" by Julia Bartkowiak, deals with a different set of tensions between religious freedom, parental rights, and the social good. While parental rights understandably extend to attempting to raise one's children in the light of one's religious views and value framework, one possible consequence is that some children might be raised with a very narrow and intolerant worldview because of parental influence. A liberal society that has a stake in, and benefits from, the existence of tolerant and open-minded citizens might be tempted to consider introducing courses on world religions in its public schools in order to ensure that its future citizens have exposure to a wider range of views than provided by their parents. Bartkowiak argues, however, that such attempts to make courses on world religions mandatory in public schools would not be a good idea, since it is questionable whether the child's interests are necessarily clearly harmed by lack of exposure to views other than those of their parents. Such lack of clear harms makes state interference with parental rights to determine their child's upbringing questionable. Furthermore, Bartkowiak doubts whether such courses would, in practice, be taught in a manner that in fact promoted the type of social good they were intended to promote. Given the impossibility of monitoring that such courses are well conducted, teachers who are not well trained in the subject matter or who are religiously bigoted or parochial in their own views might do more harm than good. Bartkowiak examines the constitutional distinction between the "teaching of religion" (which is constitutionally unacceptable in public schools) and "teaching about religion" (which is constitutionally acceptable) and argues that this distinction is dangerously vague and unclear and would result in world religions courses that taught religion under the guise of teaching about religion. Bartkowiak points out that making world religion courses optional or allowing for parental exemptions would be less objectionable than making them mandatory but concludes that there are better alternatives to promoting tolerance among citizens than world religions courses in public schools.

The essays within this volume provide interesting insights into, and clarifications of, issues pertaining to families having and raising children and explore the difficult legal and social choices that emerge as a result of tensions between the competing claims of parents, children, and the social good. Collectively, they reveal the degree to which these real-life problems have entered into the theoretical concerns of philosophers, political theorists, and legal scholars. Each of the essays takes a clear and distinctive position on the topic it examines, thus constituting both an exploration of, and an intervention in, these ongoing debates pertaining to families and children. While committed to the positions they endorse, they reveal a measured awareness of competing points of view and support their positions with clearly expressed arguments.

We would like to thank the many people who have helped bring this volume into existence. Hugh LaFollette was especially helpful in suggesting authors who were currently working on those issues of interest to us. Sandy Thatcher encouraged and supported this project. Marc

Bartkowiak and B. Thomas King III typed and provided computer assistance. Gideon Oliver assisted with the completion of the manuscript. Finally, we would like to thank our partners, Jim Hill and Thad Bartkowiak, for their input on our essays, for assistance with computer-related problems, and for their patience, encouragement, and support. Without the assistance of these individuals and the cooperation of all the authors represented within this anthology, this collection would have been much more difficult to complete.

1

Mothers, Citizenship, and Independence

A Critique of Pure Family Values

IRIS MARION YOUNG

In recent years in the United States many liberals have joined conservatives in espousing "family values" as the moral foundation of peace and prosperity. This philosophy says that the "intact" two-parent heterosexual family is the preferred family form. While this is not good news for gay men and lesbians, it also devalues single mothers and by implication all mothers. In this essay I assess the implications of family values discourse for the citizenship status of mothers by examining the writing of one its most articulate and liberal proponents, William Galston.

In his book *Liberal Purposes*, Galston argues that law and public policy cannot and should not be neutral among ends and legitimately ought to encourage in its citizens the virtues consistent with the social good.[1] He infers from this general position that the liberal state ought to privilege the "intact two-parent" family. This particular family structure,

1. William Galston, *Liberal Purposes* (Cambridge: Cambridge University Press, 1991), chaps. 1–7.

I am grateful to David Alexander, Ronald Beiner, Lisa Brush, Gerald Dworkin, Steven Elkin, Robert Goodin, Carole Pateman, and Kenneth Winston for helpful comments on earlier versions of this paper. An earlier version of this paper was published in *Ethics* 105 (April 1995): 535–56.

he argues, best promotes the welfare of children and enables them to become good citizens. The state is therefore justified in implementing policies that encourage marriage and discourage divorce and single motherhood. Galston's argument for the moral preeminence of the intact two-parent family has both an empirical and a normative aspect. I first examine some of his empirical claims that divorce and single motherhood have bad social consequences and show that the evidence is much more ambiguous than he allows. I then concentrate on the normative dimensions of Galston's argument, which hinge on the citizen virtue of independence. Review of the role of the norm of independence in modern political theory reveals it as male biased and instrumental in relegating dependent people and their usually female caretakers to an inferior status. Contrary to Galston, promoting equal citizenship requires abandoning the idea that those who are not self-sufficient are of lesser worth. On the contrary, public policy should provide social support to promote the autonomy of the people who need help from others. Only such an abandonment of the norm of independence understood as self-sufficiency can grant equal citizenship to at-home caretakers and people who, for whatever reason, are unable completely to support or take care of themselves. Liberals must affirm a plurality of family forms as valid ways of life. By virtue of its structure, no one family form is inherently better at realizing the values of family life. I conclude by discussing some general implications of this argument for public policy.

ARE DIVORCE AND SINGLE PARENTHOOD CAUSES OF POVERTY AND DISABILITY?

In arguing for the moral superiority of stable marriage, Galston distinguishes what he calls intrinsic traditionalism from functional traditionalism. Intrinsic traditionalism promotes particular institutional forms and individual behavior simply because they conform to past practice, the precepts of religion, or the commands of some other authority adhered to without reason or criticism. Functional traditionalism, on the other hand, "rests its case on asserted links between certain moral principles and public virtues or institutions needed for the successful functioning of a liberal community. So, for example, an intrinsic traditionalist might deplore divorce as a violation of divine law, whereas a functional traditionalist might object to it on the grounds (for which considerable empirical evidence can be adduced) that children in divorced families tend to suffer the kinds of economic and psychological damage that reduce their capability to become independent and contributing members of the community" (280).

If a plausible link can be established between a particular family form and the ability of children to take their place as good citizens—independent and contributing members of the community—Galston asserts, then this justifies the state's preference for that family form and perhaps even limits the liberty of adults to raise children under other conditions. Just as parental freedom does not include the right to beat or starve your child or to treat your child in a manner that will impede normal development, so "you are not free to act in ways that will lead your child to impose significant and avoidable burdens on the community" (252). Consequently, the freedom of parents should be subordinate to the state aim of raising good citizens: "My focus is on what must be a key objective of our society: raising children who are prepared—intellectually, physically, morally, and emotionally—to take their place as law-abiding and independent citizens. Available evidence supports the conclusion that on balance, the intact two-parent family is best suited to this task" (285).

The divorce rate in the United States jumped very significantly between 1970 and 1975, peaked in 1981, and since then has been declining to the 1975 level of 4.7 divorces per 1,000 married couples per year.[2] The number of children affected by divorce has remained roughly constant since 1975 at around one million each year. Galston claims that there is strong evidence to support the claim that divorce causes lasting emotional distress in children. He cites a study by Wallerstein and Blakeslee, who followed about sixty children of divorce for ten years and claimed to find that the experience of divorce in adolescence causes a lack of confidence and an inability to sustain relationships in adulthood.[3] This study has been criticized for its small sample, for the fact that all the subjects were in therapy at the start of the study, and for the fact that there are no comparisons with children from intact families.[4]

A wider look at the literature reveals a much more ambiguous picture of the effects (or lack of effects) of divorce on the capacities and character of children. Some demographic studies show greater risk of school

2. U.S. Bureau of the Census, *Statistical Abstract of the United States, 1993–94* (Austin: Reference Press), 101–2.

3. Judith S. Wallerstein and Sandra Blakeslee, *Second Chances: Men, Women, and Children a Decade After Divorce* (New York: Ticknor & Fields, 1989).

4. Andrew Cherlin and Frank Furstenburg, "Divorce Doesn't Always Hurt the Kids," *Washington Post,* 19 March 1989, C3.

drop-out, career and income disadvantage, and teen pregnancy for children of divorce than for children of stable marriages, but others find few differences on a range of academic, developmental, emotional, and health measures. Some longitudinal studies find poorer adjustment for adolescent children of divorce, but others find no relationships.[5] Where differences between children of divorce and those from intact families on measures of well-being are found, they are usually rather small. One meta-analysis of ninety-two mostly American studies finds children of divorce to have only slightly lower levels of well-being than those from intact families.[6]

Where children of divorce do suffer emotional damage, moreover, it may be that family conflict rather than divorce itself is the cause. A ten-year study recently released in Australia found no significant differences between children of divorce and children of continuing marriage in levels of academic achievement, career success, or ability to enter and maintain intimate relationships. It found that emotional distress tended to be associated with family conflict, whether it resulted in divorce or not, and that even the effects of conflict are offset by a strong relationship between the child and at least one of the parents.[7]

One of the policy recommendations that Galston makes for regulating family life for the sake of raising good citizens is to make divorce more difficult to obtain. Given the very mixed record on the effects of divorce on children, surely it is questionable that the state has a legitimate right to limit the liberty of unhappily married adults to sever their relationship. Moreover, if family conflict instead of divorce itself is a likelier cause of emotional distress in children, encouraging parents to stay together when they do not want to may cause more harm to children than allowing parents to divorce in as simple and peaceful a manner as possible.[8]

5. See Rosemary Dunlop and Alisa Burns, "The Sleeper Effect—Myth or Reality? Findings from a Ten-Year Study of the Effects of Parental Divorce at Adolescence," paper presented at the Fourth Australian Family Research Conference, Manly, NSW, February 1993.

6. P. R. Amato and B. Keith, "Parental Divorce and the Well-Being of Children: A Meta-analysis," *Psychological Bulletin* 110 (1991): 26–46.

7. Dunlop and Burns, "The Sleeper Effect"; Andrew Cherlin also finds that the adverse effects observed in children are often prior to divorce and can be attributed to a hostile family environment ("Longitudinal Studies of Effects of Divorce on Children in Great Britain and the United States," *Science*, 7 June 1991, 1386–89).

8. Dunlop and Burns suggest that one reason they find lower levels of emotional distress in their study of children of divorce than do some American studies may be that Australian divorce procedures rely on family court counseling and mediation much more than do those in the United States, which rely on a highly charged adversarial system of divorce settlement.

Galston argues that not only divorce but also single parenthood, whether the parent has been married or not, is bad for children. In 1992, 26 percent of families with children in the United States were headed by single parents; only 4 percent of all families were headed by unmarried men, whereas 22 percent were headed by unmarried women.[9] Many single-parent families are created by divorce; in fact, in 1992, 14 percent of American children lived with a divorced or separated mother only. Because so much of family values discourse is laced with race, I will note that 22 percent of black children were living with a divorced or separated mother, and 13 percent of white children.[10]

Recent discussions of family values, however, focus more on single-mother families created by births to unmarried women. Galston is not alone in suggesting that "illegitimacy" is on the rise and is destroying the moral fabric of society. So let us dwell for a moment on the facts about births to unmarried women. In 1990, 26 percent of all births in the United States were to unmarried women. Contrary to the image that "illegitimacy" is a black phenomenon, 56 percent of these women were white and 41 percent were African American.[11] Again contrary to popular image, the rate of births to unmarried black mothers has been falling in the last twenty years and rising very significantly among white mothers. The proportion of births to unmarried African American mothers is still far higher than to unmarried white mothers, but the gap has been steadily narrowing. The proportion of births to unmarried mothers in relation to all births has been rising significantly in the last decade largely because married couples are having significantly fewer children.[12]

Popular imagery also assumes that most unwed mothers are black teenagers. There was a significant decline in births to unmarried black teenagers from 1970 to 1986, however, and births to unmarried white teenagers more than doubled during the same period. The proportion of teens among unwed mothers has been declining steadily, moreover; in 1990 more than two-thirds of births to unwed mothers were women twenty years and older. Birth rates among unmarried white women between the ages of thirty and thirty-four have doubled between 1980

9. *Statistical Abstract,* 61. These statistics may obscure the fact that unmarried parents may nevertheless be co-parenting with other adults in the household. Lesbian parents, for example, usually appear as single mothers in statistics even when they live in long-term partnerships.

10. *Statistical Abstract,* 64.

11. Ibid., 77–78.

12. Christopher Jenks, *Rethinking Social Policy: Race, Poverty, and the Underclass* (New York: Harper Perennial, 1992), 198; Herbert L. Smith and Phillips Cutright, "Thinking About Change in Illegitimacy Ratios: United States, 1963–1983," *Demography* 25 (1988): 235–47.

and 1987; among all other races there was only a modest increase in this age bracket.[13]

Thus unwed motherhood has become a mainstream American phenomenon, not confined to any particular age, race, or educational attainment. Divorce when children are present increased significantly in the 1970s but has leveled off in the 1980s and occurs among all races, ages, regions, and income groups. As a result of all these trends, some people estimate that, among children born in the late 1970s, 42 percent of whites and 86 percent of blacks will spend some time in a single-parent family.[14] The single-parent family form, primarily of single mothers, is common in American society and increasingly common in many other societies in the world today.

Galston claims that the single-parent family is bad for children. He and others suggest that children of single parents receive less emotional and intellectual support and less supervision than do children in two-parent families.[15] It is certainly plausible to claim that parenting is easier and more effective if two or more adults discuss the children's needs and provide different kinds of interactions for children. It does not follow that the second adult must be a live-in husband, however, and some studies have found that the addition of any adult to a single-parent household, whether a relative, lover, or friend, tends to offset single-parent tendencies to relinquish parental decision making too early.[16]

While Galston claims that the evidence is clear that single-parent families are worse for children than intact two-parent families, many others find the evidence to be more ambiguous. It seems more likely that single-parent families are better for children in some respects and not better in others. For example, while adults in single-parent families tend to spend less time supervising homework, they are less likely to pressure their children into social conformity and more likely to praise good grades.[17] Children in single-mother households may suffer disadvantages associated with stress on that one parent, but there may also be advantages to single-parent families, such as a greater closeness between parent and child or greater emotional maturity than children

13. *Statistical Abstract,* 78.

14. Larry Bumpass, "Children and Marital Disruption: A Replication and Update," *Demography* 21 (February 1984): 71–82.

15. See, e.g., Amitai Etzioni, *The Spirit of Community* (New York: Crown, 1993), chap. 2.

16. Nan Marie Astone and Sara McLanahan, "Family Structure and High School Completion: The Role of Parental Practices," discussion paper, Institute for Research on Poverty, University of Wisconsin, Madison, 1989, 905–9.

17. Stephanie Coontz, *The Way We Never Were* (New York: Basic Books, 1992), 224.

have in two-parent families.[18] Growing up in a single-parent family may be a handicap, but having numerous siblings in a two-parent family can also be a handicap. Since single parents have fewer children, these two family forms may be comparable in their consequences for children.[19]

Galston's main reason for claiming that single parenthood is bad for children, however, is less contestable. Children in single-mother families are much more likely to be poor than families headed by men. In 1990, 44.7 percent of women-maintained households with children were in poverty compared with about 7.7 percent of male-headed households. Black single mothers are more likely to be poor, but white single mothers are also at high risk. In 1990, 48 percent of black female-headed households and 27 percent of white female-headed families were poor.[20] More than half of single mothers with a high school education or less are poor, regardless of their race or age.[21]

The primary income for most of these children comes from their mothers. Court-ordered child support awards averaged only $2,100 per family in 1985, and many fathers failed to pay.[22] The primary cause of the poverty of children in single-parent households is women's lack of earning power. In 1990 the median weekly earnings for women twenty-five years and over was $400, compared with $539 for men.[23] About 40 percent of women maintaining households alone are full-time, year-round workers, and another 27 percent work seasonally or part-time. But more than 21 percent of families headed by employed women have incomes below poverty, compared with 4 percent of families headed by an employed man.[24] Jenks estimates that if we wanted to ensure that every full-time employed single mother could live a life of minimum subsistence for herself and two children on her earnings alone, we would have needed a minimum wage of $9.00 per hour in 1988. Unless a woman has a college degree, she is more likely to earn $6.50 per hour,

18. Sharyne Merritt and Linda Steiner, *And Baby Makes Two: Motherhood Without Marriage* (New York: Franklin Watts, 1984), 160.

19. Sara McLanahan, "The Consequences of Single Parenthood for Subsequent Generations," *Focus* (University of Wisconsin, Institute for Research on Poverty) 11 (1988): 16–24.

20. Diana Pearce, "Welfare Is Not *for* Women: Why the War on Poverty Cannot Conquer the Feminization of Poverty," in *Women, the State, and Welfare,* ed. Linda Gordon (Madison: University of Wisconsin Press, 1990), 265–79.

21. Laurence E. Lynn, Jr., "Ending Welfare Reform As We Know It," *American Prospect* (Fall 1993): 88.

22. Pearce, "Welfare Is Not *for* Women," 265–79.

23. *Statistical Abstract,* 131.

24. Pearce, "Welfare Is Not *for* Women."

and if she does not have a high school diploma, she earns an average of $4.10 per hour.[25]

One-third of all single mothers do not participate in the official labor force. (There is no way of telling how many of these earn income in informal markets, and many of them do.) Some cannot get jobs, either because jobs are not available to match their skills or because they lack skills. Some believe that they will be better mothers if they can nurture and supervise their children at home, even though they will be poor. Many lack access to decent child care or cannot afford it at the low wage they can earn. Some reason that living on state subsidy will be better for their children than accepting employment at or near minimum wage with no benefits, especially since as workers they must pay for clothes, transportation, child care, and other expenses they would not have if they did not have paid employment. Even so, less than 60 percent of poor children were subsidized by welfare in 1986, down from nearly 86 percent of poor children in 1973.[26] Despite racist myths, only about 31 percent of welfare recipients are African American, a proportion that has remained constant in the last twenty years.[27]

Because of the undeniable fact that children of single-mother families are economically disadvantaged, many of them severely, Galston argues that the single-parent family is itself a bad family form. He recommends marriage as the cure for childhood poverty. "It is no exaggeration to say that the best anti-poverty program for children is a stable, intact family" (285). Given that over 40 percent of poor families are married couple families, this certainly is an exaggeration.

Still, on average adult men of all races earn more than women, and white men earn, on average, about one and one-third times what white women earn.[28] Galston is right, moreover, to claim that most families today need two wage earners "to maintain even a modestly middle class way of life" (285). Most children who are economically well-off, therefore, depend on two adult incomes. Because couples usually choose to allocate household and child-rearing responsibilities to women, however, many married women work only part-time. This fact, in combination with the fact that men are usually able to earn significantly more than women, means that most economically well-off women and children depend on a male wage to keep them out of poverty.

25. Jenks, *Rethinking Social Policy*, 235.
26. Teresa L. Amot, "Black Women and AFDC: Making Entitlement out of Necessity," in *Women, the State, and Welfare*, ed. Gordon.
27. Jenks, *Rethinking Social Policy*, 149.
28. *Statistical Abstract*, 133.

MARRIAGE PREFERENCE REINFORCES THE SUBORDINATION OF MOTHERS

Galston's normative argument for the superiority of the intact two-parent family warrants examination. Single-parent families are a less desirable family form, according to Galston, and public policy ought to take action to discourage their existence. Galston takes pains to deny that his position is an attack on single parents. Such a proposition would be "insulting to the millions of single parents who are struggling successfully against the odds to provide good homes for their children" (285). Nor does he believe that mothers ought to have primary responsibility for child welfare. Indeed, he rightly believes that fathers who leave mothers alone with children and pay little or no child support are a major social problem. In evaluating Galston's arguments about desirable family structure, however, I will focus on single mothers, because the vast majority of single-parent households are headed by women. I will assume that the only empirical case to be made for the claim that single-parent families are undesirable is that they are more likely to be poor than are two-parent families.

Many women parent alone because they have inadequate access to contraception and abortion or because their husbands have chosen to leave the household. Many women of all ages, however, choose to bear children without husbands. Women initiate an increasing proportion of divorces, moreover, and increasing numbers of divorced mothers are not seeking remarriage. Galston's position on the moral superiority of the two-parent family implies that the choices of these mothers are morally wrong, not for reasons of intrinsic traditionalism, but for the functional traditionalist reasons concerning the duty of parents to maximize the welfare of children.

I reconstruct Galston's argument to that conclusion thus: Society, through the state, has a direct and fundamental interest in the raising of good citizens. A good citizen possesses liberal virtues, which are courage, law-abidingness, loyalty, independence, tolerance, willingness to work and to delay gratification, adaptability, and the ability to discern the rights of others (221–24). Two-parent families are best able to inculcate these virtues, whereas single-mother families are less likely to do so. Therefore, women should refrain from having children out of wedlock, and mothers should put the interests of their children above their own and not divorce their husbands in order to pursue greater happiness for themselves. In circumstances where they have not chosen single motherhood, mothers should try to get husbands. Thus, public policy should regulate family behavior, providing disincentives for less worthy lifestyles and actions, and incentives for the more worthy. In what follows, I will show that this argument entails continuing the patriarchal tradition, which denies women, and in particular mothers, full citizenship.

Galston identifies *independence* as one of the primary liberal virtues because the liberal society is characterized by individualism. Public policy should prefer intact two-parent families because these best nurture such independence:

> To individualism corresponds the liberal virtue of independence—the disposition to care for, and take responsibility for, oneself and to avoid becoming needlessly dependent on others. Human beings are not born independent, nor do they attain independence through biological maturation alone. A growing body of evidence suggests that in a liberal society, the family is the critical arena in which independence and a host of other virtues must be engendered. The weakening of families is thus fraught with danger for liberal societies. In turn, strong families rest on specific virtues. Without fidelity, stable families cannot be maintained. Without a concern for children that extends well beyond the boundaries of adult self-regard, parents cannot effectively discharge their responsibility to form secure, self-reliant young people. In short, the independence required for liberal social life rests on self-restraint and self-transcendence—the virtues of family solidarity. (222)

This is a rather thin and vague description of independence, but from this and other passages I infer that independence here means primarily having a well-paid, secure job sufficient to support oneself and one's children at a level that can enable them to develop the capacities and acquire the skills to achieve such jobs themselves and can also provide enough savings so that one does not become dependent on those children or others when one is too old to work.

The major problem with single motherhood, as I construe Galston's argument, is that single mothers tend not to be independent in this sense; that is, they are often poor or close to poor and depend on government subsidy to meet some or all of their needs and those of their children. I noted earlier that the primary reason for this is that women's wages frequently are far lower than men's and that affordable child care is often unavailable. I have no doubt of Galston's commitment to sexual equality, including pay equity. Nor do I doubt that he deplores men who dominate women in the household. An argument for the superiority of intact two-parent families, he says, does not entail a return of women to the status of barefoot in the kitchen; sound families today need mothers as well as fathers in the workforce. He does not note that in most families with two wage earners there is a great disparity between the male and the female wage, either because the mother's full-time work is less well paid than the father's, or because the mother works part-time so that she can also take primary responsibility for caring for the children and doing household work. Most economically well-off women and children are economically dependent on a man.

In the absence of explicit attention to the facts of gender inequality and male domination and their implications, Galston's argument for the moral superiority of stable marriage comes to this: Mothers should subordinate themselves to, and be dependent on, men even if they would rather parent on their own, for the sake of nurturing the independence of their children. Independence is a paragon virtue of liberal citizenship, but a mother's virtue entails dependence on a man. The independence they nurture, moreover, is primarily in their male children, since their female children are likely to grow up to be mothers. This argument implies that mothers are less than full citizens in the liberal society.

Now Galston would surely deny that he intends that mothers should subordinate themselves to men. But in the absence of explicit consideration of gender inequalities in earning power and household division of labor, preferring stable marriage over divorce and single motherhood amounts to calling for mothers to depend on men to keep them out of poverty, and this entails subordination in many cases. As Susan Okin powerfully argues, men and women tend not to have equal power in families, and the unequal power derives to a significant extent from the unequal wages that men typically bring into the household.[29] Men fail to take equal responsibility for housework and child care, often doing little of either, because they have the power not to. Women therefore often work many more hours than their husbands at tasks that are undervalued. More often than not men are the primary decision makers in a household, not because the women are passive and traditional, but because they depend on their husband's income. For example, women's lives are often disrupted and friendships torn by following the male wage earner to another job. Finally, their subordination and dependence puts women at risk of battery and rape, which far too many suffer at the hands of their husbands. Many women nevertheless stay in battering relationships for a long time because they economically depend on their batterers and believe it is best for their children to keep the family "intact."

29. Susan Okin, *Justice, Gender, and the Family* (New York: Basic Books, 1989).

A gender-neutral theory of family values ignores the fact that in the current gender structure stable marriage means that women are often dependent on men and often suffer power inequality and various degrees of domination by men both inside and outside the home. It ignores the fact that for many mothers leaving marriage and choosing not to enter marriage is not a frivolous and selfish pursuit of pleasure but a matter of escaping unjust subordination.

In the absence of attention to this unjust gender structure, Galston's argument replicates the male-centeredness of modern political theory's conception of citizenship. Liberal and republican political theorists in the early modern period more explicitly recommended the subordinate and dependent status of wives and mothers.[30] The actual unit of liberal or republican society is the household, not the individual person. The male head of household exhibits the virtue of independence, supporting dependent mothers and children. The citizen virtue of mothers does not entail independence but, rather, the virtues of caring and sacrifice necessary for nurturing children to be good citizens.

INDEPENDENCE, DEPENDENCE, AND CITIZENSHIP

In the tradition of modern political theory, independence is the citizen virtue of the male head of household and property owner. The bourgeois citizen meets his own needs and desires and those of his dependents by means of self-sufficient production on his property and by means of independent contract to buy and sell goods. This social organization depends on a distinction between private and public. Productive activity of meeting needs and desires is organized privately, with dependent wives overseeing their day-to-day provision and the raising of children. This frees the male head of household to conduct the contract business that will enlarge his property and to meet with other independent citizens to discuss affairs of state.[31]

30. For an account of the role of "republican motherhood" in American history and its continued effects on reinforcing the inequality of women, see Rogers M. Smith, "'One United People': Second Class Female Citizenship and the American Quest for Community," *Yale Journal of Law and the Humanities* 1 (1989): 229–93.

31. On the masculinity of independence as a citizen virtue, see Carole Pateman, "The Patriarchal Welfare State," in *The Disorder of Women* (Cambridge: Polity, 1989); see also Anna Yeatman, "Beyond Natural Right: The Conditions for Universal Citizenship," *Social Concept* 4 (1988): 3–32.

Independence is an important citizen virtue in the modern democratic republic because it enables citizens to come together in public on relatively free and equal terms. If every citizen meets the needs of himself and his dependents through his own property, then citizens are immune to threats or particularist influence by others on whom they depend for their livelihoods. With independence in this sense they may deliberate on equal terms and consider the merits of issues in terms of the general good.[32]

Thus the citizen virtue of independence also entails personal autonomy, a sense of self-confidence and inner direction, as well as the ability to be reflective, not swayed by immediate impulse or blind emotion in the making of political argument. Paradoxically, such autonomy and personal independence is thought to require the loving attention of particularist mothers who devote themselves to fostering this sense of self in their children. Attentive love disqualifies the nurturers of the individuality and autonomy of citizens from the exercise of citizenship, however, because the character of mothers tends to be emotional and oriented to particular needs and interests instead of to the general good. A sexual division of labor is thus appropriate and fitting between noncitizen women who are emotionally attached to men and children whose autonomy they foster by nurturing their particular individuality, and citizen men, who have became autonomous and independent thinkers, thanks to the loving care of mothers, and who exercise autonomous political judgment for the general good.[33]

Galston's statement of the virtue of independence departs from this modern understanding of the importance of independence as a virtue. As I quoted earlier, he defines independence as "the disposition to care for, and to take responsibility for, oneself and avoid becoming needlessly dependent on others" (222). Unlike the tradition, Galston does not construct independence as a means to the end of promoting rational political judgment by free and equal citizens. His picture of the polity distinguishes between leaders and citizens, and it seems that only leaders will

32. Jeremy Waldron well summarizes this rationale for independence as a virtue of early modern citizenship in "Social Citizen and the Defense of Welfare Provision," in *Liberal Rights* (Cambridge: Cambridge University Press, 1993); see also Susan James, "The Good-Enough Citizen: Female Citizenship and Independence," in *Beyond Equality and Difference: Citizenship, Feminist Politics, and Female Subjectivity,* ed. Gisela Bock and Susan James (London: Routledge, 1992).

33. On the paradoxes of women's incorporation into the modern polity and their implications for women's contemporary standing, see Carole Pateman, "Equality, Difference, Subordination: The Politics of Motherhood and Women's Citizenship," in *Beyond Equality and Difference,* ed. Bock and James, 17–29.

make public policy decisions. The primary virtue of citizens in this division is that they be moderate in their demands on leaders; they should demand no more from their government than they are willing to pay for in taxes and be self-disciplined enough to accept painful measures when their leaders judge that they are necessary (see 224–25).

Instead of a means to the end of political autonomy, in Galston's account it seems that the primary purpose of independence is to minimize public spending. Divorce and single parenthood, he suggests, cause the poverty, crime, and disability that make people depend on public spending to meet their needs: "The consequences of family failure affect society at large. We all pay for systems of welfare, criminal justice, and incarceration, as well as for physical and mental disability; we are all made poorer by the inability or unwillingness of young adults to become contributing members of society; we all suffer if our society is unsafe and divided" (286).

Although it is a far cry from the old property-based meaning of economic independence, as I noted above, Galston appears to follow contemporary liberal common sense in identifying independence with having a well-paid, secure job. On his scheme of liberal virtues, persons who are independent in this sense are more virtuous than those who are not. However, I wish now to question this commonsense valuation of independence as a measure of the value or virtue of citizens.

Normatively privileging independence in this sense, and making it a primary virtue of citizenship, implies judging a huge number of people in liberal societies as less than full citizens. First, there are those unable to care for themselves alone and who thus depend on others to meet some or all of their needs: children, frail old people, many people with physical and mental disabilities, sick and injured people. Most of us are dependents of this sort at some time of our lives, and many of us for a good part of our lives. Second, there are those people, usually women, who care for dependents of this sort: dependency workers. Most dependency work takes place outside paid employment, in the home. Thus those who do this work must be supported by others to have their material needs met. Though they do vital, often difficult and time-consuming work, dependency workers are often not independent in Galston's sense. Privileging independence as a citizen virtue thus amounts to defining dependency workers as second-class citizens.[34]

Holding independence as a norm not only renders dependent people and their caretakers second-class citizens, but it also tends to make them

34. See Eva Feder Kittay, "Equality, Rawls, and the Dependency Critique," in *Love's Labor* (New York: Routledge, 1998).

invisible. Dependent people and their caretakers come to be defined outside public social relations, marginalized to a private realm beyond the
interaction of free and full citizens with one another. Such marginalization renders dependent people and their caretakers more abjectly dependent than they would be if they were acknowledged as equal citizens
and received the kind of social support that would enable them to be as
independent as possible and participate in civic and political life.

As women have joined the labor force in large numbers, the expectation that every person should be an independent worker has become
more general. Thus the stigma attached to dependency has increased.[35]
Ironically, during this same period it has become increasingly difficult
for many people to have well-paid secure jobs, because employers have
closed down basic manufacturing enterprises and rely increasingly on
part-time and seasonal work.

Independence, I suggest, should not be thought of as a basic citizen
virtue. But this contradicts many people's stated values. If you ask children, or people in wheel chairs, or old people, or women on welfare,
what they want for their lives, they will all say that they wish to be independent. In order to respect their experience and at the same time recognize people's needs for support, I suggest that we must distinguish two
meanings of independence.

The first is autonomy: within the bounds of justice, to be able to make
choices about one's life and to act on those choices without having to
obey others, meet their conditions, or fear their threats and punishments.
The second is self-sufficiency: not needing help or support from anyone
in meeting one's needs and carrying out one's life plans. The modern
republican linkage of citizenship with independence tied these two. If
you were not a self-sufficient property holder, then you were subordinate to a property holder in order to have your needs met and thus could
not be a full citizen. But egalitarian social movements claimed equal citizenship for servants, wage workers, and wives. The extension of citizenship to formerly subordinate people meant that the link between self-
sufficiency and autonomy had to be broken. The ability of workers and
wives to think for themselves in politics and make their own decisions
about their lives and actions, however, had to be guaranteed by laws
that protected them from the power of employers and husbands on
whom they were dependent for their livelihoods.

35. For an important account of the changes in the meaning of dependence and the way
the term is increasingly confined to single mothers, see Nancy Faser and Linda Gordon, "A
Genealogy of *Dependency*: Tracing a Key Word of the U.S. Welfare State," *Signs: A Journal of
Women in Culture and Society* 19 (1994): 1–29.

Autonomy should be considered an important moral value in the liberal society. Respecting individuals as full citizens means granting and fostering in them liberties and capacities to be autonomous—to choose their own ends and develop their own opinions. It also means protecting them from the tyranny of those who might try to determine those choices and opinions because they control resources on which citizens depend for their living.[36]

In contemporary society, however, most people experience this kind of dependence. Most people depend directly or indirectly on the owners of capital for their living. Whole communities depend on employment in a local manufacturing plant and the retail markets that employment generates. When the owner shuts down the plant, furthermore, he says that he is dependent on the world market, on the relation of the dollar to the yen, and that he must compete with cheaper goods made in Korea. The ideal of independence as self-sufficiency, perhaps a worthy ideal in Thomas Jefferson's America, has become inoperative in today's world of intricate economic interdependence.

Independence as self-sufficiency has come to mean, in most people's minds, what I have suggested that it means for Galston—having a well-paid secure job—even though this is not self-sufficiency in Jefferson's sense. I have suggested that privileging independence in the newer sense has the consequence of marginalizing many people: women who take care of children or old people at home, sick people, people who for whatever reason cannot find work or whose wages are too low to provide subsistence. Wealthier liberal societies usually do not allow these people to starve or die of exposure, but they usually limit the autonomy of those to whom they provide aid and support. People who depend on public subsidy or private charity to meet some or all of their needs must often submit to other people's judgments about their lives and actions—where they will live, how they will live, how they will spend money, what they will do with their time. Thus citizens judged self-sufficient have a right to autonomy, but those who are not independent in this sense often have their autonomy limited in many ways. I submit that this makes them second-class citizens. Too many single mothers fall in this category, and contemporary rhetoric and policy proposals seem determined to deprive them further of their autonomy.

In a liberal polity, independence as being able to make choices about one's life without coercion or threat should be thought of as a liberal

36. For an important account of a concept of autonomy along these lines, see Jennifer Nedelsky, "Reconceiving Autonomy," *Yale Journal of Law and Feminism* 1 (1989): 7–35.

right, respected equally in all citizens. Independence, in the sense of thinking for oneself and making rational judgments about the public good, should be thought of as a liberal virtue; the society is likely to be better governed and more democratic if its citizens think critically and express themselves honestly. Contemporary liberal welfare societies still often tend to recognize a right of autonomy only for those who can meet their needs entirely through private employment. But a humane liberal society should affirm that in order to be autonomous in both the sense of deciding what to do with one's life and formulating one's own opinions most people require material and social support, and that some people require more support than others.[37]

CITIZEN RESPONSIBILITIES TO CONTRIBUTE TO SOCIETY

Galston would be likely to criticize my claim that independence of choice and thought requires social support for focusing too much on citizen rights and not enough on citizen responsibilities. He thinks that a client, demand-oriented view of citizenship has weakened the expectation that citizens will attend to the public good as well as their own. Although citizens have rights to basic liberty, respect, and tolerance from their fellow citizens and from the state, they have the reciprocal responsibility to contribute meaningfully to the social fabric. The state can rightfully expect such contributions from healthy adult citizens and can rightfully punish and stigmatize noncontributors.

Galston is quite right to expect that citizens should contribute to the social good and should be given equal opportunity to contribute. He is wrong, however, to identify making a social contribution with being independent in the sense of having a job. The following passages suggest this identification of making a contribution with having a job:

> This conception of contribution opportunity applies not only to the availability of jobs for adults but also to the availability of adequate opportunities for children and youth to develop their capacities to contribute. (185)

37. In "Social Citizen and the Defense of Welfare Provision," Jeremy Waldron gives an important normative argument for this idea of social citizenship originated by Marshall. See also Barry Hindess, "Multiculturalism and Citizenship," in *Multicultural Citizens: The Philosophy and Politics of Identity,* ed. Chandran Kukathas (Canberra: Center for Independent Studies, 1993), 31–46.

> Contribution has both quantitative and qualitative dimensions.
> Key quantitative variables include sacrifice, effort, duration, and
> productivity. The key qualitative variable is the importance of dif-
> ferent functions as defined either by the community as a whole or
> (more typically) by some socioeconomic entity within the commu-
> nity. (186)

In other words, the worth of a person's social contribution is usually
measured by how much wage or salary that person earns at a job. Galston
is hardly alone in identifying making a significant social contribution
with having a good job. This is the stuff of popular common sense. It is,
however, an incorrect and unjust identification.

Although they do overlap, having a good job and being a contributing member of society are not equivalent concepts. Most of us can think
of lucrative jobs and businesses that we judge contribute little to society,
except perhaps notches in the gross national product, and that may be
positively harmful. Two examples are designing sugary cereal ads to be
aired on Saturday morning cartoons and working as a lobbyist for the
tobacco industry. Just what sorts of activities count as contributing is of
course contestable, but most people would agree that some jobs do not
contribute to the social good even though they may contribute to some
particular ends.

Perhaps more important, most of us would agree that people can make
important social contributions that either do not get paid or receive a
token payment disconnected from their social worth. Good art, literature,
and philosophy, for example, are notoriously poor sellers in the market.
Every society must publicly subsidize its cultural production.

Most relevant to the citizen status of mothers, dependency work makes
a vast and vital social contribution. As already mentioned, most caring for
children, sick people, old people, and people with disabilities is performed
unpaid by women in the home. In American society, as in many others,
when these usually female dependency workers are paid in social services
agencies, the wages often keep the workers below the poverty line. A just
society would recognize dependency work as the significant social contribution it is by giving those who do it decent material comfort.[38]

Community organizing and service provision represent a final category of social contribution outside the labor market. Much of the infra-
structure of civic life in American society today, which keeps the society
minimally democratic, participatory, and critical and also does much to

38. Deborah A. Stone, "Caring Work in a Liberal Polity," *Journal of Health Politics, Policy, and Law* 16 (1991): 547–52.

preserve what social bonds there are, is done by volunteers or very low-paid and dedicated workers: neighborhood crime watches, rape crisis centers, environmental clean-up crews, AIDS prevention and support groups, consumer information lobbies, political issue and advocacy groups, and so on. Poor people, especially poor single mothers, participate in such service providing and organizing activity to an extent that seriously belies the stereotype of the welfare loafer.[39] Many people believe that having the state directly organize political participation and social service provision is both inefficient and tends wrongly to infringe on civil and political freedom. Thus people who do these things—and a healthy liberal democratic society needs a great many more people doing them than we have in the United States today—must depend on public resources for their ability to make these social contributions.

I agree with Galston that society ought to encourage all its citizens to engage in useful social contributions to the extent that they are able. Many children, old people, people with little training, and people with physical and mental disabilities would be able to contribute more to social life than their circumstances allow them today if the norm of the self-sufficient, hale and hearty, male adult worker did not hold sway. A more just society would provide the home help, child care, transportation, workplace accommodation, and flexible work hours that would enable more of these people to make meaningful contributions. Many people should contribute through private paid employment. But many of the activities that are basic to a healthy liberal democratic society—cultural production, caretaking, civic and political organizing, the building and maintenance of decent affordable housing—are not and never will be profitable in the private market. Many of these activities, moreover, are not best performed in state bureaucratic jobs. They are best performed privately and autonomously, but the people who do them must be socially supported in a decent life.

PLURALIST FAMILY VALUES AND PUBLIC POLICY

I have agreed with Galston that the idea of liberal neutrality is a fiction and that it is appropriate for public policy to promote particular ends and goods. Among such ends and goods, some belong to family life: privacy, intimacy, responsibility, caring for particular others, and leisure-time

39. See Harry Boyte, *Community Is Possible* (New York: Harper & Row, 1984).

play. In addition to these, there are particular family values important for children's welfare: attentive love; nurturance to emotional, intellectual, and moral maturity; relative stability; and orderly change.

There are family values, the ends and purposes of family life, and individual virtues that enact them. There is no doubt that some families better instantiate them than others. Along with many others using family values rhetoric today, however, Galston is wrong to assert that a particular *kind* of family best embodies these values for children—the intact, two-parent, by implication heterosexual, family. These family values can be and often are realized in a plurality of family forms: gay and lesbian families,[40] single-parent families, blended families, nuclear families, extended families.

Public policy should promote and encourage the ends and purposes of families. Contrary to what Galston argues, however, public policy should not *prefer* particular means of realizing these ends. It is wrong, that is, for public policy to encourage particular family forms and discourage others. For the sake of protecting children and other household members, the state can properly intervene in or punish particular actions or inactions within families, especially violence and serious willful neglect, but this is quite different from punishing or favoring families based on their composition alone. Such preference is simply discrimination, inconsistent with liberal pluralist principles of giving citizens equal respect whatever their culture or way of life.

Attitudes and institutional assumptions that are unfairly biased toward heterosexual two-parent families put burdens and stresses on many families that others do not face, which sometimes make it more difficult for them to raise children well. Injustices in the economic system and workplace structures prevent many families, including many single-parent families, from giving their children material comfort and the resources they need to develop their capacities. In light of such prejudices and unjust inequalities, the primary way that public policy should promote family values is by facilitating material and social supports to enable all families to be as excellent as possible. I will conclude by briefly discussing several policy areas affected by this argument.

Reproductive Freedom

Many people respond to calls for appreciation and support for single-mother families by asserting that women simply should not have babies

---

40. See Frederick W. Bozett, ed., *Gay and Lesbian Parents* (New York: Praeger, 1987).

that they cannot raise in material comfort on their own. Many single women who do have babies, of course, have inadequate access to contraception and abortion. Policies that truly enabled women to be heterosexually active without having to bear unwanted children would thus probably reduce the need for publicly supporting children.

Reproductive freedom goes both ways, however. People should be free to have children as well as not to have them. In a crowded world each additional child makes for social costs; thus everyone has a moral obligation to ask whether they should bring another child into the world. The decision of an upper-income married couple to have their third child may be morally questionable from this point of view. A liberal society that claims to respect the autonomy of all its citizens equally should affirm the freedom of all citizens to bear and rear children, whether they are married or not, whether they have high incomes or not.

Father Obligations

Many argue that it is unfair for mothers to bear responsibility for financial support of children alone and that fathers ought to be made to pay. In principle I agree. Court-ordered child support obligations of divorced fathers should be much more vigorously enforced, and children-first divorce policies should make these awards larger than they usually are now when the father earns a good income. Forcing unwed mothers to name fathers of their children is problematic under liberal principles, however, because it may subject the women to harassment or threat of violence from the man she names or force her into a long-term relationship with a man she wishes not to see. Trying to force low-income fathers to pay child support they do not have, moreover, will not raise the standard of living of children.

Welfare Reform

In 1996 the U.S. Congress passed the most sweeping changes in public assistance programs since the 1930s, the Personal Responsibility and Work Opportunity Reconciliation Act. For the first time in its history, Aid to Families with Dependent Children is no longer guaranteed as an entitlement for parents who meet eligibility criteria. The legislation allows states to limit welfare receipt to 24 consecutive months, and five years lifetime. Most relevant for the purposes of this essay, the law requires most AFDC recipients to work at jobs as a condition of the receipt of benefits.

Already many questions have arisen about whether states are capable of implementing this law as intended, given their politics and budgetary constraints. When issues of child care, transportation, job creation, and viable training programs are included, it turns out to be far more complex and costly to expect welfare mothers to work for their check than most had thought. I do not have the space to address these questions here. The philosophy behind this legislation clearly expresses the fictional value of independence through a job and inattention to the contribution of child raising that I have criticized in this essay. I think that the effect of the reform is to encourage policies that punish women and children for not attaining to a norm of independence. At the same time, it does little to help make mothers independent in the sense of having a secure job at a decent wage. Instead, it forces more people into the status of working poor, a group whose numbers swell annually. Thus the legislation further limits the autonomy of many poor mothers at the same time that it fails to address the dependence of tens of millions of Americans on a labor market where full-time employment at living wages is increasingly scarce. The equation of independence with having a job thus allows both the public and private sectors to avoid responsibilities to parents and children.

Full Employment and Guaranteed Income

Capitalism has some virtues, but after three hundred years it should be clear that one of them is not employing all able-bodied people at decent wages. A liberal capitalist society can expect all citizens to make contributions only if it makes opportunities available to everyone at a level of compensation sufficient to support themselves and their children in a decent life. Where the private labor market does not have enough jobs for all those able and willing to work, the public sector should provide useful work at a decent wage.

Either employers should be required to raise their wages so that every worker can live at least a minimally decent life or public funds should supplement the incomes of poorly paid workers.[41] Part of any such wage adjustment policy should be efforts to raise wages for typically female jobs to levels of decently paid men's jobs. A liberal democratic society

---

41. A number of writers have pointed out that a consistent commitment encouraging all able-bodied people to make meaningful social contributions entails expanding welfare supports to the working poor rather than reducing welfare supports. That is, because so many people's wages are too little to give them a decent life, justice requires that they be dependent on public support. See Sar A. Levitan, Frank Gall, and Isaac Shapir, *Working but Poor*, rev. ed. (Baltimore: Johns Hopkins University Press, 1993).

that gives equal respect to all citizens, moreover, would institute a guaranteed income policy that guarantees public support to all able-bodied persons to make social contributions that the private market only poorly supports: for example, care of dependents, whether inside or outside the home, provision of social services, building and maintaining affordable housing, community enhancement and empowerment organizing, and the facilitation of citizen participation in civic and political activities.

Within such a full employment and guaranteed income framework, dependency work done in the home ought to be recognized as a social contribution. As much as possible, families ought to be able to choose to care for their young children, elderly or disabled relatives, and close friends in their homes; they should not be forced to do so, however, by lack of good affordable alternative care. People who do dependency work, whether inside or outside the home, should be materially supported. Public policy should promote flexible work hours in private and public jobs, moreover, so that dependency workers can combine their home-care responsibilities with out-of-home contributions. If dependency work were recognized and supported in these ways, many men would probably do more of it.

Mothers' Houses

People who parent alone by choice or circumstances should be respected as equal citizens. Even with adequate material support, however, it is more difficult for many people to raise children on their own than cooperatively with others. One way to recognize and appreciate single-mother families is to promote living arrangements for them that ensure privacy and at the same time facilitate cooperation and support in child-rearing responsibilities. Some liberal democratic governments have promoted or supported such cooperative living arrangements among single mothers.[42]

CONCLUSION

I have argued that a family-values rhetoric that finds married-couple families the most morally valuable fails to recognize mothers as equal

42. Delores Hayden, *Redesigning the American Dream* (New York: Norton, 1984), 137–38; Gerda R. Wekerle, "Responding to Diversity: Housing Development by and for Women," in *Shelter, Women, and Development: First and Third World Perspectives*, ed. Hemalata C. Dandekar (Ann Arbor: George Wahr, 1991), 178–86.

citizens. Holding independence in the sense of self-sufficiency as a primary norm of citizenship accounts for this devaluation of women, who in the current gender structure are doubly disadvantaged by poor wages and primary responsibility for society's dependency work. A society that recognizes all of its members as equal citizens and expects them all to make meaningful contributions must recognize and support the contribution of dependency work and publicly support many other opportunities for making social contributions.

2

Fathers' Rights, Mothers' Wrongs?

Reflections on Unwed Fathers' Rights and Sex Equality

MARY L. SHANLEY

In the early 1990s the case of *Baby Girl Clausen*, involving a custody dispute between biological parents, Cara Clausen and Daniel Schmidt of Iowa, and adoptive parents, Roberta and Jan DeBoer of Michigan, over who should be recognized as the legal parents of baby Jessica focused attention on the issue of what rights biological unwed fathers may have to custody of their infant offspring. When Cara Clausen, at the time unmarried, gave birth to a baby girl, she gave her irrevocable consent to the child's adoption two days after its birth as did the man she named as the child's father on the birth certificate. Within weeks, however, Clausen regretted her decision and informed Daniel Schmidt that he was the baby's father. Schmidt responded by filing a petition to establish

I wish to thank Julia Bartkowiak, Joan Callahan, Ann Congleton, Stephen Ellmann, Nancy Erickson, Leslie Goldstein, Mona Harrington, Alice Hearst, Wolfgang Hirczy, Martha Minow, Uma Narayan, Susan Okin, and Joan Posner for helping me to think about the issues raised in this article. I began work on this article while a Fellow at the Center for Human Values at Princeton University, for whose support I am very grateful. This essay was originally published in somewhat different form in *Hypatia* 10 (Winter 1995): 74–103, and in *Reproduction, Ethics, and the Law: Feminist Perspectives*, ed. Joan C. Callahan (Bloomington: Indiana University Press, 1995), 219–48.

paternity and initiating legal action to block the adoption. Schmidt contended that a biological father has a right to custody of his child unless it is shown that he is "unfit" to be a parent. After some two years of litigation, Michigan declared it did not have jurisdiction in the matter and Iowa proceeded to enforce its decree that Schmidt's parental rights had never properly been terminated and the child had to be returned to his physical custody.[1]

Many of those who commented on the case asked whether Daniel Schmidt's alleged rights should be enforced in the face of the trauma Jessica, now a toddler, would suffer in being removed from the only family she had known. While this matter merits serious attention, I want to focus on a different issue raised by the case, namely the basis and nature of an unwed biological father's right to veto an adoption decision of an unwed mother. This question was obscured in the case of *Baby Girl Clausen* because Daniel Schmidt initiated his action with the full cooperation of Cara Clausen, who had come to regret her decision. But it was his rights that the Iowa courts upheld, holding that an unwed biological father had a right to preclude an adoption initiated by the biological mother or the state.

There have been a significant number of cases in which an unwed biological father has sought to reverse the biological mother's decision to allow a child to be adopted, and legal thinking on the matter is quite unsettled.[2] Many courts continue to apply the traditional rule that they must consider the "best interest" of the child in making any decision about custody. Supporters of biological fathers' rights, by contrast, argue that when the biological mother does not wish to retain custody, the biological father's claim automatically takes precedence over that of some "stranger" or potential adoptive parent.[3] Interestingly, some

---

1. *In the Interest of B.G.C.*, Supreme Court of Iowa, No. 207/91–476, 92–49, 23 September 1992; and *In the Matter of Baby Girl Clausen*, Michigan Court of Appeals, No. 161102, 29 March 1993.

2. A summary of the different statutory provisions in all fifty states regarding who must give consent to an adoption and under what conditions is found in *Adoption Laws: Answers to the Most-Asked Questions* (Rockville, Md.: National Adoption Information Clearinghouse, n.d.).

3. Jeffrey S. Boyd, "The Unwed Father's Custody Claim in California: When Does the Parental Preference Doctrine Apply?" *Pepperdine Law Review* 17 (1990): 969–1010; Elizabeth Buchanan, "The Constitutional Rights of Unwed Fathers Before and After Lehr v. Robertson, *Ohio State Law Journal* 45 (1984): 311–82; Laurel J. Eveleigh, "Certainly Not Child's Play: A Serious Game of Hide and Seek with the Rights of Unwed Fathers," *Syracuse Law Review* 40 (1989): 1055–88; John R. Hamilton, "The Unwed Father and the Right to Know of His

advocates of women's rights have also criticized the best interest standard as too subject to the biases of individual judges but have argued that women's unique role in human gestation and childbirth, as well as various aspects of their social and economic vulnerability, dictate that an unwed biological mother must be able to make the decision to have her child adopted without interference by the father or the state.[4] According to this view, neither the biological mother nor the state has an obligation to seek the biological father's consent to the adoption decision or even to inform him of his paternity. From such a perspective, statutes that require biological mothers, but not biological fathers, to consent to the adoption of their newborn infant do not deny men equal protection. The debate between advocates of these two perspectives takes us to the difficult issue of what, indeed, should be the grounding of *anyone's* claim to parental rights.

From my perspective, neither the "fathers' rights" nor the "maternal autonomy" position provides a fully satisfactory basis for thinking about the custodial claims of unwed biological parents. I am persuaded by considerations advanced by advocates in both camps that the best interest standard is unsuitable for cases involving newborns surrendered by their mothers for adoption, in part because that standard does not adequately recognize the claims of biological paternity, and in part because it is difficult to guard adequately against the biases of individual judges. But almost all arguments for unwed fathers' rights are based

Child's Existence," *Kentucky Law Journal* 76 (1987–88): 949–1009; Jennifer J. Raab, "Lehr v. Robertson: Unwed Fathers and Adoption—How Much Process Is Due?" *Harvard Women's Law Journal* 7 (1984): 265–87; Claudia Serviss, "Lehr v. Robertson's 'Grasp the Opportunity': For California's Natural Fathers, Custody May Be Beyond Their Grasp," *Western State University Law Review* 18 (1991), 771–90; Rebecca L. Steward, "Constitutional Rights of Unwed Fathers: Is Equal Protection Equal for Unwed Fathers?" *Southwestern University Law Review* 19 (1990): 1087–111; Daniel C. Zinman, "Father Knows Best: The Unwed Father's Right to Raise His Infant Surrendered for Adoption," *Fordham Law Review* 60 (April 1992): 971–1001. Wolfgang Hirczy argues that the law should insist that the paternity of every child be established at birth, a necessary prerequisite for an unwed father's assertion of paternal rights; see "The Politics of Illegitimacy: A Cross-National Comparison," paper presented at the Annual Meeting of the American Political Science Association, Chicago, 3–6 September 1992.

4. Mary Becker, "The Rights of Unwed Parents: Feminist Approaches," *Social Service Review* 63 (December 1989): 496–518; Nancy S. Erickson, "The Feminist Dilemma over Unwed Parents' Custody Rights: The Mother's Rights Must Take Priority," *Journal of Law and Inequality* 2 (1984): 447–72; Nancy S. Erickson, "Neither Abortion Nor Adoption: Women Without Options," paper presented at the American Association of Law Schools (AALS), San Francisco, 6 January 1990, 39 n. 22; Barbara Katz Rothman, *Recreating Motherhood: Ideology and Technology in a Patriarchal Society* (New York: W. W. Norton, 1989).

on a notion of gender-neutrality that is misleading, due not only to women's biological experience of pregnancy but also to the inequality inherent in the social structures in which sexual and reproductive activity currently take place. Many arguments in favor of a mother's right to decide on the custody of her child, by contrast, expose the ways in which gender-neutral rules applied to situations of social and economic inequality may in practice perpetuate male privilege. These insights might suggest that one good way to compensate for the present social and economic inequalities would be to give women complete or at least preponderant decision-making authority about reproductive matters until present social and economic inequalities based on sex diminish. But such a policy would run the risk of reinforcing the gender stereotype that women, not men, are the natural and proper nurturers of children. Law and social policy in the area of parental rights must walk a very fine line between adopting false gender neutrality by treating men and women identically on the one hand, and reinforcing gender stereotypes on the other.

The theoretical question of who should have parental rights and on what grounds is complicated by the practical consideration of what will prove to be the best means of moving toward both greater sexual equality and acceptance of diverse family forms. (I am, for example, concerned that any principles I develop here be compatible with enabling lesbian life partners to parent a child free from threats by a known sperm donor to seek full parental rights.) I am also influenced by my belief in the desirability of sexual equality in both the public and private spheres, which requires not only access to jobs and public activity for women but also the assumption of concrete, day-to-day, "hands on" responsibility for child rearing by men.

I argue here that a liberal polity interested in protecting the possibility for intimate association and family life for all its members should articulate norms that ground parental claims in a mixture of genetic relationship, assumption of responsibility, and provision of care to the child (including gestation). In the case of a newborn, this means that the biological father must take concrete steps to demonstrate his commitment to the child prior to the biological mother's relinquishment of the child for adoption and that courts must have the authority to judge both his efforts and the mother's objections to his claim. Only some such standard, I believe, recognizes the complexity of the sexual, genetic, biological, economic, and social relationships between adults and among adults and children that are involved in human reproductive activity.

UNWED PARENTS' CUSTODY RIGHTS IN COMMON LAW AND CONSTITUTIONAL LAW

The Patriarchal Construction of the Common Law Regarding Custody

A frequent theme in much of the literature advocating unwed fathers' rights is that unmarried fathers have been treated unfairly as a result of widespread social hostility toward them. Arguing that an unwed biological father has a right to be informed of the birth of his child under any circumstances, John Hamilton complains that "[u]ntil a few years ago, unwed fathers were ignored or received virtually no protection from either the United States Constitution or the statutes of most states. Indeed, courts and legislatures traditionally have been openly hostile to the recognition of parental rights of unwed fathers."[5] Commentaries that assume that laws placing custody of nonmarital children in their biological mothers' hands reflected hostility to biological fathers display a profound misunderstanding of the patriarchal roots of family law as well as a stunning indifference to the devastating social and economic consequences of unwed motherhood for women.

The common law, which largely regulated legal aspects of family relationships in America well into the nineteenth century, was profoundly patriarchal; legal definitions of who is a father and the extent of paternal responsibilities governed not only a man's relationships with his children but also with women both inside and outside his family. Under the common law a man had complete custodial authority over any children born of his wife and no legal relationship at all to children he sired out of wedlock. The child of his wife took his surname; the nonmarital child did not. The marital child had a right to financial support from him; the nonmarital child did not. The marital child had the right to inherit from him if he died without a will; the nonmarital child did not.[6]

The husband's authority over the marital child was an extension of his authority over his wife. Under the common law doctrine of coverture, a wife's legal personality was subsumed in that of her husband during marriage. A wife could not enter into contracts, sue or be sued, or engage in other legal transactions without being joined by her husband. He owned outright her moveable property and had control of (although he could not alienate) her real estate. So complete was the husband's custodial authority that during his lifetime he had the power to convey

---

5. Hamilton, "The Unwed Father and the Right to Know of His Child's Existence," 949–50.
6. Becker, "The Rights of Unwed Parents: Feminist Approaches," 498.

his parental rights to a third person without the mother's consent and could name someone other than the mother to be the child's guardian after his death.[7]

Thus, under the common law a man's legal relationship to his offspring was governed by his relationship to their mother. If the woman was his wife, a child was "his," so much so that he exercised exclusive custodial authority. If the mother was not his wife, however, the child was *fillius nulli*, the child of no one. While the father was shielded from financial responsibility for his "spurious" offspring, a woman who bore children outside of marriage was "ruined"; unmarried mothers' desperate attempts at suicide and infanticide dot the pages of social histories and nineteenth-century novels. Although the nonmarital child could inherit from no one, in order to keep children off public support, Poor Laws assigned mothers financial responsibility for their offspring and gave them custodial rights as long as they did so. A woman's responsibility for her nonmarital children punished her for sex outside of marriage and increased women's incentives to join themselves to men through marriage.

During the nineteenth century, in part due to women's rights advocacy, legislatures began to replace common law rules with statutes that granted wives equal custodial rights with their husbands. By the early twentieth century, when parents divorced, judges began to prefer mothers as custodians of marital children of "tender years" (usually under seven or ten years of age).[8] Eventually the standard of the "best interest of the child"—which did not automatically prefer either spouse and which purported to recognize the needs of the child as paramount— replaced any presumption explicitly favoring the custodial claim of either married parent when they divorced.

With respect to the custody of nonmarital children the law changed more slowly, and the impetus came mainly from children's rights advocates who wanted to get rid of the legal disabilities of "illegitimacy," such as the inability to collect survivors' benefits, receive child support,

7. William Blackstone, *Commentaries on the Laws of England,* 9th ed. (1783), ed. Berkowitz and Throne (1978), 1:453. On coverture in general, see Mary L. Shanley, *Feminism, Marriage, and the Law in Victorian England* (Princeton: Princeton University Press, 1989). On laws governing custody in the early United States, see Michael Grossberg, *Governing the Hearth: Law and the Family in Nineteenth-Century America* (Chapel Hill: University of North Carolina, 1985).

8. Also important was the rise in both social and judicial attention to childhood and its particular needs. See Jamil S. Zainaldin, "The Emergence of a Modern American Family Law: Child Custody, Adoption, and the Courts, 1796–1851," *Northwestern University Law Review* 73 (1979): 1038–89, and Grossberg, *Governing the Hearth.*

and inherit from the father.[9] Thus the common law protections of fathers against the claims of nonmarital children and their mothers have been largely dissolved, and paternal responsibility for out-of-wedlock children established. But the common law history provides no basis for paternal rights to such children. Some advocates of unwed biological fathers' rights have argued, however, that while unrecognized in the common law, the ability to raise one's biological child is a fundamental interest protected by the United States Constitution and that under the Constitution men and women must have equal rights to claim custody of their nonmarital offspring.

The Emergence of Unwed Fathers' Constitutional Rights

Over the past twenty years, five decisions of the Supreme Court—*Stanley v. Illinois, Quilloin v. Wolcott, Caban v. Mohammed, Lehr v. Robertson*, and *Michael H. v. Gerald D.*—laid down some guidelines for thinking about unwed fathers' rights. These decisions have established that at least in those instances where an unmarried biological father has established a relationship with his child by an unmarried woman, the father's right to continue the relationship may be constitutionally protected. Although these decisions do not by any means resolve all the dilemmas surrounding the custody of infants born to unmarried biological parents, they provide a useful starting point for thinking about those issues.

The Court first considered the custodial rights of unmarried biological fathers in 1972 in *Stanley v. Illinois* [405 U.S. 645 (1972)]. Mr. Stanley had lived with his three biological children and their mother, to whom he was not married, intermittently for eighteen years. When the mother died, Illinois declared the children wards of the state and placed them with court appointed guardians. This was done without a hearing as to Stanley's fitness as a parent. Stanley protested, arguing that Illinois law denied him equal protection of the laws since neither unwed mothers, nor married fathers or mothers, could be deprived of custody of their children unless they were shown to be unfit. The state argued that Stanley's fitness or unfitness was irrelevant because an unwed father was not a "parent" whose existing relationship with his children must be considered; an unwed father was presumed unfit because he had not married the mother. The Supreme Court rejected Illinois's argument and stated that "[t]he private interest here, that of a man in the children he has sired and raised, undeniably warrants deference and, absent a

9. *Weber v. Aetna Casualty & Surety Co.*, 406 U.S. 164 (1972); *Gomez v. Perez*, 409 U.S. 535 (1973); and *Trimble v. Gordon*, 430 U.S. 762 (1977).

powerful countervailing interest, protection."[10] Failure to provide a hearing on parental fitness for an unwed father violated both the due process and the equal protection clauses of the Fourteenth Amendment.

In cases after *Stanley,* the Court drew distinctions between biological fathers who, like Stanley, had been involved in raising their biological children and those who had not assumed day-to-day practical responsibility for them. In *Quilloin v. Walcott* [434 U.S. 246 (1978)], Leon Quilloin sought to prevent the adoption of his eleven-year-old biological child by the child's stepfather, Mr. Wolcott. The Court upheld a Georgia statute that stipulated that a biological mother alone could consent to the adoption of her child; the consent of the unwed biological father was required only if he had legitimated the child. The Court said that no due process violation occurred when contact between the biological father and child had been only sporadic.

The next year, hearkening back to *Stanley,* the Court said in *Caban v. Mohammed* [441 U.S. 380 (1979)] that a New York statute that required unwed biological mothers, but not biological fathers, to consent to the adoption of their children was unconstitutional when an unwed biological father's relationship to his child was "fully comparable" to that of the mother. Caban, like Stanley, had been involved with raising the children, having lived with their mother and supported them for several years. The case arose when the mother's new husband sought to adopt her children. Mr. Caban, who had previously lived with the children and their mother for several years, argued that the law that required only the biological mother's consent to adoption violated the equal protection clause. Caban also claimed that biological fathers had a due process right or liberty interest "to maintain a parental relationship with their children absent a finding they are unfit as parents."[11] New York argued that the distinction between biological mother and biological father was justified because of the fundamental difference between maternal and paternal relationships with their children. The Supreme Court agreed with Caban, holding that "maternal and paternal roles are not invariably different in importance," but it explicitly reserved any opinion about whether a distinction such as New York had made would be valid with regard to newborn adoptions.[12]

Lehr v. Robertson [463 U.S. 248 (1983)] also concerned a biological father's effort to block the adoption of his child by her stepfather, but unlike Mr. Stanley and Mr. Caban, and like Mr. Quilloin, Jonathan Lehr

10. *Stanley v. Illinois,* 405 U.S. 645 (1972) at 651.
11. *Caban v. Mohammed,* 441 U.S 380 (1979) at 385.
12. 441 U.S. 380 at 392, n. 11.

had had almost no contact with his biological daughter, Jessica. Lehr claimed, however, that he had a liberty interest in an actual *or potential* relationship with Jessica and that the State's failure to provide him notice of her pending adoption violated due process. He also asserted that the New York statute violated equal protection because it required the consent of the biological mother, but not the biological father, for an adoption. The majority held that the biological connection alone is not sufficient to *guarantee* an unwed father a voice in the adoption decision, although it affords him an *opportunity* to be heard: the "biological connection . . . offers the natural father an opportunity that no other male possesses to develop a relationship with his offspring. If he grasps that opportunity and accepts some measure of responsibility for the child's future, he may enjoy the blessings of the parent-child relationship," but if he fails to grasp the opportunity, "the Equal Protection Clause does not prevent a State from according the two parents different legal rights."[13]

The rule that the Supreme Court seemed to be developing in these cases, namely, that an unwed biological father who had established a substantial relationship with his child had a constitutionally protected interest in maintaining that relationship, was sidelined in the Court's most recent decision dealing with an unwed biological father's rights. In *Michael H. v. Gerald D.* [491 U.S. 110 (1989)], the Court found that a California statute creating an irrebuttable presumption that a woman's husband was the father of a child she bore was constitutional. A biological father, Michael H., who had lived intermittently with and provided care to his biological daughter and her mother even though the mother was married to and intermittently lived with her husband as well, argued that he had a right to a hearing to establish his paternity when the husband and wife sought to cut off his contact with the child.

The case produced no fewer than five opinions from a deeply fractured Court. The plurality decision, written by Justice Scalia and joined in full only by Chief Justice Rehnquist, rejected Michael's claim. Scalia contended both that the state had an interest in preserving the "unitary family" and that neither Michael nor his genetic daughter had a constitutionally protected liberty interest in maintaining their relationship.[14] Justices O'Connor and Kennedy agreed with Scalia's conclusion but not

---

13. *Lehr v. Robertson,* 463 U.S. 248 (1983) at 268.

14. 491 U.S. 110 at 113–32. Justice Scalia argued that the proper methodology of discerning what interests are protected by the due process clause is to look at "the most specific level at which a relevant tradition protecting, or denying protection to, the asserted right can be identified." 491 U.S. 110 at 127–28, n. 6.

his reasoning.[15] In a concurring opinion, Justice Stevens asserted, without much apparent basis, that Michael could have obtained visitation rights as an "other person having an interest in the welfare of the child," and so did not need further protection.[16] Two dissenting opinions supported Michael's right to a hearing, but used quite different grounds to do so. Justice White, joined by Justice Brennan, reiterated the view he expressed in *Lehr* that biology itself creates a presumptive parental right. Justice Brennan, joined by Justices Marshall and Blackmun, argued that the combination of biology and nurture establishes the liberty interest Michael claimed.[17]

It is important to note that despite the fact that they arrived at opposite conclusions, both Scalia's and White's opinions adopted male-centered models of the basis of parental rights. Scalia looked to the law to protect the paternal rights of married men by basing those rights on a man's legal relationship with the child's mother. White grounded paternal rights in a biological tie established by blood tests, regardless of a man's legal ties to the mother. Both opinions made it unnecessary for the law to ascertain the *mother's* wishes or intentions with respect to paternal claims to her child. By contrast, and although they too reached opposite conclusions, both Stevens and Brennan considered the interests and actions of the mother to be relevant to establishing paternal claims. For Stevens, the inherent biological and sociological differences between care of the fetus by a woman and a man justified different treatment of parental rights at the time of birth. Brennan suggested that once a relationship between father and child exists, the mother cannot then exclude an otherwise fit father from being heard with respect to his paternal rights. Brennan's opinion left open the question of to what extent Michael's situation was like or unlike that of an unwed biological father of a child born to an unmarried woman.

These decisions do not tell us whether under the Constitution an unwed biological father has a right to veto the adoption of a newborn even if he has had no opportunity to establish the kind of relationship and provide the kind of care that the Court has declared protects parental rights.[18] Advocates of fathers' rights insist that unwed biological fathers

15. Justices O'Connor and Kennedy disagreed with Justice Scalia's attempt to identify "the most specific level" of a "tradition" to discover what interests are protected by the due process clause (491 U.S. 110 at 132).

16. 491 U.S. 110 at 133.

17. 491 U. S. 110 at 157–63 and 136–57.

18. Jonathan Lehr raised this issue, but it was not definitively answered in *Lehr v. Robertson* since the majority of the Supreme Court rejected evidence Lehr offered to support his contention that his early efforts to know his daughter had been rebuffed by her mother.

do have such a constitutional right and that when the biological mother has decided to relinquish her parental rights, a biological father, unless shown to be "unfit," is entitled to assume custody of his offspring without a hearing on the best interest of the child.

FIT FATHERS AND COMPETENT MOTHERS: WHO SHALL DECIDE WHEN BIOLOGICAL PARENTS DISAGREE?

An Unwed Father's Right to "Grasp the Opportunity" to Become a Parent: The Pursuit of Abstract Equality

Should a biological father have the opportunity to veto an adoption regardless of the wishes of the mother? Should adoption proceedings be precluded until the father has been heard? What considerations should guide us as we try to evaluate such issues? To answer these questions we need to think about both the basis of claims for custodial rights and the relative claims of biological mothers and fathers outside of marriage.

The argument that the biological father must be given custody when the biological mother chooses not to raise the child is grounded first of all in the conviction that parenthood is a significant good in the lives of men as well as women. Fathers might wish to raise their children for the same reasons mothers do—sharing intimacy and love, nurturing a child to adulthood, seeing one's genetic inheritance survive into the next generation, and passing on ethnic and religious traditions. A commitment to gender neutrality led most states to abandon an automatic maternal preference if mother and father, married or unmarried, each sought custody, and the same commitment would suggest that the law require the consent of *both* parents, if known, before the child can be adopted.

Various commentators support an unwed father's right to veto the adoption of his child on the grounds that fathers have a fully comparable interest to that of mothers in exercising parental rights and responsibilities. Claudia Serviss says all parents have "a constitutionally-protected opportunity interest in developing a parent-child relationship."[19] John Hamilton argues that all unwed fathers have a right to be notified by the state of the existence of their offspring and be heard before any adoption can proceed and that the state may therefore require the biological mother to identify the biological father, whereas Daniel Zinman

19. Serviss, "Lehr v. Robertson's 'Grasp the Opportunity,'" 788.

insists that the state must allow a biological father to take custody of his child when the biological mother has relinquished her rights unless he is shown to be unfit.[20] In *In the Matter of Kelsey S.*, the California Supreme Court appeared to agree that a gender-neutral standard should prevail. It held unconstitutional a statute that gave unwed mothers and legally recognized or "presumed" fathers a greater say in pre-adoption proceedings to terminate parental rights than it gave to unwed biological fathers. The Court declared that the statute rested on a "sex-based distinction" that bore no relationship to any legitimate state interest once the child was outside the mother's body and she had decided to relinquish custody.[21]

The presumption of fitness for biological parents also avoids the dangers of subjective judgment and cultural prejudice that seem unavoidable in attempts to determine the child's best interest.[22] One supporter of an unwed father's right to custody argues that the best interest determination "is subject to abuse and may lead to paternalistic infringement on the parent-child relationship in the name of the child's welfare. Given the long waiting list of adoptive parents that exists today and the traditional preference for rearing a child in a two-parent home, a best interest test is a no-win situation for the unwed father of a newborn with whom he has not yet had the opportunity to develop an emotional tie."[23] In 1987 the Georgia Supreme Court explicitly rejected the best interest test in favor of a fitness standard and held that "If [the father] has not abandoned his opportunity interest, the standard which must be used to determine his rights to legitimate the child is his fitness as a parent to have custody of the child. If he is fit he must prevail."[24]

Use of the best interest test in cases of an infant who has lived with no adult caregiver for any appreciable period of time should be changed not only in the interests of sex equality but of family diversity as well. A "fitness" standard applied to unwed biological fathers would avoid the

20. Hamilton, "The Unwed Father and the Right to Know of His Child's Existence"; Zinman, "Father Knows Best."

21. "Having My Baby," *ABA Journal*, May 1992, 84–86, 84.

22. Katharine Bartlett, "Re-expressing Parenthood," *Yale Law Journal* 98 (1988): 293–340, 303.

23. "Recent Developments: Family Law—Unwed Fathers' Rights—New York Court of Appeals Mandates Veto Power over Newborn's Adoption for Unwed Father Who Demonstrates Parental Responsibility—In re Raquel Marie X . . . ," *Harvard Law Review* 104 (January 1991): 807. Martha Albertson Fineman, "Dominant Discourse, Professional Language, and Legal Change in Child Custody Decisionmaking," *Harvard Law Review* 101 (1988): 770; and Eveleigh, "Certainly Not Child's Play," also express strong reservations about the best interest test in custody adjudication.

24. *In re Baby Girl Eason*, 257 Ga. 292 at 297, 358 S.E. 2d 459 at 463 (1987), quoted in Zinman, 993–94.

possibility that an adoption decision might rest on a judge's preference that a child be raised in a two-parent household rather than by a single male, or a judge's prediction that middle-class professionals will give a child more "advantages" than the child would receive in a working-class home. If no action (or failure to act) by the biological father shows that he should not be entrusted with custody, then value judgments concerning different lifestyles and household arrangements should be precluded from inappropriately influencing the custody decision concerning the placement of a newborn infant.

The question of whether an unwed biological father shall have a right to custody of his newborn infant is not simply about a biological father's "fitness," however, but also or alternatively about an unmarried woman's authority to decide who shall take custody of her newborn child. For the biological father to assume custody, the biological mother's expressed wishes concerning the child's placement will of necessity be overridden. Arguments that a biological father should be able to veto the adoption decision of the biological mother and assume custody unless proven to be unfit run up against counter-arguments that the courts should defer to an unwed biological mother with respect to placement of her child. To these considerations I now turn.

An Unwed Mother's Claim to Decisional Autonomy:
Taking Context Seriously

Arguments in favor of the "fitness" standard for unwed biological fathers falsely assume that once a biological mother has surrendered the child for adoption she has no further relevant wishes with respect to custody. The image of the "bad mother" and the assumption that if the mother chooses not to raise the child she must be indifferent to its fate hover just beneath the surface of such depictions. The notion that once a mother decides to relinquish her child for adoption she can have no further relevant concerns distorts and denigrates both her experience of pregnancy and the nature of her decision. But relinquishment of the newborn for adoption may reflect any of a wide array of circumstances: lack of money or job prospects, youth or immaturity, feelings of inadequacy or isolation. While some women may be indifferent to the placement of their children, in most cases relinquishment is not a sign that the biological mother does not care for the child; in most cases women agonize over the adoption decision and try to make certain to do what is best for their offspring.[25]

25. Maureen A. Sweeney, "Between Sorrow and Happy Endings: A New Paradigm of Adoption," *Yale Journal of Law and Feminism* (Spring 1990): 329–70; Erickson, "The Feminist

A woman's decision to place her biological child for adoption also does not mean that she is indifferent about the question of who raises the child. The argument that an unwed biological father should be preferred to adoptive parents because they are "strangers" to the child inappropriately ignores the biological mother's preference that the child be adopted through an agency or private placement rather than placed with a guardian or in the father's custody. If the mother has had very little contact with the father beyond the act of intercourse that led to her pregnancy, the father may be as much a social "stranger" to her and the child as the adoptive parents, and his claim rests on genetics alone. Contrasting the biological father's rights to those of strangers obscures the fact that the fundamental or precipitating disagreement about custody is not between the adoptive parents and the biological father, but between the two biological parents. And if the mother has known the father over a considerable period of time, her unwillingness to make him the custodial parent needs to be examined to see why she feels as she does, just as it would be if the parents were married.

Are there any reasons to weigh the biological mother's wishes about who shall (or shall not) take custody of the child more heavily than those of the biological father? At the time of birth, the relationship of biological father and mother to the child is neither biologically nor socially symmetrical. She has borne the child for nine months, activity for which there is no precise male analog; indeed, no one else can perform functions analogous to those of gestation.[26] The biological mother's "expectant" state has affected both her own physiological experience and the ways in which others view and interact with her.[27] To what extent should asymmetry of biological function during gestation affect the right to make custodial decisions concerning a newborn?

According to sociologist Barbara Katz Rothman, parenting is a social relationship and parental rights are established by caregiving. In her view, the biological difference between mother and father is crucial and conclusive in establishing their respective claims for custody of newborns: "Infants belong to their mothers at birth because of the unique

Dilemma over Unwed Parents' Custody Rights," 459 and n. 65, and "Neither Abortion Nor Adoption," 39 n. 22.

26. The uniqueness of pregnancy has implications for the custodial claims not only of unwed fathers but also for those of a lesbian partner who had planned to co-parent a child, as well as those of a genetic mother who might turn to a "surrogate" to bear a child on her behalf.

27 On the social construction of the experience of pregnancy and childbirth, see Emily Martin, *The Woman in the Body: A Cultural Analysis of Reproduction* (Boston: Beacon Press, 1987); and Barbara Katz Rothman, *In Labor* (New York: W. W. Norton, 1982).

nurturant relationship that has existed between them up to that moment. That is, birth mothers have full parental rights, including rights of custody, of the babies they bore."[28] By the same token, other persons with a genetic tie to the child do not have such rights. Rothman would have the gestational mother's absolute claim last for six weeks after giving birth, so the adoption decision would rest solely in the mother's hands during that period. After six weeks "custody would go to the nurturing parent in case of dispute."[29] Rothman emphasizes that her preference for the gestational mother rests on her understanding of pregnancy as "a social as well as a physical relationship," and that "*any* mother is engaged in a social interaction with her fetus as the pregnancy progresses."[30] Neither the physical interdependence nor the social relationship between mother and fetus can be fully shared by any other adult, no matter how attentive. Actual caregiving, not genetic connection, creates familial bonds, and in this case, Rothman argues, custodial rights.

Others also have argued that parental rights usually are not symmetrical. Nancy Erickson argues that the liberty interest that a parent has "to control the care, custody, and upbringing of the child" pertains only to the mother (not the father) of a newborn because of her role during pregnancy.[31] Thinking about custody of older children of parents who divorce, Mary Becker argues that mothers are so frequently the primary caregivers of their children that it makes sense to adopt an automatic "maternal deference" standard rather than hold a hearing to try to determine what arrangement would be in the child's best interest. Becker is not terribly worried that giving primacy to the mother's wishes might in some instances permit a woman to deprive a caring father of custody: "A maternal deference standard would recognize that mothers, as a group, have greater competence and standing to decide what is best for their children . . . than judges, fathers, or adversarial experts. . . . Mothers will sometimes make wrong decisions, but in the aggregate they are likely to make better decisions than the other possible decision makers."[32] Becker's reasoning applied to custodial decisions affecting newborns suggests that courts should defer to a biological mother both because the woman has provided direct nurture to the fetus during pregnancy and

28. Rothman, *Recreating Motherhood,* 254.

29. Ibid., 255.

30. Ibid., 97.

31. Erickson, "The Feminist Dilemma over Unwed Parents' Custody Rights," 461–62.

32. Mary Becker, "Maternal Feelings: Myth, Taboo, and Child Custody," *Review of Law and Women's Studies* 1:972.

because, on average, biological mothers' decisions are likely to be as good as, or better than, those of anyone else.

Martha Fineman, similarly very critical of the best interest standard, would replace it with a "primary caregiver" standard.[33] Fineman argues that the best interest of the child standard frequently disadvantages mothers by looking to the likely future financial resources of father and mother. It would be more appropriate (both in terms of fairness to the parents and of the child's emotional well-being), Fineman asserts, to look instead at who has actually given the child physical and emotional care up to the present. In most but not all instances, this will be the mother. Although Fineman does not discuss custody of newborns, if courts were to apply the primary caregiver standard to the kinds of disputes I am discussing, it would suggest that the mother who has borne and given birth should make the custody decision concerning the infant.

Many arguments for giving an unwed biological father custody of an infant child whom a biological mother wishes to have adopted not only ignore the physical and social experiences of pregnancy but invite no inquiry at all into the conditions under which the woman became pregnant. Just as inquiry into the biological father's actions during the mother's pregnancy is permissible to encourage paternal nurturance and to counter notions of male ownership of children, so attention to the circumstances under which conception took place is reasonable to ensure that the child was not conceived as the result of abusive behavior toward the mother. In trying to determine which parent's wishes concerning adoption should prevail, it would not be unreasonable for the law to regard an unmarried biological father who had been in a long-term relationship with the mother or shared living expenses with her and their offspring differently than one who engaged in casual or coercive sex (perhaps a "date rape" that the woman did not prosecute), deceived the woman (perhaps saying he was single when he was in fact married), or willfully ignored the fact that the girl was under the age of consent.

While they refute the patriarchal premise of many fathers' rights arguments, some arguments that mothers should have the exclusive right to place their offspring for adoption run the risk of treating some men unjustly and of locking both women and men into traditional gender roles. If parental claims are properly grounded in the first instance in a *combination* of biological ties and nurturance, then although a father's

---

33. Martha Albertson Fineman, *The Illusion of Equality* (Chicago: University of Chicago Press, 1991).

genetic link per se does not give him parental rights, it becomes a reason *to look to see* if he has attempted to assume responsibility for the child and has done so without interfering with the mother's well-being. If, and only if, he has acted accordingly, should a court recognize his claim to custody.

RETHINKING THE BASES OF PARENTAL RIGHTS: RESPONSIBILITY, RELATIONSHIP, AND CARE

If unwed biological fathers should have some custodial claim to their children but not the extreme claim qualified only by "fitness," what standards should define the extent of their rights? The law needs to adopt stringent criteria for assessing the biological father's intention to take responsibility for, and act as a parent to, his child even prior to birth. Such criteria will require us to shift our thinking and mode of argumentation away from an emphasis on parents as owners to parents as stewards, from parental rights to parental responsibilities, and from parents viewed as individuals to parents as persons-in-relationship with a child.

Many discussions of the "rights" of biological mothers and fathers reveal the inherent tension in liberal theory and legal practice between protecting individuals and their freedoms and protecting and fostering those relationships that in fundamental ways constitute every individual.[34] The language of parental rights emphasizes the parent's status as an autonomous rights-bearer, and invoking individual rights has proved useful in minimizing the role of the state in people's procreative and child-rearing decisions. For example, begetting, bearing, and raising children are for many people part of the good or fulfilling life that the liberal state is obligated to protect. No one seriously proposes that

34. Excellent discussions of the ways in which classical liberal theory pays insufficient attention to the ways in which individuals are constituted in and by their relationships to others are found in Virginia Held, *Feminist Morality: Transforming Culture, Society, and Politics* (Chicago: University of Chicago Press, 1993); Jennifer Nedelsky, "Reconceiving Autonomy" and "Law, Boundaries, and the Bounded Self," *Representations* 30 (1990): 162–89; Sara Ruddick, *Maternal Thinking: Towards a Politics of Peace* (Boston: Beacon Press, 1989); and Joan C. Tronto, *Moral Boundaries: A Political Argument for an Ethic of Care* (New York: Routledge, 1993).

Issues involving children raise in a particularly acute manner the tension between protecting people as individuals and protecting family associations or family ties. On the dilemmas inherent in using privacy language to afford protection to both individuals and families, see Kenneth L. Karst, "The Freedom of Intimate Association," *Yale Law Journal* 89 (1980): 624–92.

children should simply be assigned at birth to the best possible or next available parents without regard to who begot and bore them. And since biological parents have a variety of incentives to care for their children to the best of their ability, assigning custody to them simultaneously protects children's rights as well as those of adults and sets important bounds to the exercise of state power.[35]

Yet in other contexts, use of the language of parental rights inappropriately focuses on the individual parent rather than on the relationships that are inherent in being a "parent." Katharine Bartlett has advocated recasting many legal disputes that involve parents and children in such a way that the language used does not pit one "right" against another but emphasizes the view that parenthood implies deep and sustained human connection and must be grounded in adult responsibility for children: "The law should force parents to state their claims . . . not from the competing, individual perspectives of either parent or even of the child, but from the perspective of each parent-child relationship." Bartlett suggests that language based more explicitly on open-ended responsibility toward children would capture the nature of the parent-child relationship better than discussions framed in terms of parental rights.

When someone is considered in the role of parent, he or she cannot be viewed apart from the child that makes him or her a parent; an "autonomous" (in the sense of unfettered or atomistic) individual is precisely what a parent is *not*. A "parental right" should not be viewed as pertaining to an individual per se, but only to an individual-in-relationship with a dependent child. It is therefore entirely appropriate for the law to require that efforts be made to establish a relationship before a parental right can be recognized.

Asking a court to determine whether a man or woman has made efforts to establish a parental relationship with a newborn is, however, fraught with difficulties that involve the different physical relationship of biological father and mother to the fetus during pregnancy, the social relationships between biological father and mother, and the need to minimize both intrusiveness by the courts and subjectivity in their judgments. Indeed, part of the attraction of both the paternal fitness test and the maternal deference standard is that each of these provides a fixed criterion for determining an unwed biological father's custodial claim. Unfortunately, however, the efficiency and clarity of each of

---

35. See Susan M. Okin, *Justice, Gender, and the Family* (New York: Basic Books, 1989), and Frances Olsen, "The Myth of State Intervention in the Family," *University of Michigan Journal of Law Reform* 18 (1985): 4, for a clear analysis of the impossibility of complete state neutrality toward the family.

these criteria are purchased at the cost of reducing legal discourse about family relationships to an assertion of either fathers' or mothers' rights.

My proposal that an unwed biological father have an opportunity to establish his intention to parent his offspring through his behavior tries to minimize the legal effects of biological asymmetry without ignoring altogether the relevance of sexual difference. I assume that an unwed biological mother has demonstrated a parental relationship with her newborn by virtue of having carried the fetus to term, whereas an unwed biological father may be required to show actual involvement with pre-natal life if he wishes to have custody of the child. The model or norm of "parent" in this case, therefore, is established not by the male who awaits the appearance of the child after birth, but by the pregnant woman.[36]

The different biological roles of men and women in human reproduc-tion make it imperative that law and public policy "recognize that a father and mother must be permitted to demonstrate commitment to their child in different ways."[37] What actions might a court accept as indications that an unwed biological father had made every effort to act as a parent to the child? Protracted attempts by the New York State leg-islature to define the extent of a biological father's right to withhold consent to the adoption of his nonmarital child show how difficult it is to identify what actions establish a man's intention to take responsibil-ity for his infant offspring. In 1990 in *In re Raquel Marie X.*, the New York Court of Appeals struck down a statute that stipulated that only a father who had established a home with the mother for six months prior to her relinquishment of the child for adoption could veto the mother's adoption decision.[38] The court held that the provision imposed "an absolute condition . . . only tangentially related to the parental relation-ship" and allowed a woman who would not live with a man the power unilaterally to cut off his constitutionally protected interest in parenting his child.[39] It instructed the legislature to find some other way to gauge a father's commitment to his unborn child's welfare and to set forth cer-tain standards that lower courts were to follow in the meantime when judging an unwed father's parental commitment. "[T]he father must be willing to assume full custody, not merely attempt to prevent the adop-tion, and he must promptly manifest parental responsibility both before

36. See Zillah Eisenstein, *The Female Body and the Law* (Berkeley and Los Angeles: Uni-versity of California Press, 1988).

37. "Recent Developments: Family Law—Unwed Fathers' Rights— . . . *In re Raquel Marie X* . . ." *Harvard Law Review* 104 (January 1991): 805 (footnote omitted).

38. *In Matter of Raquel Marie X*, 76 NY 2d 387 (1990).

39. 76 NY 2d at 405, 559 NE 2d at 426, 559 NYS 2d at 863.

and after the child's birth."[40] In assessing the father's demonstration of responsibility, judges should look at such matters as "public acknowledgment of paternity, payment of pregnancy and birth expenses, steps taken to establish legal responsibility for the child, and other factors evincing a commitment to the child."[41]

Although courts in New York have used these guidelines in resolving cases involving unwed fathers' efforts to block mothers' adoption decisions in the years since *In re Raquel Marie X.*, by the end of 1997 the New York legislature had not yet passed a new statute governing an unwed father's right to veto an adoption. Two different approaches were evident in proposed legislation, reflecting a widely shared uncertainty over what considerations were appropriate in determining the nature and extent of an unwed biological father's custodial rights.

One approach was found in A 1518, introduced to the Assembly during the 1997–98 Session and referred to the Committee on the Judiciary. The bill listed a number of actions an unwed father of an infant under six months might take to establish his right to consent to the adoption. The bill would make his consent necessary if he openly lived with the child or the child's mother prior to the placement of the child for adoption; *or* held himself out to be the father of such child during such period; *or* paid or offered to pay a fair and reasonable sum, consistent with his means, for the medical expenses of pregnancy and childbirth; *or* initiated judicial proceedings to obtain custody of the child; *or* married the child's mother.[42] Since the father needs to have taken only one of these actions, and may have initiated judicial proceedings after the child was born, this bill applies a simple "fitness" test and requires no showing of interest prior to the child's birth.

By contrast with the minimal expectations put on unwed fathers by A 1518, legislation proposed by the Family Court Advisory and Rules Committee in its 1997 Report to New York State's Chief Administrative Judge requires that a father have demonstrated his commitment to his offspring in a number of ways, and have done so both prior to and after the birth of the child.[43] In place of the *or's* in A 1518, the proposed bill of the Family Court Advisory and Rules Committee uses the conjunctive

40. "Recent Developments," 803.

41. 6 N.Y. 2d at 428, 559 N.E. 2d at 428, 559 N.Y.S. 2d at 865.

42. New York State Legislature, Asssembly, A. 1518, 15 January 1997, introduced by Member of the Assembly Lopez and referred to the Committee on the Judiciary. Mr. Lopez had supported such legislation at least since May 1993, when he introduced a similar bill, A. 8028, which died in committee.

43. *1997 Report of the Family Court Advisory and Rules Committee to the Chief Administrative Judge of the courts of the State of New York* (December 1996).

and. This wording makes it clear that a biological father must have supported the mother or baby financially, held himself out as the father, *and* taken steps to initiate legal proceedings to establish paternity and assume custody of the child. This bill clearly means to grant the right to consent to an adoption only to unwed fathers who demonstrate that they have been and will be actively engaged in the care and upbringing of their offspring, and who themselves wish to assume custody; the stipulations rest on an image of father as caretaker and nurturer, not simply as progenitor.

The bill proposed by the Family Court Advisory and Rules Committee is clearly more consistent with the principles set forth in this essay than is A 1518, but a fully adequate statute would go further. A court should be required to hear a mother's objections to a father's assuming custody of the child, if she has any, both because the birth of a child has resulted from a web of social interactions and relationships and because the mother's relinquishment of the child for adoption should be viewed as the last in a series of actions meant to provide care for the child, not as an act of abandonment that gives her no interest in the child's placement. In cases in which the mother objects to the father's assumption of custody, a court should listen to the *reasons* the mother opposes placing the child in the biological father's custody. Because parental rights must be grounded in the provision of care and the assumption of responsibility, if an unwed mother demonstrated that her pregnancy was a result of force, coercion, or deception, or that she had been under the age of consent when intercourse occurred, the father would be held to be "unfit."

Finally, a statute should provide that a pregnant woman who wishes to make plans for her child should be able to ascertain early in the pregnancy whether or not the father will step forward later to oppose the adoption. The law should provide that she be able to notify him in writing of the pregnancy and preclude him from a veto if he fails to act soon after receipt of such notification. Similarly, if a father is found to be entitled to veto an adoption, a mother should be able to negate her consent to the child's adoption and be put back in the same position she was in prior to her consent, that is, as one of two unwed parents each of whom seeks custody.[44]

One purpose of spelling out what actions the father needs to take to establish his claim would be to ascertain as early as possible during the pregnancy or after birth whether or not he wished custody so that infants could be definitively freed for adoption. Where the mother objected to

---

44. Nancy Erickson, "Proposal for a Model Law on Unwed Fathers' Adoption Rights," unpublished paper, Brooklyn, N.Y., n.d. [1991].

the father assuming custody, a hearing would be necessary. A hearing would, of course, take more time than assigning custody based on a rule that any "fit" biological father prevail or that a mother be able to make the decision to place her child for adoption unimpeded by the biological father. But a hearing to ascertain whether an unwed biological father has grasped the opportunity to parent his newborn should not cause more delay than a best interest hearing. Such a hearing would be to ascertain facts about the unwed father's behavior and the mother's considered opinion concerning custody, not to try to project what custodial arrangement might be in the child's best interest.

These considerations leave unresolved the thorny issue of how the law should deal with cases in which a biological mother lies to the biological father about his paternity or otherwise hides her pregnancy, making it impossible for him to take any action to signal his willingness to take care of his offspring. In 1992 the New York Court of Appeals addressed the question of what effect a lack of knowledge of a woman's pregnancy should have on a biological father's right to seek custody after learning of the child's existence. In *Matter of Robert O. v. Russell K.*, an unwed biological father sought to overturn the adoption of his son on the grounds that either the mother or the state had a duty to ensure that he knew of the child's birth and that their failure to inform him denied him his constitutional rights. The New York court acknowledged that "the unwed father of an infant placed for adoption immediately at birth faces a unique dilemma should he desire to establish his parental rights." His opportunity to "shoulder the responsibility of parenthood may disappear before he has a chance to grasp it." But although the father, Robert O., acted as soon as he knew of the child's existence, the adoption had been finalized ten months previously. "Promptness," said the Court, "is measured in terms of the child's life, not by the onset of the father's awareness." Robert O., having failed to determine in a timely fashion whether the woman with whom he had lived was pregnant, lost the right he would have had to an opportunity to manifest his "willingness to be a parent."[45] The responsibility to know of a child's existence should fall on the man who would assume responsibility for raising the child.[46] A biological father aware of a woman's pregnancy should be required to act prior to birth and soon after he suspects his

45. *Matter of Robert O. v. Russell K.*, 80 NY 2d 252 (1992) at 262.
46. By contrast, one defender of unwed fathers' rights proposes a jail sentence of up to two years for a woman who refuses to name the father of her child when surrendering the infant for adoption; I find this outrageous. John R. Hamilton, "The Unwed Father and the Right to Know of His Child's Existence," *Kentucky Law Journal* 76 (1987–88): 1103 n. 406.

paternity; a biological father who is actively kept ignorant might be allowed to step forward for some specified period after birth (probably not less than eight weeks nor longer than six months), but thereafter the importance of establishing a firm parent-child relationship would preclude his advancing a parental claim.[47] The child's need for such a relationship should also lead to requirements that courts hear and decide disputes concerning the adoption of infants expeditiously.

Although the reflections set forth in this essay suggest various reforms in the laws governing the custody of nonmarital children, they do not in and of themselves answer the question of whether the case of *Baby Girl Clausen* was decided correctly. I find that very hard to do because neither side grounded its position in the kinds of principles I have put forward here. The Iowa statute that Daniel Schmidt invoked to claim that the adoption could not be finalized required the biological father's consent, but no proof that he had demonstrated his commitment to the child prior to (or even subsequent to) birth. The father's mere opposition to the adoption was a sufficient basis upon which to grant him custody. The DeBoers, for their part, based their claim that they should be allowed to adopt Jessica on the best interest standard. Under existing law, placing the child with the Schmidts reinforced the notion that a biological tie between man and child automatically creates a custodial claim. On the other hand, under existing law, a decision favoring the DeBoers would not only have reinforced the best interest standard but might have been viewed as rewarding them for prolonging legal proceedings after Schmidt raised his claim.

The outcome consonant with the principles advanced here would have granted a hearing to Schmidt, recognizing that while his biological tie alone did not guarantee him custodial rights, his claim that he was deceived as to his paternity during Clausen's pregnancy and that the baby was less than four weeks old when he acted provided grounds for a hearing. That hearing would not have attempted to determine whether the child's best interest would be better served by granting custody to Schmidt or the DeBoers, but whether Schmidt's actions were sufficient to establish a claim to custody. To establish his right to consent to the adoption, he would have to demonstrate that he had had good reason to

---

47. I discuss the "Baby Richard" case from Illinois, in which a biological father claimed parental rights contending that he had been kept in ignorance of the baby's existence by the mother and her family, in "Unwed Fathers' Rights, Adoption, and Sex Equality: Gender-Neutrality and the Perpetuation of Patriarchy," *Columbia Law Review* 95 (January 1995): 201–44. The court rulings are found in *In re Doe* (Baby Boy Janikova), 627 N.E.2d 648 (Ill. App. Ct. 1993) and *In re Doe* (Baby Boy Janikova), 638 N.E.2d 181 (Ill.), cert. denied, 63 U.S.L.W. 3313 (U.S. Nov. 7, 1994) (No. 94–615), and cert. denied, 63 U.S.L.W. 3109 (U.S. Nov. 7, 1994) (No. 94–236).

believe that the child Cara Clausen was carrying was not his offspring, that he acted immediately and decisively to assume full custody after learning that he was Jessica's biological father, and that he had done so within the statutory limit for advancing such a claim. It seems to me likely both that Schmidt's claim would have been recognized and that the likelihood of a ruling in his favor would have been much clearer to the DeBoers and their lawyer than was the case under the law then in effect.

The main lesson to be drawn from cases like *Baby Girl Clausen* is that it is imperative that states formulate adoption laws that reflect the principle that parental rights are established in the first instance by a combination of biology and the provision of care, a principle already articulated by the Supreme Court. Another lesson may be that in some instances it would make sense to allow some form of legal recognition to the fact that a child may have more than two "parents": genetic parents (sperm and egg donors), biological parents, stepparents, adoptive parents, social parents (that is, those who actually provide care), and legal guardians. Some such recognition might avoid cases in which it seems that unwed biological fathers try to block the adoption out of fear of losing all opportunity to know their biological offspring. Adoption registries that allow adopted children and birth parents to contact one another by mutual consent seem to have been helpful to biological parents, adoptive parents, and children alike and might offer unwed fathers an alternative to blocking an adoption.

Cases like *Matter of Robert O. v. Russell K.* and *Baby Girl Clausen* should also lead us to try to understand the circumstances, such as fear of violence or harassment, or shame over an unwanted sexual relationship, that might lead an unwed mother to lie about or conceal the paternity of her child. Working toward justice in family relationships requires struggling to eliminate the social conditions that give rise to such fear and shame, and also requires making sure that all citizens have access to the resources that allow family relationships to survive and flourish so that no biological parents will be forced by economic factors to relinquish custody of children they would prefer to raise themselves had they the resources to do so.

CONCLUSION

This analysis of disputes over paternal custody of nonmarital newborns makes it abundantly clear that the language of individual rights, so central to liberal political theory and to the due process and equal protection guarantees of the U.S. Constitution is not well suited to dealing with complex issues of parent-child relationships. While notions of maternal or paternal rights are not useless (for example, they allow us to think about limits to state intervention), they tend to focus attention on an adult individual, whereas parental issues involve adults and a child, and the relationships among them.[48] Legal and social discourse alike must put the lived relationship between parents and between parent and child, not the rights of individuals alone, at the center of the analysis of parental claims. In particular, the language of a father's "right" to custody of his infant child based on his genetic tie obscures the complexity of the relationships involved in human reproductive activity.

Because parenting involves being in a relationship with another dependent person, a parental "right" cannot properly be conceived of as something independent of the relationship. An individual can exercise a parental right, but the existence or the nature of the right cannot be explained by reference to that individual alone. Only by taking account of the interpersonal dependency, reciprocity, and responsibility involved in family relationships will we be able to approach a world dedicated to achieving both lived equality between men and women and committed parents for every child.

---

48. Cases concerning contract parenthood, artificial insemination by donor, or embryo transfer may involve different adults in the roles of genetic, biological, and intentional parents, and so involve more than two adults claiming the legal status of parent.

3
Family Ties

Rethinking Parental Claims in the Light of Surrogacy and Custody

UMA NARAYAN

Family arrangements today are as multiple and various as they have ever been. The existence of a plethora of family arrangements and a variety of relationships within which people have and raise children pose new challenges for the law and invite rethinking in a number of areas that pertain to the relationships between children and their parents. This essay attempts two connected but discrete projects. The first project is to provide a moral assessment of surrogacy in both its commercial and noncommercial forms, leading to a consideration of three legal alternatives for regulating surrogacy and disputes over children arising from surrogacy arrangements. I will argue in favor of handling disputes over children who result from surrogacy as custody disputes. This will bring me to the second project of this essay, which is to critically rethink some assumptions that currently structure custody decisions. In so doing,

I would like to thank Pat Boling, Mary Lyndon Shanley, and my colleagues in the Vassar philosophy department for helpful comments on an earlier version of this paper. I would also like to thank Julia Bartkowiak for her generous assistance and helpful comments on this version. A number of the ideas in this essay were initially developed in my article "The 'Gift' of a Child: Commercial Surrogacy, Gift Surrogacy, and Motherhood," in *Expecting Trouble: Surrogacy, Fetal Abuse, and the New Reproductive Technologies*, ed. Pat Boling (Boulder, Colo.: Westview Press, 1995).

I hope to clarify the criteria that I think should provide legal bases for claiming parental relationships to children and to prescribe some general rules that would render the resolutions of custody disputes more fair and equitable to all concerned. Although my exploration of custody will be prompted by my reflections on disputes over children resulting from surrogacy arrangements, my conclusions on custody will have implications for a wide range of custodial disputes over children.

Because my interest in the moral and legal problems concerning surrogate motherhood was triggered by the Baby M. controversy, my initial worries focused on the moral and legal ramifications of the practice of *commercial surrogacy* under a *legally enforceable contract*, and I was sympathetic to feminist arguments against such contracts.[1] I gave little thought to gift surrogacy and assumed that it was a benign and even a laudable practice. On reflection, I have come to think that, along a number of moral dimensions, instances of gift surrogacy may be as problematic as instances of commercial surrogacy. I have also come to think that many of the moral and legal problems with commercial surrogacy do not seem unique to such arrangements or *necessarily* connected to the commercial and contractual aspects of paid surrogacy. They appear rather to be the results of women bearing children under conditions of powerlessness, whether as gift or commercial, surrogates or simply as women having children within patriarchal relationships. I will consider a number of moral criticisms that have been made about commercial surrogacy and point to the ways in which related criticisms can be made of both gift surrogacy and ordinary motherhood, and I will argue that it is a mistake to see commercial surrogacy as always radically discontinuous with both gift surrogacy and ordinary motherhood.

INTRUSIONS INTO WOMEN'S PRIVACY AND AUTONOMY

A popular moral objection to commercial surrogacy contends that such commercial transactions permit serious intrusions into women's repro-

---

1. See, for instance, Martha A. Field, "The Case Against Enforcement of Surrogacy Contracts," *Politics and the Life Sciences* 8, no. 2 (1990): 199–204; Mary Gibson, "Contract Motherhood: Social Practice in Social Context," *Women and Criminal Justice*, 1–2 (1991), also published in *Criminalization of a Woman's Body*, ed. Clarice Feinman (New York: The Haworth Press, 1992), 55–99; Susan Muller Okin, "A Critique of Pregnancy Contracts," *Politics and the Life Sciences* 8, no. 2 (1990): 205–10; and Mary Lyndon Shanley, "'Surrogate Mothering' and Women's Freedom: A Critique of Contracts for Human Reproduction," *Signs: Journal of Women in Culture and Society* 18 (Spring 1993): 1–22.

ductive autonomy and privacy. Many versions of this argument have focused on the sale of women's reproductive services under an *enforceable surrogacy contract* whereby women may be *contractually* bound to refrain from abortion; to undergo various intrusive medical procedures, such as amniocentesis; to be vulnerable to surveillance regarding matters of diet, exercise, and lifestyle; and to be subject in a variety of ways to serious intrusions on their autonomy and privacy and their decisions regarding their own bodies. However, even where commercial surrogacy contracts are not legally enforceable, as is currently the case in a number of states, commercial surrogacy may not disappear as a practice. Some people might consider a genetically related child worth the risk of hiring a commercial surrogate even in the absence of an enforceable contract, leaving commercial surrogates vulnerable to such intrusions both from the commissioning parents and from legal or psychological professionals hired by them.

Such vulnerability to intrusions on autonomy and privacy are not, however, unique to commercial surrogates. There may be similar or greater risks of such intrusions in some cases of gift surrogacy. Gift surrogates who have prior ties of family or friendship with the receiving parents may be as economically or psychologically vulnerable to pressures to submit to intrusive procedures and regulations as are some commercial surrogates. Their not being paid does not foreclose the possibility that they are economically dependent on members of their family. The existence of personal and familial ties may also make it easier for the receiving parents to impose conditions and engage in surveillance of the gift surrogate's lifestyle. It would be naive to assume that families, which often exercise an oppressive degree of control over women, are necessarily freer spaces for women's choices than commercial relationships.[2] Cases like that of Alejandra Munoz, a poor and illiterate nineteen-year-old Mexican woman who was deceived into being impregnated with her cousin's husband's sperm after being illegally brought into the United States by her relatives, confirm the legitimacy of such worries. Alejandra Munoz was initially told that the embryo she conceived would be implanted into the womb of her infertile cousin. When this failed to happen, she wished to terminate the pregnancy, but

2. For a similar argument, see Sharyn L. Roach Anleu, "Reinforcing Gender Norms: Commercial and Altruistic Surrogacy," *Acta Sociologica* 33 (March 1990): 63–74; and Janice Raymond, "Reproductive Gifts and Gift-Giving: The Altruistic Woman," *Hastings Center Report* 20 (November–December 1990): 7–11.

she was threatened with being exposed as an illegal alien and was forcibly confined to the house by her relatives until she gave birth.[3]

Such risks of reproductive coercion and manipulation are not unique to women who are commercial or gift surrogates. For a great many women around the world, decisions about whether to have children, how many children to have, and under what conditions are controlled by the husband and his family or are made in the context of overwhelming cultural pressures. Many women in countries like India and China, who are under heavy pressures to bear sons, are induced by families to undergo amniocentesis and to abort if the fetus happens to be female.[4] It is women who tend to be blamed for both fertility and infertility in a variety of contexts and subject to physical and mental abuse as a result. U.S. studies indicate that abusive husbands become more violent when their partners become pregnant, putting both the women and their fetuses at risk at a time when deciding to leave the marriage may be additionally difficult.[5] For many women, inability or unwillingness to conform to the reproductive choices of their husbands could result in the breakdown of the marriage. A study of voluntarily childless American couples found that when the wife wanted a child and the husband did not, they stayed childless; and when the husband wanted a child and the wife did not, they often divorced.[6]

My point is thus not only that gift surrogates are vulnerable to the intrusions on autonomy and privacy to which commercial surrogates are vulnerable, but that vulnerabilities to such intrusions mark, in different degrees, *all* women who bear children under conditions of powerlessness in patriarchal contexts. It does not take commercial surrogacy or the marketplace to reduce women to reproductive vehicles enabling men to acquire genetically related children. Marriage often suffices, giving men control over wombs they do not have to rent since the class and power differentials that may exist between commercial surrogates and receiving couples often exist between husbands and their wives, whose lack of

3. For a discussion of the Munoz case, see Phyllis Chessler, *Sacred Bond* (New York: Times Books, 1988), chap. 3.

4. Viola Roggencamp, "Abortion of a Special Kind: Male Sex Selection in India," in *Test-Tube Women: What Future for Motherhood?* ed. Rita Arditti et al. (London: Pandora Press, 1989), 266–78.

5. Pregnant women's risk of violence is 60.6 percent greater than that of nonpregnant women. See Murray A. Strauss and Richard J. Gelles, eds., *Physical Violence in American Families* (New Brunswick, N.J.: Transaction Publishers, 1990), 282.

6. It has been argued that the dominant partner in a relationship controls a variety of reproductive decisions and that in most societies the dominant partner is likely to be a man. See Judith Lorber, "Choice, Gift, or Patriarchal Bargain: Women 's Consent to In Vitro Fertilization in Male Infertility," *Hypatia* 4 (Fall 1989): 32.

control over their reproductive choices may differ in degree but not in kind from the fictional situation of the handmaid in the *Handmaid's Tale*.[7]

SURROGACY AND EXPLOITATION

Commercial surrogacy has also been criticized on the grounds that it involves the economic and gender-role exploitation of women. However, these problems are also not unique to commercial surrogacy, and instances of both gift surrogacy and ordinary motherhood are subject to these criticisms. That commercial surrogacy involves the *economic* exploitation of women seems a plausible claim, since the average com mercial surrogate is paid $10,000—not very generous payment for all the effort and inconvenience involved. That women enter such arrangements voluntarily does not render the arrangements nonexploitative,[8] and we need to think about the contexts that make such transactions attractive to women.

While commercial surrogacy may well involve economic exploitation, many instances of "ordinary motherhood" also involve the economic exploitation of women. Many mothers do most of the work involved in child care and child rearing, as well as the bulk of associated domestic work, as unpaid labor. Furthermore, their domestic and child-rearing activities are often perceived as "gifts of love"—activities done out of a mother's emotional care for her family—and not perceived as unremitting hard work or as "real" economic contributions.[9] Ordinary mothers, unlike commercial surrogates, are not paid, however badly, to have children. Yet they often bear a disproportionate share of the economic costs of having and raising children. They are more likely than fathers to compromise their careers, to drop out of the labor force, or to opt for part-time work while raising their children. Such decisions often reduce their economic earning power over a lifetime, leaving them economically dependent on their spouses and vulnerable to poverty if the marriage breaks up.[10] In

7. Margaret Atwood, *The Handmaid's Tale* (London: Virago Press, 1985).

8. I am sympathetic to Sara Ann Ketchum's point that we cannot assume that "the presumed or formal voluntariness" of the arrangement makes it nonexploitative. See "Selling Babies and Selling Bodies," *Hypatia* 4 (Fall 1989): 121.

9. Anleu, "Reinforcing Gender Norms."

10. For an extended analysis of the economic, social, and personal price women pay for mothering, see M. Rivka Polatnick, "Why Men Don't Rear Children: A Power Analysis," in *Mothering: Essays in Feminist Theory*, ed. Joyce Trebilcot (Totowa, N.J.: Rowman & Allenheld, 1983), 21–40.

many social contexts, motherhood and economic marginalization work to reinforce each other. Lack of attractive economic and career opportunities for women help make motherhood an appealing avenue for feeling a sense of achievement; and being a mother, with primary responsibility for children, perpetuates economic marginalization. As with commercial surrogacy, that women choose to be mothers does not vitiate the claim that motherhood under such conditions involves the economic and gender-role exploitation of women.

Commercial surrogacy has been criticized for involving forms of gender-role exploitation linked to dominant norms of "femininity." Aspects of "femininity" that glorify motherhood and portray ideal women as loving, nurturing, and self-sacrificing seem deeply involved in motivating women to be commercial surrogates. When surrogacy initially became an issue of public interest, many articles and interviews stressed that most commercial surrogates were in fact *altruistically* motivated and that payment was only a peripheral incentive. The motivations frequently expressed by commercial surrogacy included a desire to help infertile couples, a love of being pregnant, a sense that having children was one of women's most important accomplishments, and a desire to resolve the guilt of having had an abortion.[11]

If, as interviews with commercial surrogates suggest, gender socialization operates so as to cause some women to feel a strong sense of obligation to help perfect strangers have children, it seems plausible that these norms would operate to make many women feel an even greater degree of obligation to help infertile friends or relatives have children. Thus gift surrogacy too might involve gender-role exploitation where the gift surrogate's emotional and familial ties make her feel strongly *obliged* to bearing a child for infertile relatives. In addition, many women's sense of obligation to have children also surfaces in the context of their *own* families, where women often feel that they "owe" their husband children and blame themselves for "failures" to be fertile or to provide a male child.

The gendered "altruism" at work in some cases of gift surrogacy seems particularly troubling. Many publicized cases of gift surrogacy have involved the gift surrogate's subjecting herself to considerably greater medical risks than the average case of commercial surrogacy. I am thinking especially of cases that have involved older women having children for their daughters—women whose age considerably increases

---

11. Similar arguments are made by Anleu, "Reinforcing Gender Norms."

the physical costs and risks of pregnancy and multiple births. One case involved a forty-eight-year-old South African woman who had four embryos transplanted into her and gave birth to triplets for her daughter.[12] A U.S. case involved fifty-three-year-old Geraldine Weslowski, who had been through menopause, and who underwent extensive treatment with hormones and three embryo transplants so that she could eventually give birth to her grandchild.[13] The wisdom of taking such risks and making such sacrifices, and the sense of priorities involved in such decisions to be gift surrogates, seem questionable at best.

The contrast between commercial surrogacy, gift surrogacy, and ordinary motherhood becomes even blurrier when we learn that many commercial as well as gift surrogates act in the hope that their "gift of a child" will lead to a reciprocal gift of acceptance and integration into a "surrogate family"—to sustained emotional bonds with the receiving parents and to a place in their family life that would be personally satisfying, as well as allowing some degree of contact and affectional ties to the child. Phyllis Chessler reports several cases like that of Debbie, who expected that being a commercial surrogate would lead to a "wonderful" and "lifelong relationship" with the receiving parents.[14] Chessler's analysis suggests that, while many receiving parents play up to these expectations while the commercial surrogate is pregnant, most surrogates soon confront the cold reality that the contract couple "want nothing more to do with her once the baby is safely 'theirs.'"[15] It is also not clear that the motivations of commercial and gift surrogates who see their "gift of a child" as a chance to secure acceptance and emotional integration into a family differ profoundly from those of many "regular" mothers, who may see having a child as an opportunity for securing their relationship to a man and for establishing familial bonds that provide a sense of emotional connection and value.

All this suggests, again, that there are no simple contrasts to be drawn among commercial surrogacy, gift surrogacy, and ordinary motherhood. I will next explore moral criticisms of commercial surrogacy that focus on wrongs or harms to the child involved and explore the degree to which gift surrogacy and ordinary motherhood escape these problems.

12. Eric Levin, "Motherly Love Works a Miracle," *People,* 19 October 1987, 43.

13. Lindsey Gruson, "A Mother's Gift: Bearing Her Grandchild," *New York Times,* 16 February 1993, B1, B4.

14. Chessler, *Sacred Bond,* 57.

15. Ibid., 60.

SURROGACY AND THE COMMODIFICATION OF CHILDREN

One general criticism of commercial surrogacy argues that it constitutes baby-selling and that it thus involves the commodification of human beings such as was involved in slavery.[16] However, many of the moral objections to the commodification of children seem prima facie to apply to gift surrogacy as well. It is not clear that treating children as "entities that can be gifted away" is less objectionable than treating them as "entities that can be sold," nor is it self-evident that an entity must be subject to market mechanisms to be commodified. Being able to "gift something away" seems to imply ownership of that entity just as much as being able to sell it. Despite these similarities, worries about the "commodification of children" have solely focused on commercial surrogacy.

There are disanalogies between commercial surrogacy and the sale of other ordinary commodities since parental claims to children are not strictly analogous to property rights. The receiving parents who acquire parental claims to the child cannot then resell it, since there are restrictions on how the child may be treated.[17] Some moral objections to commercial surrogacy argue that the practice uses children as means to others' ends and fails to treat them as ends-in-themselves. For example, Elizabeth Anderson argues that children "are to be loved and cherished by their parents, not to be used or manipulated by them for merely personal advantage."[18] She goes on to argue against commercial surrogacy on the grounds that the surrogate:

> deliberately conceives a child with the intention of giving it up for material advantage. Her renunciation of parental responsibilities is not done for the child's sake, nor for the sake of an interest she shares with the child, but typically for her own sake (and possibly, if "altruism" is a motive, for the intended parents' sakes).[19]

I agree that it is wrong not to respect persons as ends-in-themselves, and that persons can be thus wronged even if they are not harmed.[20] However, the Kantian injunction on which such arguments rely only requires

16. See Sarah Boone, "Slavery and Contract Motherhood: A Racialized Objection to the Autonomy Arguments," in *Issues in Reproductive Technology I: An Anthology,* ed. Helen B. Holmes (New York: Garland Press, 1992); and Ketchum, "Selling Babies and Selling Bodies."

17. John Robertson, "Surrogate Mothers: Not So Novel After All," *Hastings Center Report* 13 (October 1983).

18. Elizabeth S. Anderson, "Is Women's Labor a Commodity?" *Philosophy and Public Affairs* 19 (1990): 83.

19. Ibid., 76.

20. Gibson, "Contract Motherhood," 78.

that we do not treat persons *merely* as means to our ends. It is not clear that such a charge conclusively applies to commercial surrogacy since the commercial surrogate could object that she is relinquishing parental responsibilities at least *partly* "for the child's sake." She has borne and relinquished the child in order that the receiving parents can establish the parental bonds they desire with the child and raise it in a manner that secures its well-being.

I suspect that an overly strict notion of what "respect for persons" requires is at work in a number of such arguments—a sense that a child must be desired "purely for its own sake" if it is not to be treated merely as a means to adults' ends. While this may constitute an ideal stance toward children, most people who have children seem to do so for a variety of motives, some more admirable than others, ranging from economic necessity, to wanting to pass on their genes, to cementing their relationship, to experiencing the pleasures of raising a child. Though these desires are not "purely for the sake of the child," they are compatible with the parents also loving the child and caring for it in ways that do treat it as an end in itself. It is therefore not clear to me that a commercial or gift surrogate or the receiving parents are necessarily treating the child "merely as a means" any more than are many regular parents.

I am sympathetic to the claim that children who result from commercial surrogacy arrangements might experience "feelings of abandonment, insecurity, and incomplete identity," even when they know they are loved and wanted by their receiving parents.[21] Children may also experience such feelings if they are products of gift surrogacy arrangements, if they are adopted, if their parents undergo a divorce, or if they are subject to emotionally distant parenting by their natural parents. In fact, many children all over the world, especially girl children in cultures where daughters are seen as burdens and sons are highly prized, go through life knowing that they were not particularly desired by their parents, even when their parents do not subject them to other forms of mistreatment. Thus, it is not clear to me that these psychological risks are unique to surrogacy or that they constitute an especially compelling moral argument against commercial or gift surrogacy. I do not see why surrogate mothers or commissioning parents should be held to considerably higher standards than large numbers of regular parents. Thus, arguments against commercial surrogacy that appeal to the commodification of children and to risks of harms to children are either uncompelling or point to problems that are not unique to commercial surrogacy.

21. Ibid, 79.

It is possible that some instances of commercial surrogacy will not manifest these problems, whereas some cases of gift surrogacy, some cases of women reproducing as wives within patriarchal families, and some cases of adoption will do so.

Given that commercial and gift surrogacy arrangements continue to occur, the practice of surrogacy needs to be legally regulated. What legal alternative might best protect the multiplicity of interests at stake in surrogacy arrangements? I will next explore three legal options that constitute the most significant alternatives that have been proposed as means to regulate surrogacy arrangements. The first option is to permit gift surrogacy while criminalizing commercial surrogacy. The second option is to permit both forms of surrogacy and to regulate the exchanges of children involved in ways that are similar to private adoption. The third option is to permit both commercial and gift surrogacy and to treat all disputes over children who result from surrogacy arrangements as custody disputes. I will explain why I do not favor the first two options. While I favor the third option, I do so only in conjunction with a rethinking of prevailing legal norms that govern both custody arrangements and accepted bases for parental claims to children.

CRIMINALIZING COMMERCIAL SURROGACY

Several people have argued that given the risks and harms to women and children that are involved in commercial surrogacy, commercial surrogacy ought to be legally prohibited under the penalty of a criminal sanction.[22] Some difficulties that I have with such proposals have to do with their intended targets and with their purported effects. Most proponents of criminalization intend penalties to apply only to the middlemen involved in these transactions[23] and find it unpalatable to extend criminal penalties to the surrogate mother and the commissioning parents.

22. See Rosemarie Tong, "The Overdue Death of a Feminist Chameleon: Taking a Stand on Surrogacy arrangements," *Journal of Social Philosophy* 21 (Fall–Winter 1990): 50; and Gibson, "Contract Motherhood," 85.

23. Mary Gibson argues only that commercial brokering should be a criminal offense ("Contract Motherhood," 85). The Surrogacy Arrangements Act in the United Kingdom penalizes lawyers, physicians, and social workers who serve as middlemen in commercial surrogacy negotiations as well as publishers and managers of publications that accept ads offering or seeking surrogacy services, but it withholds penalties from the surrogate mother or contracting parents (Department of Health and Social Security, United Kingdom, Report of the Committee of Inquiry into Human Fertilization and Embryology, London, HMSO, July 1984, 47).

I am not convinced that this position is a morally consistent one. If a commercial transaction is legal for two parties to engage in, it is difficult for me to see why it should be illegal for a third party to engage in the business of making these transactions possible.

Furthermore, criminal sanctions for the middlemen alone seem unlikely to work as a significant deterrent to the practice. It seems just as likely to have the opposite effect. On average, middlemen are paid at least as much as a surrogate mother.[24] Criminalizing the mediation of middlemen without criminal penalties for nonmediated commercial surrogacy arrangements may considerably reduce the costs, making the practice more affordable for many. There is also the possibility that criminalizing commercial surrogacy will merely drive the practice underground.

My central reason for opposing criminal prohibition with respect to surrogacy is connected to the general argument made earlier: that the moral concerns that are aroused by commercial surrogacy also pertain to some cases of gift surrogacy and to cases of reproduction within the confines of patriarchal familial relationships. Yet, most of those who advocate criminalizing commercial surrogacy do not argue for the concomitant criminalization of gift surrogacy or of motherhood under patriarchal conditions. If none of these dangers are unique to commercial surrogacy, I do not consider them a justification for criminalizing commercial surrogacy *alone*. If we routinely permit people to enter into some alienating and exploitative relationships and transactions but prohibit others that have exactly the same features, this raises questions of fairness in that certain life choices are denied the protection routinely accorded to others. Such inconsistencies reinforce a problematic picture that portrays commercial reproduction alone as the site of alienation, commodification, and exploitation. Several feminist analyses of marriage and the family have gone a long way in showing that this picture is not accurate.[25]

There is another set of commonalties between commercial surrogacy, gift-surrogacy, and regular motherhood in patriarchal contexts that make prohibitory legislation solely against commercial surrogacy problematic. For every commercial or gift surrogate or regular mother who

---

24. While surrogates are usually paid $10,000, the total costs of the fees paid to the surrogate, the commercial broker, the physicians, psychiatrists, and attorneys involved in many surrogacy arrangements range from $30,000 to $50,000. See Alta Charo, "Legislative Approaches to Surrogate Motherhood," in *Surrogate Motherhood: Politics and Privacy,* ed. Larry Gostin (Bloomington: Indiana University Press, 1990), 92.

25. See, for instance, Michele Barrett and Mary McIntosh, *The Anti-Social Family* (London: Verso Editions/NLB, 1982), and Trebilcot, ed., *Mothering.*

acknowledges that her reproductive experiences have involved exploitation, coercive intrusion, and the like, there are many who sincerely deny
that they have experienced these problems. The degree to which these
problems manifest themselves in *particular cases* of commercial or gift
surrogacy, or in cases of ordinary motherhood, may indeed vary widely.
Take gift surrogacy for instance. For every horrible instance involving
outright coercion and exploitation, such as the Munoz case, there are
undoubtedly instances that are benign and unproblematic.[26] While it
would be a mistake to regard any of these reproductive contexts as in
general devoid of problems, it would also be a mistake to ignore significant differences in the degree to which these problems manifest themselves in different cases. I believe that areas such as surrogacy, where not
only our experiences but also our *assessments* of our experiences vary
widely, are not good areas for prohibitory state legislation.

SURROGACY ARRANGEMENTS AS PRIVATE ADOPTIONS

Some people, since they do not see much difference between arranging
to adopt a mother's baby soon after it is conceived and arranging to do
so prior to conception, have advocated that all surrogacy arrangements
should be handled as private adoptions.[27] They have argued that prior to
surrendering the child for adoption, the surrogate mother alone should
be regarded as the parent of the child regardless of whether she is the
genetic mother of the child or a nongenetic gestatory surrogate.[28] On
the private adoption model, it would only be legally permissible to pay
the mother "reasonable medical expenses," and the mother would have
a period of time after birth in which to decide whether she really wished
to relinquish the child.

   This approach is attractive to many because it seems to restrict the
amount of money paid to the surrogate, making the transaction seem

26. For instance, see some of the Dutch cases of gift surrogacy mentioned in Juliette Zip-
per and Selma Sevenhuijsen, "Surrogacy: Feminist Notions of Motherhood Reconsidered," in
Reproductive Technologies: Gender, Motherhood, and Medicine, ed. Michelle Stanworth
(Oxford: Polity Press, 1987), 118–38.
27. See Lori B. Andrews, "Alternative Modes of Reproduction," in *Reproductive Laws for
the 1990's,* ed. Sherill Cohen and Nadine Taub (Clifton, N.J.: Humana Press, 1989), 384. Rosemarie Tong ultimately supports this approach, see Tong, "The Overdue Death of a Feminist
Chameleon."
28. George J. Annas, "Regulating the New Reproductive Technologies," in *Reproductive
Laws for the 1990's,* ed. Cohen and Taub, 414.

less like baby-selling. However, it is not clear how profound a monetary difference is actually involved when the commissioning parents are legally permitted to pay the birth mother's hospital and medical expenses and other "provable necessary expenses," such as her food and rent. Given that the average commercial surrogate receives $10,000, it is not clear to me that surrogacy arrangements that work as private adoptions will necessarily involve a smaller amount of money changing hands over a nine-month period under the rubric of "necessary expenses." And, while it *might* limit payment to the surrogate mothers, the private adoption approach to surrogacy would potentially be no less lucrative to middlemen, especially lawyers, who would continue to be crucial to many of these arrangements.

Another feature that seems attractive about this proposal is that it would protect the parental claims of gestational mothers and would provide them time for a reflective assessment about whether to surrender the child. The question it raises, however, is whether it is fair to the genetic commissioning father or couple, who would have no valid legal claims to the child until the gestatory mother surrendered it for adoption. The argument that the disappointment the genetic father or parents sustain is no more than the disappointment would-be adoptive parents sometimes sustain[29] is not wholly convincing, since would-be adoptive parents usually have no genetic relationship to the child they hoped to parent. This raises the question of why, under the proposal that would treat surrogacy arrangements as private adoptions, genetic mothers and genetic fathers have no parental claims to the child even though they do in other contexts. Why, for instance, should genetic paternity constitute a basis for legal claims to a child within the institution of marriage but not in surrogacy? Why should married women who have gestated their children have *less* of an exclusive claim to their children than surrogate mothers?

The proposal to treat surrogacy as private adoption needs to account for why gestation should be the *sole basis* for parental claims to a child. The gestational relationship is certainly a unique one, and no one else stands in that particular relationship to a child, but that in itself is not an argument. However, if gestation is seen as a basis for parental claims on the grounds that it involves providing care for the child before its birth, spouses or partners who have significantly supported the mother economically and psychologically during her pregnancy, thus indirectly providing for the care of the child, may have a basis for parental claims

---

29. Tong, "The Overdue Death of a Feminist Chameleon," 43.

on grounds not altogether different from the gestational mother. Unlike anonymous sperm donors and some genetic fathers of the children of unwed mothers, who desire no contact with or responsibility for the child, the commissioning genetic father or couple strongly desire parental connections to the child and have assisted the gestational mother in providing for the child's well-being. This makes it harder to justify the position that they should have no legally recognized parental claims until they secure the child through adoption.[30] If gestation confers parental claims because the gestatory mother has undergone effort and risk in securing the child's existence, the same may hold for some genetic commissioning mothers. Producing ova for in vitro fertilization involves subjecting the woman to hormonal treatment that ripens her eggs and to surgical procedures that enable the removal of the eggs from her body.

In addition, the privileging of gestation as a basis for parental claims in surrogacy makes some feminists nervous. Lori B. Andrews argues, "If gestation can be viewed as unique in surrogacy, it can be viewed as unique in other areas. Pregnant women could be held to have responsibilities that other members of society do not have—such as the responsibility to have a Cesarean section against their wishes in order to protect the health of a child."[31] I share these reservations and do not think that considering the gestational relationship to be the *sole* basis for parental claims in surrogacy cases is any wiser than refusing, as courts have done, to see it as *a valid basis at all.*

The legal approach I favor would permit both commercial and gift surrogacy and would handle disputes concerning children not as contract violations but as regular custody disputes. While broadly speaking, this is how such disputes are currently handled, I would make significant changes with respect to how matters of parental claims and custody are currently handled by the law. In what follows, I will set out these changes and my reasons for advocating them. The changes I advocate in the legal norms governing custody and parental relationships to children have implications for a wide range of parental relationships to, and disputes over, children. Hence, the discussion that follows will not center on surrogacy even though it will clarify the manner in which I think disputes over children resulting from surrogacy should be treated as custody disputes.

---

30. These problems are acknowledged by Tong (ibid., 52).

31. Lori B. Andrews, "Surrogate Motherhood: The Challenge for Feminists," in *Surrogate Motherhood: Politics and Privacy,* ed. Larry Gostin (Bloomington: Indiana University Press, 1990), 179.

GENETICS, GESTATION, CARE-GIVING: RETHINKING BASES FOR PARENTAL CLAIMS TO CHILDREN

In custody disputes, the law decides between competing claims on the part of those who have standing to assert parental rights to a child. I shall begin by arguing that genetic connections, gestation, and sustained caregiving should each confer prima facie bases for the standing to claim legal recognition of parental relationships to children. By this I mean that each of them should suffice in its own right for the law to *consider* the relationship to be a parent-child relationship that *might* warrant legal recognition and to provide bases for claims to custody or visitation relationships between adults and children. However, each of these bases can be legally overridden or fail to be granted legal weight where there are good reasons for so doing and would not always result in legal outcomes where the relationship between the adult and the child would be legally endorsed and maintained as a parental relationship. But genetic connections, gestation, and sustained caregiving ought each to give an individual *standing* to claim a parental relationship to the child in the eyes of the law in distinction from parties who satisfy none of these criteria and are appropriately treated as "legal strangers" with respect to the child.

In what is taken to be the "standard" parental relationship, genetic, gestational, and caregiving relationships to a child tend to overlap and coincide. The genetic mother is also the gestational mother, and the genetic parents each contribute to the care and raising of the child. However, in an increasing number of cases, including surrogacy arrangements, these relationships do not neatly coincide. Some caregiver parents may not be genetically related to the child; some genetic parents may not be caregivers to their children; some gestational mothers, such as nongenetic gestational surrogates, may lack genetic connections to the child; and so forth. Given these divergences, I think it is useful to consider *why* each of these relationships—genetic, gestational, and caregiving—might warrant being considered prima facie bases for legally recognized parental relationships.

I will begin with the genetic connection. The law currently gives a significant amount of weight to the genetic relationship in determining parental claims and responsibilities towards children. Biological paternity suffices in most cases (with some exceptions like anonymous sperm donors) to generate legally recognized parental rights and obligations. Biological fathers who have neither gestated nor cared for their children are liable for child support, may have a say in the placement of the child for adoption, and have the standing to legally request custody or visitation in virtue of the genetic connection alone. Biologically connected relatives, such as grandparents, aunts, or uncles, may have the standing to request custody of a child whose biological parents are dead or incapacitated even if they have not previously been caregivers to the child.

Why should such genetic connections be taken seriously and treated as prima facie bases for parental relationships to children? This is not an easy question to answer. While many people might not be able to *explain* why they value genetic connections to others, it is the case that genetic connections are valued by many, and not only in the case of children. Many of us maintain relationships to relatives with whom we do not have much in common, or that we do not even like a great deal, because we perceive them to be "family." The deep-seated desire of some adopted children to know their family of origin even when they love and have been well cared for by their adoptive family is undoubtedly a result of the cultural weight our society assigns genetic relationships. The value assigned to genetic ties often means that people feel a degree of responsibility for relatives and accept obligations to assist them in situations where they may not act to help strangers. These are not *reasons* for valuing genetic relationships, but an acknowledgment that we live in a world where such connections are, in fact, often valued.

The legal recognition of genetic connections as providing individuals a standing to claim parental relationships to children is a response to the fact that such relationships are valued in our society and are taken to be meaningful and significant not only by adults but often also by children. In a number of cases, the recognition of genetic connection alone as bases for parental claims yields good results. Take a U.S. soldier who fathers a child overseas by a woman he is not married to, is unaware of the child's existence, and therefore has in no way contributed to the child's care or support. If the individual is informed five years later that he is the biological father of a child and that the child's mother is deceased, the recognition of genetic fatherhood as constituting a basis for legal claims to the child would permit him to bring the child to the United States and to assume the responsibilities of being the social parent of the child. In such cases, or in cases of relatives wanting to assume responsibilities for a child whose parents are dead, recognizing genetic connections as a basis for parental claims to children may well work in the best interests of the child. In these examples there are no disputes between adults for rights to a relationship with the child, and the genetic connection functions as a motivation for adults wishing to care for the child. Allowing the genetic connection to confer legal standing to claim parental relationships to the child may allow such children to acquire familial relationships and support they may otherwise not easily have.

While I believe the law should recognize such genetic ties as giving people a *standing to claim* legal parental relationships to children, I am *not* arguing that genetic connections should *always* confer legally binding parental relationships to children. There may be a variety of situations where the law may, with good reason, refuse to grant the claim, as in the case of *Thomas S. v. Robin Y.* discussed by Katherine Arnup and Susan Boyd.[32] Robin Y. and her lesbian partner each had a daughter through assisted insemination with the sperm of known donors who were gay men. The mothers and donors had a verbal agreement that the donors would have no parental rights or obligations and that the two women would be each child's co-parents. Some years later one of the donors sought recognition of parental status and visitation rights to his biological child. Even though Thomas S. was the child's biological father, I believe that the judge did the right thing in denying Thomas S.'s parental claim on the grounds that the child did not want to visit him and that her sense of security and her sense of her family as comprised of her two mothers and her sister was threatened by his demands. Thus, while I believe genetic relationships ought to confer *standing* to claim parental relationships to children, I also believe this standing may be overridden by a variety of considerations pertaining to the well-being and welfare of the child.

I shall move on to argue that a gestational relationship to a child should, like genetic relationships, constitute a basis for standing to claim legal parental relationships to a child without being decisive. The only cases where a woman might gestate a child without it being genetically related to her are cases of nongenetic gestational surrogacy or cases where a woman bears a child as a result of an egg donated by someone else. Why should gestation confer a basis for parental claims to a child? A gestational mother undergoes considerable discomfort, effort, and risk in the course of pregnancy and childbirth, and gestation is an intimate process during which a woman could quite understandably develop a deep attachment to the child she carries and gives birth to. If genetic connections, which often do not involve either the effort or the emotional sense of connection that may result from gestation, are taken to be grounds for legal parental claims to children, there seems little reason not to consider the gestational connection as an equally compelling ground.

32. Katherine Arnup and Susan Boyd, "Familial Disputes: Sperm Donors, Lesbian Mothers, and Legal Parenthood," in *Legal Inversions: Lesbians, Gay Men, and the Politics of Law,* ed. Didi Herman and Carl Stychin (Philadelphia: Temple University Press, 1995).

It is probably easiest to see why sustained relationships of caregiving should form a basis for parental claims to a child. The everyday tasks of caring for children and meeting their physical, emotional, and social needs involves a substantial amount of labor and commitment and often leads to very close bonds between the child and the caregiver. Children often feel close attachment to their caregivers, and these ongoing bonds play a significant role in their sense of security and identity. Consequently, sustained efforts at caring for the child and functioning as a *social parent* can create emotional ties that are valued by both adult and child, ties that deserve to be given legal weight.

While sustained relationships of social caregiving philosophically seem the most *compelling* basis for the recognition of parental claims to children, legal practices have tended to recognize and favor genetic connections over connections of caregiving as a basis for parental claims to children. As Shelley A. M. Gavigan points out, "a biological father has an easier time establishing his claim to be a parent within the current legal framework than does a lesbian social parent."[33]

The position I am advocating would require the law to consider genetic and gestational connections as well as the relationship of caregiving each as a compelling prima facie basis for parental claims to children. If there are conflicts or disagreements between parties who have a variety of such bases for parental claims to children, decisions about custody and visitation must be determined according to the best interests of the child. While it would be possible that awarding primary custody to a parent who is the primary caregiver might well be in the best interests of the child in a majority of cases, this would be a rebuttable presumption, and awarding custody to the primary caregiver must be determined to be in fact in the best interest of a *particular* child.

My position differs from established legal norms determining parental standing in that it explicitly recognizes the gestational relationship per se as a basis for parental claims. Gestational surrogates who had no genetic connection to the child have often been legally regarded as having no valid basis for parental claims to the children they gestate. My position would permit nongenetic gestational surrogates as well as genetic surrogates in both commercial and noncommercial arrangements to assert legal claims to the children who result from surrogacy agreements, and both sorts of cases would then have to be handled as custody disputes. My position also differs from established legal norms

33. Shelley A. M. Gavigan, "A Parent(ly) Knot: Can Heather Have Two Mommies?" in *Legal Inversions: Lesbians, Gay Men, and the Politics of Law,* ed. Herman and Stychin, 108.

in permitting a variety of nonbiological social parents who have been involved in sustained relationships of caregiving to have standing to assert parental claims to children.

The latter move would benefit a variety of people. For instance, gay men and lesbian women who work at parenting children who are biologically related only to their partners would have a basis for maintaining parental bonds with those children even if their relationships broke up, instead of being treated as legal strangers with respect to these children. Unmarried heterosexual partners who are not genetically related to the children they help their partners raise would also have legally recognized claims to maintain their parental bonds to those children, as would married partners who have helped raise children from their partner's previous relationships but have not legally adopted the child. A variety of relatives or friends who have functioned as sustained social caregivers to children as a result of various contingencies, but whom the law would currently treat as legal strangers, would have bases for parental claims to these children.

RETHINKING THE "TWO PARENTS OF OPPOSITE SEXES" MODEL

I would reform our current custody practices in two other important ways that jointly constitute a rethinking of what I shall call the "Two Parents of Opposite Sexes Model." I believe the courts should rethink the prevailing normative assumptions that (a) a particular child can have no more than two legal parents at any given time and that (b) the two parents must be of opposite sexes. The need to rethink the second assumption is underscored by the increasing presence of children raised by same-sex parents. Increasing numbers of lesbian women are having children through donor insemination or through adoption as single parents, and many of them have and raise these children with the sustained cooperation of a same-sex partner who functions as a co-mother to the child and is recognized as such by the child. Rethinking this assumption would also help protect the interests of both adults and children in cases where two people of the same sex who are not sexual partners, say a mother and daughter or two sisters, actively co-parent a child due to a variety of contingencies.

In any case where people of the same sex provide sustained social care for the child and function as its social parents, both should have standing to be recognized as the child's legal parents. The standing to be recognized as a legal parent of the child should not be overridden *purely* on the arbitrary and discriminatory presumption that the child cannot have more than one legal parent of the same sex. It is even more arbitrary to deny both parties legal parental standing in cases where both favor such recognition for a variety of good reasons, such as enabling the nonbiological co-parent to provide medical coverage for the child or to have legal standing as the child's parent were the biological parent to die. In custody conflicts, both co-parents should have standing to claim and maintain parental connections to the child.

The presupposition that no more than two persons at any given time can be granted legal recognition of their parental claims to a particular child seems clearly anachronistic given the complexity of contemporary reproductive and parental relationships. Rethinking this presupposition would benefit both adults and children in a number of different types of family relationships. Take the case of children whose biological parents divorce and remarry when the child is young and both share custody of the child in family contexts where their current partners both also function as social parents of the child. Rethinking this presupposition would permit both the nonbiological social parents to have legally recognized parental bonds to the child in cases where the biological parent dies, instead of being treated as legal strangers despite their sustained roles as social parents. It would permit legal recognition of the parental status of all adults in families comprised, for example, of two lesbian co-mothers and a gay male parent, or of a couple who function as social co-parents of their daughter's biological child.

Permitting particular children to have more than two legal parents at any given time would, in many of the sorts of cases mentioned above, both comport with the desires of all the adults involved in parental relationships and serve the best interests of the child. Such a policy would also make more options available to the parenting adults and not force them to make harsh and unpalatable choices. It would make it possible for parents to grant parental rights to others without necessarily completely surrendering their own. A young woman whose child is co-parented by her sister and brother-in-law, or a man whose former spouse and her current partner function as primary social caregivers to his biological child, would have the option of retaining parental visitation rights while surrendering primary custodial parental rights to the primary caregivers. Right now, people in these situations are often confronted with making the hard choice of completely surrendering parental claims to the child in order that the primary caregivers can gain parental rights.

I believe that permitting a child to have more than two legal parents would also result in better outcomes in a number of cases involving surrogacy and that this option would be preferable to the previously discussed private adoption approach. The private adoption approach, despite its advantages, is still an "all or nothing" approach. The gestatory mother has *all* the parental claims before ceding the child for adoption, and *no* claims whatsoever after the "change of mind" period has passed. The commissioning parents have *no* parental claims until the child is ceded for adoption, and thereafter have the *only* recognized parental claims to it. The reformed custody approach I advocate potentially allows for a wider range of parental relationships to be preserved through shared custody and visitation rights. A surrogate mother who did not wish to fully relinquish her parental claims to the child would, on the reformed custody model, have a good chance of maintaining parental bonds to the child by sharing in its custody or by having parental visitation rights. This might be a more welcome option for a surrogate mother than being forced to choose between the burdens of assuming full responsibility for the child and surrendering all ties to it, as the private adoption model requires.

My approach would give the surrogate and the commissioning parents the option of agreeing that the surrogate would not totally surrender all parental claims but would legally share custody or maintain visitation rights, and it would do so in a way that does not, as a consequence, prevent the spouse of the commissioning father who is genetically unrelated to the child from acquiring legally recognized parental claims to the child she helps raise. Both the private adoption model and our current custody practices make it impossible for such a spouse to acquire recognized parental claims to the child except via adoption, and she cannot adopt the child unless the genetic surrogate mother completely relinquishes her parental claims. This makes it impossible to protect the parental interests of both women simultaneously and raises the commissioning parents' stake in making sure that they have "exclusive possession" of the child.

I believe that the policy I recommend also has the virtue of privileging a child's interests above those of competing parents, treating children more as ends-in-themselves than as objects of property-like disputes between contending parents. It is often arguably in the child's "best interests" to maintain as many of these parental connections with adults who wish to maintain these bonds as is practically feasible in any given case. I am not arguing that in *every instance* it is in the child's interest to uphold the parental rights of all adults who have parental

claims. In some instances, the nature of the conflicts between contending parties or a variety of other circumstances might well make it in the
child's interests *not* to award custodial or visitation rights to one or more
of the parties. All I am arguing for is that such an option should not be
arbitrarily foreclosed for all cases, including those where it might well
suit the child's best interest. It would be arbitrary to foreclose this option
simply on the grounds that it does not fit dominant pictures of
parent-child relationships—pictures that have arguably failed to keep
pace with changing family structures and child-raising arrangements.

I have not attempted anything like a complete account of how a good
legal system would function with respect to parental rights and issues of
custody. I have not addressed, for instance, the ways in which economic
criteria may figure in determinations of "best interests" in ways that
may be unfair to women,[34] or the ways in which sexist and heterosexist
criteria are often used in prejudicial ways.[35] I have simply attempted to
argue that the specific changes I have described would be a fair and
principled way to protect a variety of parental claims that may arise not
only in surrogacy cases but also in a number of other parent-child contexts, and to protect the interests of the children involved. Legally recognizing a plurality of parental relationships may go a long way toward
valuing and validating a variety of relationships valued by both adults
and children and may move us away from viewing children as entities
over whom adults should be driven to seek exclusive possession.

---

34. Tong, "The Overdue Death of a Feminist Chameleon," 44.

35. For instance, commercial surrogates may run the risk of being stigmatized as "unfit
mothers" merely by virtue of the fact that they entered such a commercial transaction in the
first place. For example, Judge Sorkow felt that Mary Beth Whitehead had proved her "unfitness" as a mother the day she signed the contract with the Sterns. This seems sexist and unfair,
given that the commissioning parents' signing the same contract is not perceived as making
them unfit parents, even though it was their desire for the child and their offer of a fee that generated the transaction in the first place (Chessler, *Sacred Bond,* 38).

4

A Parent(ly) Knot

Can Heather
Have Two Mommies?

SHELLEY A. M. GAVIGAN

There is a children's book entitled *Heather Has Two Mommies*. It is the story of a little girl whose parents are a lesbian couple–Kate and Jane. Kate is a doctor, and Jane is a carpenter. Kate and Jane are blissfully happy, but they want to have a child in their lives. Following a joint decision, Jane becomes pregnant through alternative insemination, and soon thereafter Heather is born. Heather regards each woman as her mother: they are called "Mama Kate" and "Mama Jane." However, when she goes to nursery school, she discovers, apparently for the first time, that she is different from other children–she doesn't have a daddy. The

The title of this essay has been taken from the children's book *Heather Has Two Mommies* by Leslea Newman and Diana Souza (illustrator) (Northampton, Mass.: In Other Words Publishing, 1989). For a Canadian story in which a little girl also has two mothers but in which the lesbian context is muted, see Rosamund Elwin, Michele Paulse, and Dawn Lee (illustrator), *Asha's Mums* (Toronto: Women's Press, 1990). I wish to thank Jill Grant and Tracy Bomberry for their technical assistance and Karen Pearlston for her research assistance. I also acknowledge with thanks the comments of Didi Herman, Susan Boyd, and Aviva Goldberg on an earlier draft. Karen Andrews, Judy Fudge, Brenda Cossman, and Dorothy Chunn endured many hours of discussions; and I thank them for their insight and stamina. Judy Deverell inspired me, and Amy Deverell decided for herself. This essay was first published in *Legal Inversions: Lesbians, Gay Men, and the Politics of Law,* ed. Didi Herman and Carl Stychin (Philadelphia: Temple University Press, 1995). It is reproduced by permission of the author.

story proceeds to illustrate, through the first-person accounts of the other children in Heather's nursery school, that there are many kinds of families. Reassured, Heather greets her two mommies at the end of the day, and she, Kate, and Jane leave together, presumably to live happily ever after with their ginger cat and black Labrador dog.

For those of us who are students of family law and perhaps of family life, Heather's story raises interesting questions, including interesting legal ones. While the story undoubtedly provides a measure of comfort to lesbian parents and a new generation of children being raised in lesbian households (my own included), the extent to which its content is regarded by many as controversial should not be underestimated.[1] This is not simply a story about a little girl being raised by two women, or even two lesbians, who, as refugees from heterosexual relationships, are raising a child from an ended marriage. This little girl does not have and has never had a daddy; she was conceived neither in a bed nor in the back seat of a car. She is a baby whose conception was made possible by a less traditional method. It is this aspect of the story, as well as perhaps the happy and ostensibly normal lives of the lesbians, Kate and Jane, that has given rise to its reception as a controversial book.

In this essay, I take this story as a departure point to interrogate and apply the concept of familial ideology. By "familial ideology," I mean the range of dominant ideas and social practices, discourses and prejudices, common sense and social science, in which relations of gender and generation are held out and generally accepted to be best organized around and through a household comprised of two adults of the opposite sex who (usually) have expressed a primary personal, sexual, and economic commitment to each other and to care for and raise any children they may have. The family is often asserted to be the basic unit of society and is celebrated by religious authorities in quasisacred terms.

---

1. I have been chided for selecting this form of fictive relationship as my focus. Heather's mommies are white, monogamous, and apparently reasonably well-off; the carpenter has landed herself a doctor. They appear to own their own home. They seem to replicate a "Leave It to Beaver" kind of nuclear family, only there are two Mrs. Cleavers, and they both appear to work outside the home. I take the point. To be sure, to the extent that the story suggests that Heather would first learn that she is different from other children in nursery school, the story is an idealized one. However, criticism of its content needs to be tempered by the fact that this book fueled an antigay, profamily campaign in the United States. As conventionally Eurocentric and class-specific as some readers may find the story, the lesbian content is deeply troubling to the profamily Right. The *New York Times* reported that *Heather Has Two Mommies* was one of the weapons used by a conservative political group in Oregon in its 1992 campaign to force a referendum on the "strongest anti-homosexual measure ever considered by a state"; see Timothy Egan, "Oregon Measure Asks State to Repress Homosexuality," *New York Times*, 16 August 1992, 1, 34.

This form of relationship is often crystallized by marriage and supported by the state as well as by a range of nonstate institutions. The naturalized privacy, independence, interdependency, intimacy, security, and domesticity of this form of relationship are also heralded and accepted.[2] In this essay, then, I examine the implications of familial ideology in the context in which family members do not resemble the dominant image of the "normal" family: lesbian parents.[3]

I explore the extent to which dominant, socially shared understandings of biological and social reproduction and the relations expressed by the terms *parent* and *child* in law may be simultaneously challenged and reinforced by the existence (and even attitudes) of lesbian parents. More specifically, however, I challenge the view that the positions and legal struggles of lesbian parents can be deciphered by "centering" lesbians[4] or explained by recourse to the concept of heterosexual privilege. Lesbians do not live outside the law in a kind of legal limbo, nor do they exist in a legal vacuum. They shape and are shaped by the legal and social relations in which they live. I am wary of any analysis that focuses only on lesbians, because it seems to me that the "centered" lesbian can easily become the abstracted, or decontextualized, lesbian. The relational nature of my inquiry and my argument means that I am

2. For general discussions of familial ideology see Shelley A. M. Gavigan, "Law, Gender, and Ideology," in *Legal Theory Meets Legal Practice,* ed. Anne F. Bayefsky (Edmonton: Academic Publishers, 1988); Dorothy E. Chunn, *From Punishment to Doing Good* (Toronto: University of Toronto Press, 1992); Susan B. Boyd, "From Gender Specificity to Gender Neutrality? Ideologies in Canadian Child Custody Law," in *Child Custody and the Politics of Gender,* ed. Carol Smart and Selma Sevenhuijsen (London: Routledge, 1989); Susan B. Boyd, "(Re)Placing the State: Family, Law and Oppression," *Canadian Journal of Law and Society* 9 (1994): 39; and Marlee Kline, "Complicating the Ideology of Motherhood: Child Welfare Law and First Nation Women," *Queen's Law Journal* 18 (1993): 306.

Informed by the work of feminist and Marxist scholars, I share the view that the concept of ideology makes "reference not only to belief systems, but to questions of power"; see Terry Eagleton, *Ideology: An Introduction* (London: Verso, 1991), 5. Eagleton, himself drawing upon the work of other students of ideology, notes that the most widely accepted understanding of the role of ideology is that it legitimates a dominant power. The question of how it does so is particularly important when one considers the family as an ideological form. Again, according to Eagleton, the process of ascendance and dominance may be accomplished through strategies that promote particular beliefs and values; *naturalize* and *universalize* such beliefs so as to render them *self-evident* and apparently inevitable; *denigrate* ideas which might challenge it; *exclude* forms of thought process; and *obscure* social reality (ibid., 15 [emphasis in original]). If one considers these strategies with respect to the socially dominant family form, one can readily make the argument that the family is a *quintessential* ideological form.

3. See also Shelley A. M. Gavigan, "Paradise Lost, Paradox Revisited: The Implications of Familial Ideology for Feminist, Lesbian, and Gay Engagement to Law," *Osgoode Hall Law Journal* 31 (1993): 589.

4. See, e.g., Ruthann Robson, *Lesbian (Out)Law: Survival Under the Rule of Law* (Ithaca, N.Y.: Firebrand Books, 1992), 136.

unable to isolate the lesbian parent from the dominant familial realm. I begin by arguing for the necessity of ideological analysis and then move on to a discussion of lesbian custody cases.

LESBIAN PARENTS: IS FAMILIAL IDEOLOGY STILL RELEVANT?

In North America, the meaning of the family until recently enjoyed an unchallenged self-evidence as well as a certain naturalized and universalized quality, thanks in part to the trumpeting of "old-fashioned" family values in the 1992 U.S. presidential campaign. It is important to remember that the celebration of "The Family" was not simply a plank in the campaigns of the official right. The Democratic party's own nominating convention managed to produce more homages to the family than theretofore one might have imagined possible: the Democratic party was family; the gay and lesbian members of the party were family within family; the metaphor extended to presumably the greatest family of all—the American people were family. In the Canadian context, we have seen self-professed profamily politicians from all parties driving stakes into the hearts and hopes of lesbian and gay citizens in a self-aggrandizing defense of the family front.

The terrain of the family is a site of struggle and challenge, a challenge that tests the universality of the family form, rejects its naturalized quality and the denigration of other forms of relationships, and blows the whistle on its claim to reflect social reality. For defenders of the traditional family, the stakes are high. One great fear, it seems, is that a mythical army of mighty homosexuals and antifamily hedonists has set its sights too close to home: gay men and lesbians now want in. They want families—chosen families, social families—they want children; they want the fact acknowledged that some already have children; and they want their relationships recognized and valued. This is understandably traumatic for the defenders of the familial status quo, who thought they had their hands full just holding back the antifamily tide. Imagine their horror: the enemy wants in.

However, the positions taken by both the defenders of the familial fortress and the righteous band hammering at the gates illustrate the tenacity, complexity, and, perhaps even more profoundly, the contradictory nature of familial ideology. This Siren we know as the family attracts and holds almost everyone who encounters it. I am inclined to the view that few of us escape the embrace of familial ideology. As

Wendy Clark once observed, "Apart from men, one thing which feminists love to hate is the family"; and yet they find it the most difficult to
leave.[5] And understandably so—because familial ideology is more than
just a pretty face. Its appeal also packs a punch, for there are tangible
material dimensions to the family. It is almost as impossible to opt out of
familial relationships and the familial forms of distribution of scarce
resources as it is to opt out of wage labor in a capitalist society.[6] It is
incumbent upon those of us in law to identify and analyze the ways in
which law is implicated in the construction, regulation, and reproduction of the dominant notion of family, while remaining alert to the extent
that law may not be the dominant site of these processes.[7] It is critical
that we analyze both the form of the legal regulation and the ideological
content that infuses that form. The utility of ideology as an analytic
device is that it helps us understand a concept's appeal and hold on our
captured hearts and constrained imaginations, and the fact that one's
sense of social reality finds resonance. As Terry Eagleton has argued:

> [S]uccessful ideologies must be more than imposed illusions, and
> for all their inconsistencies must communicate to their subjects a
> version of social reality which is real and recognizable enough not
> to be rejected out of hand. . . . Any ruling ideology which failed
> to mesh with its subjects' lived experience would be extremely
> vulnerable and its exponents would be well advised to trade it in
> for another. But none of this contradicts the fact that ideologies
> quite often contain important propositions which are absolutely
> false.[8]

This, then, is not a form of false consciousness; the success of an ideology is its resonance with some aspect of experience or aspiration.

---

5. Wendy Clark, "Home Thoughts from Not So Far Away: A Personal Look at Family," in
What Is to Be Done About the Family? ed. Lynne Segal (Harmondsworth, Middlesex: Penguin,
1983), 168.

6. Although, paradoxically, the family has been invoked and used to offer (or force upon)
some family members (notably wives and children) a one-way ticket out of wage labor. The
work of scholars (feminists, labor historians, social policy analysts, and economists) who have
studied the emergence of calls for the "family wage" in the trade union movement has illustrated its gendered and generational implications. See the discussion of this work in Gavigan,
"Paradise Lost," 598–600.

7. Postmodernist scholars influenced by the work of Michel Foucault characterize this as
decentering law. See Carol Smart, *Feminism and the Power of Law* (London: Routledge, 1990).
As Boyd has illustrated recently in "(Re)placing the State," the decentering project is completely compatible with socialist feminist analysis.

8. Eagleton, *Ideology,* 15.

As Douglas Hay has illustrated, successful ideologies have an elastic-
ity and cogency that allow the gaps and contradictions to be glossed
over.[9] We need to be able to explain, for instance, when and why the law
holds an appeal for people. For if we do not appreciate this important
dimension of ideology, we will not be able to explain why people—even
courageous oppressed and marginalized people—continue to turn to the
law, continue "to take their lives to court"[10] and to the legislature to
press for redress or change.

If (as I believe) ideology as an analytic concept requires us to look as
well to the hearts, minds, and hopes of the subordinate, can we be
confident that the hearts and minds of the mothers who lose custody of
their children to ex-husbands or of the aboriginal parents whose children are taken from home and community are "held" by the dominant
ideology of mother or family? Do these parents turn to the courts for
assistance and support? Do they, as condemned felons on eighteenth-
century public scaffolds were importuned to do, accept the rightness or
justness of the results? Or might they rather offer an instance of the elas-
ticity of familial ideology being stretched to its limits—an instance of
resistance?

We must be prepared to do more than analyze the judges and lawyers.
We need to look to the litigants, the positions they take, and why (if we
can discern this) they take them. And, as academics, we must be prepared to take a hard look at ourselves (as Eagleton has intimated, ideological thought, like halitosis, may be more readily detectable in
another[11]). We do not have the luxury of idle critique.[12] In other words, if
we are prepared to be rigorous in a decentering project, we will admit
that the courts have not been alone nor necessarily even principally
implicated in the denial of lesbian families. Surely, some of the lesbian
parenting cases discussed below suggest that a fundamental denial
occurs long before the lesbian parents/partners find themselves in court.

Here, then, is the paradox that reveals the contradictory nature of
family and familial ideology: A commitment to familial ideology, to the
dominant notion of family, may be found in the positions of those who

9. Douglas Hay, "Property, Authority, and the Criminal Law," in *Albion's Fatal Tree:
Crime and Society in Eighteenth-Century England* (New York: Pantheon, 1975), 15.

10. Brenda Cossman, "Family Inside/Out," *University of Toronto Law Journal* 44 (1994): 2.
See Didi Herman's account of the perspectives of the key litigants in the Andrews and Mossop
cases in her *Rights of Passage: Struggles for Lesbian and Gay Legal Equality* (Toronto: University of Toronto Press, 1994).

11. Eagleton, *Ideology*, 2.

12. 1 am forever indebted to Mary McIntosh's wisdom: "Feminism and Social Policy," *Critical Social Policy* 1 (1980): 32.

go to lengths (and to court) to deny that their relationships are familial as well as those who expressly embrace the family. What must be examined is who turns to the law, who invokes what, and to what end?

HEATHER AND HER MOMMIES MEET THE LAW

The circumstances of Heather's conception and birth give rise to a large set of questions, some of which again have been raised and examined in a preliminary way in a few cases and commentaries. At the very least, it is clear that it is increasingly difficult, if not problematic, to apply either common sense or traditional legal definitions of parent and child to new forms of parenting and child-rearing relationships and arrangements. What makes a person a parent? What makes a child one's child? Who is a father? Is the contribution of sperm to a pregnancy enough to qualify?

The legal contexts in which these questions have been touched upon to date vary. In the adoption context, some Canadian judges have offered a less than sympathetic assessment of the right of a male "casual fornicator" to be regarded as a parent whose consent to a child's adoption is required.[13] In a famous Canadian abortion injunction case, a man who attempted to prevent his former girlfriend from terminating her pregnancy was told by the Supreme Court of Canada that his was not a "father's rights case": his "seminal" contribution to pregnancy did not make him a father, only a *potential* father.[14] A small line of American cases is suggestive that a sperm donor may well be able to press a claim for access to any child born as a result of an alternative method of conception[15] (*quare* whether this may suggest that the casual ejaculator tends to enjoy a more protected legal position than the casual fornicator). If a man enters into a preconception agreement with a woman in which he agrees to cover her expenses during a pregnancy if she will be inseminated with his sperm, does that make him a father or a purchaser

---

13. *Re Attorney-General of Ontario and Nevins et al.* [19881 64 O.R. 311 (Div. Ct.).

14. *Daigle v. Tremblay* [198912 S.C.R. 530, 572. Recently the British Columbia Supreme Court has rejected a Vancouver man's bid for custody of a fetus prior to birth. He claimed to be the sperm donor, and, with the consent of the pregnant woman, he attempted to obtain a custody order in his favor in an apparent attempt to avoid the baby's apprehension by child welfare authorities at birth: *Re Fink* [19941 B.C.J. No. 485 (S.C.).

15. *Jhordan C v. Mary K. and Victoria T.*, 179 Cal. App. 3d 386 (1st Dist. 1986).

of the baby eventually born?[16] Does this woman cease to be a mother if she enters into such an agreement or contract?[17]

As Heather's story suggests, the legal definition of parent and mother is challenged even further by a child-rearing lesbian household. What makes a woman a mother? Is biological maternity enough? If a biological mother has not relinquished her child through adoption, is biological maternity a necessary precondition to motherhood or to parenthood? Does the Heather of our story (legally) have two mothers? Can such a Heather ever have two mothers? Could she have more than two mothers? If Jane gave birth to Heather, can Kate be her mother too, or is Kate simply a biological stranger?[18] Could Kate register Heather in day care or school, claim her as a dependent, authorize her medical care, or leave the country on a holiday with her? If Jane and Kate separate, would Kate be able to advance an argument for custody or access to Heather? Should she ever have to? Could they jointly apply for and obtain a court order for joint custody? Should they have to? Could Jane obtain a court order for child support? Should she have to? Could Kate adopt Heather without Jane having to relinquish her parental relationship? If Jane died, could Kate be confident that her relationship with Heather would not be altered or ended? Could Kate under a will specify conditions for Heather's custody in the event of her own death?[19]

The answers to the questions of what makes a man a father and what makes a woman a mother once seemed to be self-evident, just as the answer to the question of what is a family may have seemed self-evident. However, as with the allure of all appearances and the frailty of self-evidence, the image can be altered and may not withstand a body blow. Just as the formal definition of family is under siege, so too are the definitions of parent. And just as the formal definitions are being

16. Note that in Ontario the Child and Family Services Act, R.S.O. 1990, c. 11, s. 175, prohibits payment or reward of any kind in connection with adoption.

17. The American case, *In the Matter of Baby M*, 537 A. 2d 1227 (N.J. 1988), suggests that while the surrogate mother does not cease to be a mother, she is not able to usurp the sperm donor's claim as biological father to custody; they may have to share custody of the child born as a result of their arrangement.

18. In some of the American cases, the nonbiological lesbian parent is described as a "biological stranger." See Elizabeth A. Delaney, "Statutory Protection of the Other Mother: Legally Recognizing the Relationship Between the Nonbiological Lesbian Parent and Her Child," *Hastings Law Journal* 43 (1991): 196.

19. The ethnocentrism of these questions needs to be acknowledged. Social parenting, social mothering, and informal adoption practices are all found in the child-rearing practices of many peoples. In other cultures, these questions might well be nonissues. On the role of "other mothers," see Stanlie M. James, "Mothering: A Possible Black Feminist Link to Social Transformation?" in *Theorizing Black Feminisms: The Visionary Pragmatism of Black Women*, ed. Stanlie M. James and Abena P. A. Busia (London: Routledge, 1993), 44–54.

challenged, so too is the mother/father dyad content that has traditionally infused them.

I raise these questions not to offer conclusive answers or to illustrate
an infinite, if irritating, imaginative capacity. Indeed, some of these
questions and issues have been raised already by lesbian litigants,[20] their
lawyers,[21] academics,[22] and nonlitigating lesbian parents themselves.[23]
We may be able to observe in a preliminary way that a biological father
has an easier time establishing his claim to be a parent within the current legal framework than does a lesbian social parent.[24]

To date lesbian parents in dispute have revealed two lines of argument. In one line, the nonbiological parent, seeking to avoid the imposition of parental responsibility, contends that she was never a mother to
the child.[25] In the other line, the biological parent, seeking to win sole
custody, argues that the nonbiological parent was never a mother to the
child.[26] I am inclined to characterize these as the "I was just being a good

20. See, e.g., *Anderson v. Luoma* [1986150 R.F.L. (2d) 127]. The most discussed American
lesbian parent cases to date seem to be *In the Matter of Alison D. v. Virginia M.*, 77 N.Y.2d 651,
572 N.E. 2d 27 (Ct. App. 1991); *Curiale v. Reagan*, 222 Cal. App. 3d 1597, 272 Cal. Rptr. 520 (3d
Dist. 1990); and *Nancy S. v. Michele G.*, 228 Cal. App. 3d 831, 279 Cal. Rptr. 520 (1 st Dist.
1991).

21. Paula L. Ettelbrick, "Who Is a Parent? The Need to Develop a Lesbian Conscious Family
Law," *New York Law School Journal of Human Rights* 10 (1993): 513. Ettelbrick represented the
social lesbian parent, Alison D., in *Alison D. v. Virginia M.*

22. See, e.g., Delaney, "Statutory Protection of the Other Mother"; Nancy D. Polikoff, "This
Child Does Have Two Mothers: Redefining Parenthood to Meet the Needs of Children in Les-
bian-Mother and other Nontraditional Families," *Georgetown Law Journal* 78 (1990): 459;
Martha Minow, "ReDefining Families: Who's In, and Who's Out?" *University of Colorado Law
Review* 62 (1991): 511; and Robson, *Lesbian (Out)law*, 129–39.

23. Rachel Epstein, "Breaking with Tradition," *Healthsharing* 14 (1993): 18; Kate Hill,
"Mothers by Insemination: Interviews," in *Politics of the Heart: A Lesbian Parenting Anthology*, ed. Sandra Pollack and Jeanne Vaughan (Ithaca, N.Y.: Firebrand Books, 1987), 1–11.

24. See, e.g., *Jhordan C. v. Mary K. and Victoria T.* This case involved a judicial determination that a man who had donated sperm to a lesbian (couple) that resulted in the birth of a
little boy was a father and entitled to access. This case also illustrates that the finding of biological paternity was not simply one of male or heterosexual privilege, since Jhordan had also
been ordered to reimburse the county for the public assistance that had been paid for the child's
support and to make future support payments. Polikoff, "This Child Does Have Two Mothers,"
and Katherine Arnup, "We Are Family: Lesbian Mothers in Canada," in *Resources for Feminist
Research* 20 (1993): 101, have also made this observation. However, note that in the Jhordan
case, Victoria T., the social parent, was granted standing as a person with an interest in the
child.

25. This is the argument advanced successfully by Arlene Luoma in *Anderson v. Luoma*.
Note that the middle name of the first daughter born into this relationship was Luoma's first
name: Erin Arlene Anderson (see *Anderson*, 134). Thanks to Karen Andrews for drawing this to
my attention.

26. This is the argument advanced successfully by the lesbian biological mothers in *Alison
D. v. Virginia M.* and *Curiale v. Reagan*. But see A. C v. C B., 113 N.M. 581, 829 P. 2d 660 (N.M.

sport" (and hence not a parent) and the "she was just being a good sport"
(and hence not a parent) arguments, respectively. It is important to note
that they have been advanced by *lesbian* litigants. And happily for them,
but not for their former partners, the courts have been receptive to the
argument that the nonbiological lesbian parent is not a parent. I hope
that a close examination of these lesbian parent/lesbian custody cases,
and the issues raised therein, may assist in elucidating some of the problems raised in other lesbian and gay legal contexts. For instance, the
debates surrounding legal rights for same-sex couples and for lesbian
and gay families have centered upon the benefits and equality dimensions. An apparent polarization, noted by others writing in this field,[27]
has emerged around the question of family status. This division, or
polarization, is sometimes characterized as either assimilationist or anti-
assimilationist.[28] This language, however, implies that one position is a
form of false consciousness, one that involves a denial of lesbian or gay
life, and a desire to imitate or mimic the more conventional heterosexual relationship—to live "white"—while the other embodies a fervent
desire to resist this impulse.

The lesbian custody cases discussed here focus not on the issue of
whether to extend the definition of family, but rather on how to resolve
or address a situation that lesbians themselves have created through
their relationships. And here the language of assimilation versus anti-
assimilation seems inapt. It is my argument that the positions taken
by both the lesbian parents asserting parental claims and those resisting
the claims are informed and framed by the dominant ideological construction of the family. In other words, I hope to illustrate that the two

---

App.), cert. denied, 113 N.M. 449, 827 P. 2d 837 (1992), holding that the lesbian co-parent had
standing to claim visitation rights under an agreement she had entered with child's mother.

27. See, e.g., Didi Herman, "Are We Family? Lesbian Rights and Women's Liberation,"
Osgoode Hall Law Journal 28 (1990): 789; Cossman, "Family Inside/Out"; and Susan B. Boyd,
"Expanding the 'Family' in Family Law: Recent Ontario Proposals on Same-Sex Relationships," *Canadian Journal of Women and the Law* 7 (1994): 545. Karen Andrews, "Ancient
Affections: Gays, Lesbians, and Family Status," paper presented at the Sexual Orientation and
the Law Program, Law Society of Upper Canada, Continuing Legal Education, Toronto, June
1994, 31–32, challenges the Ontario Law Reform Commission's expressed concern that the lesbian and gay community is divided deeply, sharply, and significantly on the issue of family
status and same-sex spousal benefits.

28. Brenda Cossman and Bruce Ryder, "Gay, Lesbian, and Unmarried Heterosexual Couples
and the Family Law Act: Accommodating a Diversity of Family Forms," paper prepared for the
Ontario Law Reform Commission, June 1993, 137–39. Cossman and Ryder characterize the
positions of some who are critical or wary of family-based strategy (including myself) as "anti-
assimilationist." I am inclined to the view that this generalized characterization is overinclusive,
and I would characterize the range of positions reflected in the literature in different terms.

apparently countervailing positions are derived from the same ideological framework.

LESBIANS TAKE EACH OTHER TO FAMILY COURT

There is clearly no singular form of lesbian custody case. Custody litigation involving lesbians who leave straight relationships or who run afoul of parental expectations illustrate what others have noted elsewhere: lesbian and gay parents are at risk in the courtroom if they do not conform to dominant notions of appropriate lesbian or gay sexual behavior, which is preferably invisible and apolitical. And even that may not be enough. Cases in which straight former spouses use sexual orientation as a weapon tend to reveal much about the social and, in particular, the gendered nature of dominant notions of appropriate parenting. The ability of lesbians to be "good' mothers is always suspect, always subject to scrutiny, but while they may be assailed as bad mothers, they are still mothers. While they may be found to be poor or unfit (social) parents, they are still (biological and hence legal) parents.

Cases involving child custody, access, or support disputes *between* lesbians seem to reveal that, paradoxically, lesbian litigants may also be using sexual orientation as a weapon when they rely on biological and hence legal definitions of parent and take the position that children born into a lesbian relationship are not children of that relationship. In this section, I shall examine the admittedly few reported cases in which lesbian partners (or former partners) take each other to court, contesting not only each other but the very basis of their relationship to each other and to their children. Here the issue could be fitness to parent, but these lesbian cases suggest a more fundamental challenge: the ability to *be* a (legal) parent.

It has become axiomatic in the literature on lesbian parenting to refer to a "lesbian baby boom."[29] The combination of the availability and use of alternative methods of insemination has opened the possibility for lesbians to conceive and bear children independent of medical and patriarchal relations. And as adoption has also become increasingly available to single parents, individual lesbians have adopted children who are then raised in a de facto two- (lesbian) parent household. Hard

---

29. Arnup, "We Are Family"; Polikoff, "This Child Does Have Two Mothers"; and Ettelbrick, "What Is a Parent?"

data are elusive; no one knows for sure how many "new" child-rearing lesbian households exist.

It follows that the few custody cases involving lesbians may tell us very little about how lesbian parents deal with the matters of raising children when together and custody and access upon separation. It is more than possible that most do not litigate; it might be fanciful to think that those who settle the issue between themselves do so based on principles of fairness and generosity. Nor is it true that every lesbian custody case necessarily involves or has to involve a denial of a relationship. There are Canadian cases of lesbian grandmothers[30] and lesbian aunts[31] winning custody of children in their care.

I am interested in revisiting the lesbian parenting cases that to date have elicited the most discussion and most criticism. In the Canadian context, one early case stands out: *Anderson v. Luoma*.[32] This case involved litigation between a lesbian couple who had lived together for ten years. During their relationship, Anderson gave birth to two children, whose conception was made possible by alternative insemination. The older of the two children was given Luoma's first name as a second name. When the children were four and two years of age, respectively, the relationship unraveled; Luoma took up with another woman. Title to houses and property shared by the two women tended to be in the name of the substantively better-off Luoma. She resisted the claim that she was responsible for spousal or child support and (unsuccessfully[33]) took the position that the property in her name was hers alone. Yet at the same time, Luoma, the nonbiological parent, had shared the lives of the children; when asked, the oldest child said, "I don't have a father, I have an Arlene."[34]

At trial, the judge noted that Luoma downplayed "her involvement [with the children] almost to the point of being a disinterested bystander" who suggested that her former partner had been on a "frolic of

---

30. *Nicholson v. Storey & Nicholson*, 19821 B.C.D. 1551-05 (Prov. Ct.). In this case, the lesbian maternal grandmother was awarded custody of her two-and-a-half-year-old granddaughter, who had been in the grandmother's care for most of her life. The trial judge noted that while the grandmother's homosexual relationship was not a bar, "it must be said at the least that a homosexual relationship is a minus factor."

31. M. (D.) v. D. (M.) [1991] 94 Sask. R. 315 (Q.B.).

32. [1986] 50 R.F.L. (2d) 127 (B.C.S.C.).

33. The trial judge applied the principle of unjust enrichment to the facts of the case and imposed the remedy of constructive trust: Luoma was required to share the property she and Anderson had acquired and/or lived in together. In other words, Anderson succeeded in her claim to a significant interest in the property held in Luoma's name.

34. *Anderson v. Luoma*, 134.

her own when she had the children."[35] The trial judge took a different view; in his words, "whatever formula was used, I do not have the slightest doubt the children were given love, care and affection in abundance. My impression is that these four people in the two years following the births worked and played as a 'family-like' unit complete with its trials and tribulations, its joy and laughter and its strengths."[36] Despite the trial judge's conclusion that this lesbian household had lived as a "family-like unit," Luoma was able to invoke the very specific statutory definitions of spouse and parent in the relevant British Columbia legislation to avoid the imposition of any financial responsibility for child and spousal support.

While this case is sometimes characterized as an instance of the judicial denial of lesbian families,[37] it is my view that the denial first occurred out of the mouth of the nonbiological lesbian parent. She decided to invoke the legal definitions available to her, including the sex-specific definition of spouse and the patriarchal definition of child. It is important to note that a man in her situation, at the end of a ten-year relationship with a woman whose children may not have been his biological children, would not have had that argument open to him. Thus, Luoma enjoyed the benefits of a legal interpretation that would not have been extended to a common-law husband.

The legal significance of this case may be limited. In Ontario, the opposite sex requirement in the legislative definition of spouse has been declared unconstitutional in cases involving lesbian couple adoptions and spousal support.[38] The Children's Law Reform Act of 1990 provides that a person other than a parent may apply for an order respecting custody of or access to a child.[39] Similarly, the Family Law Act of 1990 defines *parent* to include a person "who has demonstrated a settled intention to treat a child as a child of his or her family."[40] While it is not likely that Arlene Luoma would have availed herself of the provisions of the Children's Law Reform Act had they been available to her, it is the case that a less "disinterested bystander" might well be able to do so. On the other hand, given the findings of fact made by the trial judge, had Luoma found herself dealt with under Ontario law, she likely would have been found to be a parent of the two girls.

35. Ibid., 135.
36. Ibid., 134.
37. Arnup, "We Are Family," 13.
38. See Re. K. (1995), 23 O.P. (3d) 679 (Ont. Ct. Prov. Div.): M. v. H. (1997), 25 R.F.L.(4th) 116 (Ont. C.A.).
39. R.S.O. 1990, c. C12, s. 21.
40. R.S.O. 1990, c. F.3.

The much discussed U.S. case, *Alison D. v. Virginia M.*,[41] illustrates essentially the same position, this time being taken by a biological lesbian parent against her former partner. In this case the biological mother relied upon the legal definition of parent in the relevant legislation to deny that her former partner had been a parent. The two women had lived together for two years when, in 1980, they decided together to have a child. The majority of the Court of Appeals for the State of New York accepted that the parties had planned for the conception and pregnancy together and had agreed to share jointly all rights and responsibilities of child rearing. When Virginia gave birth to a baby boy in 1981, he was given Alison's last name as his middle name, and for the next two years the women jointly cared for and made decisions about the child. When Virginia left the relationship late in 1983, she initially agreed to access by Alison. By 1986, however, she had begun to limit access, and in 1987, she terminated all contact between the child and Alison, notwithstanding, as the court noted, that a "close and loving relationship" between them had been nurtured. Although the majority of the court was not inimicable to Alison's argument that she was a de facto parent, the fact that she was a "biological stranger" was enough to satisfy them that the legal definition of parent in the governing New York statute did not contemplate her relationship with the child. What is striking about this case, and others like it,[42] is that no issue was raised by either party with respect to fitness. The definition of parent in the legislation allowed the biological mother to trump the other partner.

Again, it is likely that in Ontario the result would have been more favorable to the social parent; at least there the threshold issue of standing, provided in Section 21 of the Children's Law Reform Act, and the statutory extension of the definition of in loco parentis to the definition of parent would have given Alison, the social parent, a running start.

41. See Minow, "Re-defining Families"; Ettelbrick, "Who Is a Parent?"

42. See also *Curiale v. Reagan* and *Nancy S. v. Michele G. Curiale v. Reagan* involved two lesbians who had been in a five-year relationship into which a child had been born. When they separated, they initially had an agreement that provided for shared custody. A year later the biological mother informed her former partner that she was not willing to share custody or even allow access. In *Nancy S. v. Michele G.*, the women had lived together for sixteen years. Two children were born into their relationship; the children were given the nonbiological mother's family name as their last name, and she was listed as their father on their birth certificates. After Nancy and Michele separated, the elder child lived with Michele (the nonbiological mother), and the younger one stayed with Nancy. After several years of this arrangement, Michele would not accede to a request for a change in the arrangement. When mediation failed, Nancy successfully invoked her biological parenthood to obtain sole custody of both children.

None of this denies the very real risk that lesbians face in the court-room. My purpose is to illustrate that the litigation postures and strate-gies of two lesbians in these two important cases have been to deny the relationship and to invoke the dominant construction of family relations as heterosexual and the legal importance of biological parenting to do so.

CONCLUSION

Heather's story ends where many lesbian parenting stories begin: fired with hope and optimism. The cases discussed above remind us that Heather's story is just that, a story. The endings for children in lesbian legal cases are not so blissfully or naively sanguine. Some real-life sto-ries of lesbian households, however, suggest that the children themselves do not buckle or tremble at the prospect of a "daddyless" life. I know and love a little girl who lived and was loved in a two-parent lesbian house-hold. Her day-care friends coped with this better than did some of her parents' "cool" friends. The day-care kids would call at the end of the day, "Your mom is here," when her (biological) parent arrived, and when her other parent would pick her up at the end of the day, they would call, "Your mom is here, the other one." When she left the sweet comfort of the day care (where her teachers had supported her in her decision to make a Father's Day card for her cat) for the new experience of kinder-garten and a new day care, she made no fuss. And after she had been in kindergarten for a month, one of her parents attended a curriculum night. For the first time, she saw the family chart that had been filled in for each child, with the headings, *mere, pere, soeur,* and *frere.* Her little girl's entry was less exhaustive than those of the other children, she having neither siblings nor a father. Squeezed under the heading of mother, however, in her teacher's printed script, were the names of the two women who were her parents. She had said nothing of this to her parents; perhaps it was not a big deal at all for her. After years of matter-of-factly telling each new little friend that, no, she didn't have a daddy, she had two mommies, she had quietly made the leap into the school system. Once again, she had encountered the assumptions of familial ideology. In her quiet and self-assured six-year-old way, she had issued her own challenge to the assumptions of familial ideology, and she de-clined to be made to fit.

The lesbian parents who deny their children or who deny their former partners access to them have much to learn. In fact, we all do. We must be clear with each other in our relationships with one another and with our children. If we are having children together, making joint decisions, sharing de facto joint custody, we must say this while we are together and not deny it upon separation. We must also be mindful that the children will decide for themselves who their parents are. And they, unlike some of their parents, may have greater courage when confronted by the apparent appeal of familial ideology.

5

Family Relationships and Reproductive Technology

BRENDA ALMOND

According to Caesar, in ancient times Gaul was divided into three parts. It appears today that the same may be true of parenthood, which has suffered three tripartite divisions. The first is the triple division of fatherhood—biological, legal, and social; the second is the tripartite notion of motherhood as genetic, gestatory (or birthing), and commissioning; and the third is a triple notion of parenthood itself as biological parenthood, legal parenthood, and the holding of parental responsibility.

At the same time, it seems there may be a developing social consensus, led by utilitarian philosophers as well as by some feminist theorists, and encouraged by certain lawyers and health economists, that technology has brought us into a new age of relationships by choice, and that this is something to be unproblematically welcomed. The latter is, however, a remarkable assumption in view of the history of family bonds in the story of the human race. It may well seem equally remarkable to anyone who has had direct experience of parenting, and in particular of

The author wishes to thank Derek Morgan and Gillian Douglas, the editors of *Constituting Families: A Study in Governments* (Stuttgart: Franz Steiner Verlag, 1994), for permission to use Douglas's contribution to that volume, "Parenthood: Fact of Nature or Social Construct?" as the basis for this essay, which was originally published in *The Family in the Age of Biotechnology*, ed. C. Ulanowsky (Aldershot, Hampshire: Avebury, 1995).

giving birth, and who takes time to reflect on these experiences. These are purely contingent considerations, of course, but it must be conceded at the outset that philosophy alone is unable to provide a challenge to such claims, and that any challenge must involve at least some reference to the kind of facts that social anthropology and related disciplines can provide as well as, perhaps, to some introspective reflection on one's own experience as child, parent, spouse, or other kin.

It is clear, however, that very different assumptions have guided human thinking on these matters in the past. Some indication of this is to be found in literature, legend, and folklore. In particular, there are those stories and traditions that center on what might be called the Cinderella experience. In the familiar version, the not-biologically-related child is used and abused by stepparent and stepsiblings alike. Similar stories abound of wicked stepmothers—or fathers—as well as the more intangible but ubiquitous myth of the changeling. It is worth asking: What is the point of this myth? What *is* a changeling? The answer must be that it is someone who lives in an intimate situation with those who are, biologically speaking, strangers—or from the other point of view, a stranger who invades a situation of close intimacy. Without any knowledge of the science of genetics, those who framed these stories had in mind a scarcely tangible web of connections and expectations—a sense or expectation that the absence of the biological link would mean an absence of what might be called psychic similarity: shared attitudes, appraisals, interests, tendencies, common qualities of character, a common *Weltanschauung*— a characteristic way of looking at the world. Of course, we all know that none of these things can be assumed, even where relationships are indisputable, but total breakdown or absence of common sympathies is regarded as extraordinary and provides the stuff of tragedy and disillusion.

It is interesting to contrast the position I have described—that relationships are and should be a matter of choice—with that put forward by Hegel in *The Philosophy of Right*:

> In substance marriage is a unity, though only a unity of inwardness or disposition; in outward existence, however, the unity is sundered in two parties. It is only in the children that the unity itself exists externally, objectively, and explicitly as a unity, because the parents love the children as their love, as the embodiment of their own substance ... a process which runs away into the infinite series of generations, each producing the next and presupposing the one before.[1]

1. G.W.F. Hegel, *The Philosophy of Right*, trans. T. M. Knox (Oxford: Clarendon Press, 1952), 117.

The contrast between natural and artificial, biological and social, is starkly presented in these two different approaches. One explanation for the emphasis on the social is that some relationships are indeed socially generated—that is to say, relationships by marriage. But even at the level of popular culture, there is recognition of the existence of relationships that are not merely social alongside those that are, and the responses these evoke are commonly quite different in quality. One may compare, for example, popular attitudes to mothers with those to mothers-in-law. Many societies, then, including both primitive cultures and complex modern ones, distinguish socially created relationships from blood relationships, seeing the latter as special and immutable. This double-sidedness is well described by Marilyn Strathern, an anthropologist with a particular interest in kinship networks:

> Family life is held to be used on two separable but overlapping principles. On the one hand lies the social character of particular arrangements. Household composition, the extensiveness of kin networks, the conventions of marriage—these are socially variable. On the other lie the natural facts of life. Birth and procreation, the inheritance of genetic material, the development stages through which a child progresses—these are naturally immutable.[2]

One might add—although this is part of what is at issue here—that even the changes made possible by new technologies cannot negate the essential *naturalness* of conception, pregnancy, and childbirth, the relationships they create and those on which they depend. So why should some people think otherwise? Why deny what to many people will seem obvious—the deep importance of human kin connections?

A possible answer to this question is provided by the British legal theorist John Eekelaar, who argues that to a very large extent parenthood is a social and not a natural concept. "All attributions of parenthood are social," he writes, "so the choice is not between 'social engineering' and 'following nature,' but between different kinds of 'social engineering.'"[3] Eekelaar's views rest on a double foundation. The first is a particular view of the role of law; the second, a commonly held assumption about the role of society in relation to the duty of care of the young. It will be useful to consider these two aspects separately before going on to consider some of the more specific issues involved here.

---

2. M. Strathern, *Reproducing the Future: Anthropology, Kinship, and the New Reproductive Technologies* (Manchester: Manchester University Press, 1992), 17.

3. J. Eekelaar, "Parenthood, Social Engineering, and Rights," in *Constituting Families: A Study in Governments*, ed. E. Morgan and G. Douglas (Stuttgart: Franz Steiner Verlag, 1993), 81.

THE ROLE OF LAW

Eekelaar sees law as active, not a passive by-product of social change—as leading, not following, social convention. In this he follows the legal historian Roscoe Pound in rejecting the Hegelian thesis—later developed into a new and more general theory of law, ideology, and society by Karl Marx—that law is a reflection of social progress and development.[4] From the point of view of moral philosophy, this theory could be said to run parallel to the emotive theory of ethics, which in a similar way portrays *moral* language as dynamic rather than descriptive, as seeking to influence others rather than to inform them—as attempting to evoke action and alter attitudes. The term used by Pound to describe this dynamic or active function of law was "social engineering"—a term that, as Eekelaar points out, is often used pejoratively today, although Karl Popper, in *The Poverty of Historicism*, used it with favourable overtones.[5] Popper's sympathetic perception, however, was based on a conception of social engineering as small-scale and limited in scope, and he chose it in order to paint a contrast between the humdrum and unambitious goals of the engineer—a kind of social repairman—and the Utopian architectural blueprints of totalitarianism. I suspect Popper would see attempts to change the natural structure and basis of the family by means of a pincer attack from medicine and law as having more in common with the latter than the former.

Eekelaar supports his general perception that law does in fact lead rather than follow in these areas by appeal to the legal ruling that a husband is presumed to be the father of a child when it is born to a woman living in a marital relationship with him. (*Pater ist quem nuptiae demonstrant.*) He speculates as to the reasons for this, in part interpreting historical attitudes by appeal to recent developments—for example, new legislation concerning surrogacy and the recent refusal by a judge to allow DNA "finger-printing" for purposes of establishing paternity. (It should not be overlooked, however, that it has become a well-established procedure in cases involving immigration applications.) He concludes that these recent judgments, like the rules that have prevailed in the past, are to be understood as expressing the primacy of social over biological parenthood. Their implication, he says, is that parenthood is indeed socially engineered.

---

4. R. Pound, *Interpretations of Legal History* (Cambridge: Cambridge University Press, 1923), 151–52.

5. K. Popper, *The Poverty of Historicism*, 2d ed. (London: Routledge & Kegan Paul, 1961).

This is to overlook, however, an important, indeed crucial point as far as an appeal to past practice is concerned—that the capacity to establish parenthood reliably through DNA fingerprinting is an entirely *new* development that was quite simply not available to earlier generations. Previously unconceived-of possibilities now exist—for example, the remarkable capability of establishing the identities of bodies thought to be those of the Russian tsar and his family by comparing their DNA to that of known descendants of the family. Indeed, in view of such possibilities, it could well be argued that both the recent legislation in the United Kingdom (e.g., Secton 30 of the Human Fertilisaton and Embryology Act 1990) and the decision of the judge in the case cited are actually ill-conceived. Whatever view one takes of the new legislation, however, it would be foolish to overlook the fact that the older approach to confirming paternity would of necessity have been based on pragmatic rather than theoretic considerations. In earlier times conclusively establishing paternity would have been, in most circumstances, an impossible task—except, of course, in those cases that the law indeed recognized, where the husband was physically apart from his wife for the relevant period. For clearly, under normal circumstances, the only way for a woman to be sure of the fatherhood of her baby would have been to have intercourse with only one man during her menstrual cycle. The law—or any outsider—would be obliged to assume that she *might* have intercourse during this period with her husband, so there could be no *better* founded claim than his, even if there was evidence of a concurrent adulterous liaison. But to suggest that what must be legally presumed is the whole of the story would be to deny common sense, which even in the past was prepared to cast a glance, whether jaundiced or ribald, at striking physical resemblances of children to persons outside the family circle. A legal convenience does not, then, require one to interpret the facts in such a way as to see the case of human procreation as totally distinct from reproduction in livestock or plants—a rose is a rose, not the alien stock on which it is grafted.

So while it is no doubt right to say that law is not invariably to be seen as merely following or describing social convention, there are limits to its scope for creativity—for molding the relationships between people by fiat. Indeed, it is often the other way around. As Marilyn Strathern points out, the very notion of a parent in Western thought evokes the idea of a social relationship. Moreover, such a conception of kinship has implicit within it an expectation of a closeness of understanding and empathy, a "crisscrossing network of similarities" of character (to lift a metaphor of Wittgenstein's out of context), and an expectation of service and sacrifice that is, more often than not, actually forthcoming. It is these natural tendencies and inclinations, on the whole, that have provided the signposts that have supplied a direction for law to follow over its long evolution.

This places a considerable weight on kin relationships, but it is hardly surprising that humans should attach importance to these—particularly the parent-child relationship—when other species defend their young to the death and when, as has been claimed, even the organically simple tadpole is able to differentiate between siblings, half-siblings, and unrelated individuals. But evidence from the animal kingdom is not essential to this case. The Greeks, whose literature and philosophy have exercised so much influence over modern thought, saw blood relationships, particularly those between parents and child, brother and sister, as absolute and as morally exigent. It is interesting to note that the Oedipus story would lose its point, its sting, if *social* relations were regarded as primary—the whole point of that story is that social relationships were being impeccably played out among people whose biological relationship made this wholly inappropriate. To kill a father—even one you have never met before—was an inexpiable crime, as it was to violate a mother, even one who had never known or nursed her child.

Eekelaar, however, in a kind of modern updating of these Oedipal possibilities, conceives of a case in which biological, legal, and responsible (or caring) fatherhood are separated. He is concerned about a case, *re O,* in which biological fatherhood was preferred over parenthood.[6] In his own hypothetical case, the biological father, A, is an anonymous sperm donor playing no further role; the legal father, B, is the man with whom the mother was living at the time of birth but from whom she has separated; and the responsible father, C, is the mother's new husband, who has been granted parental responsibility. For Eekelaar, the significant person in this situation is C. Parental right and responsibilities should go to him, for "[p]arental responsibility should always be associated with exercise of social parenthood."[7] He argues, therefore, that the United Kingdom's Children Act (1989) is wrong in its underlying presumption that biological parents have responsibility for their children and in its attempt to attach social and legal responsibility to biological parenthood.

Eekelaar's view, in contrast, amounts to an assertion that biological parenthood is in itself negligible. But if this is what is being claimed, it has wide implications. To begin with, it involves endorsing a common but simplistic view of artificial insemination by a donor as a simple

6. 1 FLR 77.
7. Eekelaar, "Parenthood, Social Engineering, and Rights."

medical procedure. And secondly, it involves seeing as unproblematic developments in *in vitro* fertilization that have led to the detachment of motherhood, too, from its biological meaning. Initially, the transfer of an egg from a willing donor to a woman desperately wanting to bear and raise a child may seem to raise few ethical difficulties, but techno-logical possibilities do not stay tidily within the bounds of this relatively uncontroversial scenario. Instead, they open up a "slippery slope" of devastating potential. Examples are not hard to find: the possibility of harvesting viable eggs from a fetus means that an aborted fetus could now be a genetic mother; eggs taken from women in their twenties have been successfully implanted and brought to term by women in their late fifties; and developments in intensive care have made possible the ges-tation and delivery of a baby to a dead woman whose womb and repro-ductive system have been kept artificially functioning. To regard any of these developments as of purely medical significance would be a mis-take. Their social implications are dramatic, and their possible psycho-logical and emotional effects as yet unknown. At a minimum, one might say that to be born under some of these circumstances would indeed be to be an orphan in a sense previously unknown to human beings. It would be to be born already an exile from the kinship network.

These considerations suggest, then, that one should pause and look very carefully at what might be called the "hard-headed" assumption that gametes are detachable, that genetic relations are negligible. Ini-tially, this is to rely on an intuitive response, a sense of ethical affront—perhaps, even, as Mary Warnock described it, a feeling of "outrage."[8] This reference to feeling is best understood in relation to her earlier defense of the role of moral sentiment in an article called "The artificial family."[9] But it is not hard to find practical arguments to lend weight to these reactions. To begin with, the consent of the donors, particularly of the young women who donated their eggs, may well have been secured on quite different tacit assumptions about the destiny of those eggs. In view of the breadth of possibilities, therefore, there is a case for inter-preting "informed consent" quite strictly in this area.

But secondly, the "hard-headed" approach may be based on some unrecognized factual assumptions about the quality of care that can be relied on where purely social connections are involved. Indeed, I would suggest that there is a need for a new judgment of Solomon here. In the biblical tale, Solomon recognized that the true—that is, the biological—

8. M. Warnock, "Do Human Cells Have Rights?" *Bioethics* 1 (1987): 1–14.
9. In *Moral Dilemmas and Modern Medicine*, ed. M. Lockwood (Oxford: Oxford Univer-sity Press, 1985).

mother would prefer even to sacrifice her own rights and her relationship with the child if that were necessary to preserve the child's life, and that it was *for this very reason* that her rights and relationship should be preserved. I would suggest that things are not intrinsically different today if one considers, for example, recent abuse cases connected with children's homes to which children have been taken, often on the grounds that this is necessary to protect them from possible abuse by their natural parents. Who can be trusted with children? Clearly parents cannot always be, and children must sometimes be removed from their care, but it is far from self-evident that other caregivers are less fallible.

THE ROLE OF SOCIETY: THE DUTY TO CARE

But for Eekelaar, the problem is compounded by the fact that he does not attribute to the parent even a direct duty to care. Instead, he sees the responsibility for looking after children as falling on the state or on society in general. Everyone, he says, has a general obligation to "promote human flourishing" and a specific obligation derived from that to care for the newborn. He concedes, however, that society may best fulfill this obligation by imposing a duty of care on biological parents. Thus, a natural duty is neatly inverted in Eekelaar's argument to become a derivative, social, or indeed legal duty, rather than a primary, ethical one. The immediate consequence of this is that society might well fulfill its duties in a number of different ways, any of which would be equally morally acceptable. These would include various kinds of social parenting.

For comment on this, we must once again turn to social anthropology. Eekelaar seems to be overly influenced by the fact that different societies may deal with the problem of child care in different ways. For example, Eekelaar would probably find useful support in the fact that in some tribes a woman's brother is responsible for a child, not its natural father. Nevertheless, while variation in social arrangements is possible, and while there have even, of course, been societies ignorant of the connection between sexual intercourse and childbearing, the idea of a blood tie has on the whole been the idea of something immutable and non-negotiable. As I have commented elsewhere, "A person's 'sisters, cousins, and aunts'—narrow-minded uncles, bad-tempered brothers, or handicapped son or daughter—are part of the baggage of life."[10]

10. B. Almond, "Human Bonds," *Journal of Applied Philosophy* 5 (1988): 3–16.

Nor is it only the parent-child relationship that is involved. For where there are "real" (i.e., blood) relationships, these have wider implications—something that Eekelaar's discussion, which remains narrowly focused on parents and children, completely ignores. These connections are not isolated facts, and their social relevance spreads out in a widening circle. Strathern writes: "In many cultures of the world, a child is thought to embody the relationship between its parents and the relationships its parents have with other kin." She adds, "Until now, it has been part of most of the indigenous cultural repertoires in Europe to see the domain of kinship, and what is called its biological base in procreation, as an area of relationships that provided a given baseline to human existence" and "It is an extraordinarily impoverished view of culture to imagine that how we conceive of parents and children only affects parents and children."[11]

This was so widely taken for granted until recently that it came as a surprising discovery to our legislators a few years ago that grandparents had no status in British law. And yet, with the ubiquitous breakdown of marriages and *de facto* partnerships, it is to be expected that contingent relationships could assume greater rather than lesser importance.

It is worth noticing too that social work practice and local authority provision in the past—together with "community care" today—work on quite the opposite assumptions from those implied by the "social construction" view. While certain philosophers promote the view that advanced reproductive medical techniques are to be welcomed as expanding *choice*—making it possible for any kind of relationship to be created or abandoned at will—social workers are routinely required to seek "real" relatives and attempt to convince them of their moral and social obligation to change the whole pattern of their lives to accommodate sick, senile, or disabled kin. And of course descent and lineage continue to be regarded as of crucial legal importance as long as inheritance is considered a just way of passing on wealth.

Eekelaar, in contrast, seems to see the primary family relationship as confined within the duality of parent and child. He does, however, recognize that certain moral and legal concepts have a part to play in this relationship. While rejecting any conception of rights as independent entities and describing them as "intellectual constructs," he nevertheless recognizes a complex of rights and reciprocal obligations involved in the parent-child relationship. In particular, he argues that children have rights, in the sense of what they "when fully informed and mature,

---

11. Strathern, *Reproducing the Future,* 31–34 passim.

would be likely to have chosen."[12] He distinguishes recognition of these rights from welfarism, which he defines as basing arrangements on some external judgment as to what is in the child's best interest.

I will not discuss this account of rights in detail since the central issues here do not depend on agreement about their analysis. Most would agree, however, that morality cannot be based entirely on rights without appeal to other moral concepts. It is true, too, that it is not necessary to invoke children's rights in order to talk about parental duties. And thirdly, Eekelaar is undoubtedly correct to point out that the attribution of a right is not to be confused with another person's judgment of where someone's interests lie. One can undoubtedly have a right to what is *not* in one's interest, and not a benefit—it is not for the football pools promoter, for example, to judge whether a prize-winner's life is likely to be ruined by his sudden access of wealth before deciding whether to award the prize. Nor is the question of what *is* in fact a benefit the same as the question of whether it is what someone *wants*. But of course it is true that one will only claim what one, at least in some sense, wants (though some people are perverse enough to claim or want something *only* because they conceive of it as their right and not because they have some independent reason for it).

Applying this to the case of a child in relation to a parent, these considerations would imply even more strongly that there is a residual notion of a right not covered by the child's best interest, benefit, or even choice. If this is so, then it would be wrong to base judicial decisions concerning a child's care simply on the child's best interest as judged by a third party. To do this, in any case, is to ignore the question of *parental* rights. Rather than being, as many believe, qualified and provisional, these are important and substantial rights, grounded in parents' duty to care for their children. This conception of parental rights can be derived from the Kantian principle that "ought" implies "can." In other words, society would be inconsistent to declare that there is a parental duty to care without conceding a parental right to do so. If this is conceded, it follows that parents have a direct moral obligation to care for their children. If society does not permit them to care for their children, it prevents them from fulfilling that duty and thus violates their rights.

Other arguments too may be advanced for the priority of parental rights. Not without weight is the quasi-biological argument derived from Hobbes that there is at least some attenuated concept of ownership of children that is analogous to people's ownership of their own bodies.

---

12. Eekelaar, "Parenthood, Social Engineering, and Rights."

Recognition of this claim can only be intuitive, for it can hardly be grounded on any extraneous considerations. Nevertheless, the biological argument need not stand alone. For it may be ranged alongside an argument of a political nature relating to the conditions necessary for cultural and religious freedom. Conceding parental rights, it can be argued, is the best and most effective way to limit the power of the state over the individual. Totalitarian projects, both philosophical and actual, have tended to encroach upon and limit parental control and family influence; and even under liberal regimes, where benign motives may be presumed, there is a continuing danger of the state usurping private prerogatives.

Ferdinand Schoeman has added a moral argument to this essentially political one: that the right of parents to exercise power over their children is based on their own justifiable moral claim to a certain kind of intimate relationship. He writes: "Why should the family be given extensive responsibilities for the development of children? Why should the biological parent be thought entitled to be in charge of a family? I believe that the notion of intimacy supplies the basis for these presumptions."[13] Schoeman's argument, then, is that close human relationships require as their setting privacy and autonomy, and that a parent's right to this type of private relationship overrides even some limited cost to the child.

It has to be admitted, however, that some situations make a choice unavoidable. In these situations, in which there is a conflict between adults' and children's wishes, there is growing willingness to involve older children themselves in the decision. Eekelaar suggests that the question of who *initiates* social care may be settled differently from decisions about later arrangements, when he proposes that the child's own wishes should play a part.

There are, however, difficulties with both halves of this strategy. First, where an early choice by others is concerned, what of the wish a child might retrospectively have for its own (genetic) mother or father? The "constructivist" view seems to involve permitting early decisions that would in effect deprive the child of this, that may indeed later come to be seen by the child as the only and important option. As for the idea of allowing a child later in life the possibility of choosing a new social family—something that has recently happened in the United States—it is unlikely that this could provide a stable base that lasts for life,

13. F. Schoeman, "Rights of Children, Rights of Parents, and the Moral Basis of the Family," *Ethics* 91 (1980): 14.

generating responsibilities as well as benefits. What, one wonders, might become of the traditional network of expectations of kin support later in life, particularly where there are adverse changes in circumstances? Would the "chooser" child, when adult, accept a member of his or her "socially chosen" family for expensive or self-sacrificing care? Would the socially chosen family, conversely, accept a child "chooser" back to their care if adult life brings that child disability or hardship?

The inclination to answer "no" to these questions is based on a perfectly sound and rational conception of the notion of choice. A "chooser" on the whole, wants only what is pleasant and rewarding—that is the whole point of choice. But life, on the other hand, is a mosaic of darker and lighter patterns. And "chooser" children are unlikely to volunteer for what is not personally satisfying. Indeed, there is a chance that such children would be unwilling to care for their elders even through social and community measures, whether taxes or charitable contributions. Nor is the loss entirely on one side. For children, too, there is the loss involved in losing the possibility of a relationship for whom their whole "narrative" is familiar—those irreplaceable persons who have known them "all their lives," in the familiar phrase.

But these are perhaps highly abstract reflections, and it might be difficult to see what they might imply in practice. In conclusion, then, it will be useful to return to some of these practical recommendations.

THE RIGHT TO BE INFORMED OF BIOLOGICAL PARENTHOOD

In Sweden a child born by AID has a right (at eighteen) to know the identity of the semen donor, but the latter has no rights of legal paternity. In Britain officially recognized agencies accepting sperm from donors must record their identities, but as things currently stand, this is to be kept confidential even from the child. In contrast, practices in France in this matter are very different. Donation is strictly limited to two or three occasions; donors are married men with children, and their offer to be sperm donors is discussed carefully with both the men and their families.[14]

If the considerations that have been advanced in this chapter have any weight, then it would seem that such donors should recognize that

14. S. Noveas, *Les Passeurs de gametes* (Nancy, Meurthe-et-Moselle: Presses Universitaires, 1994).

they are indeed fathering *children*, and that children should be guaranteed access to information about them. This said, it has to be recognized, of course, that the procedures involved are simple and in the end impossible to regularize or police. People might, however, be less willing to assist with "irregular" donation if they were aware that this might have legal implications.

The issue of fatherhood, however, may seem straightforward when compared with the new complexities involved in the notion of motherhood. Sections 27 and 28 of the 1990 British Act referred to earlier define a mother as the "carrier" of a child, whether or not that child is genetically hers. However, under Section 30, a woman who carries (gestates) a child but hands it over to a couple as a result of a surrogacy agreement ceases to be the legal mother, just as in the case of adoption. This ambiguity is hard to resolve practically. As far as intuitive judgment between the claims of a genetic and a gestatory mother are concerned, there is much force in Raimond Gaita's view that it is inconceivable that a child conceived *in vitro* would have the same interest in seeking out his natural parent as one conceived in the ordinary way.[15] I think, however, that the genetic connection might continue to exert some fascination, or at least curiosity, were someone aware of an origin of this sort. This unavoidable conflict, however, should alert us to the unprecedented severing of links that may be a consequence of such procedures. The least that is required here of the law is that it should not lend its weight to the suppression of information about biological parenthood, and in particular that it should ensure that, as far as possible, records are maintained and are accessible to those desiring information—possibly without direct identification—of their origins.

WHOSE RESPONSIBILITY IS IT TO CARE FOR CHILDREN?

In general, most people would probably agree that parental responsibility should be associated with the exercise of social parenthood. This means that it should, in many cases, be extended to long-term cohabitees and stepparents. But there may be tension here between the early claims of the mother and the long-term claims of the father. Indeed, there are some grounds for saying that modern European and North American societies are moving toward matriarchy as a result of insensitive

15. R. Gaita, "Parental Rights and Responsibilities," *Quadrant* (September 1991): 42.

taxation policies that make little or no allowance for family responsibilities and of social provisions that are unintentionally destructive of family life—for the more provision is made for single parents, the less need there is for partnership between the sexes. A single mother in a recent interview remarked, "If it weren't for the help I get from my mother and grandmother, I don't know what I'd do"—a remark that was revealing in that it pointed to a demographic shift in the source of reliable support. It uncovers a situation that research might well show to be far more common than is generally acknowledged, and the social consequences of which are wider than the immediate family unit.

CONCLUSIONS

Variations in the traditional family are not unique to modern times. In particular, stepparents and stepsiblings are no new phenomenon, although the reasons for their existence have changed. In the past, women's high mortality rate, particularly in relation to childbirth, was the cause of remarriages and new relationships; whereas today the cause is more commonly a matter of the breakdown of relationships, divorce, and remarriage. It is worth noticing in relation to this observation that for children, parental mortality would almost certainly have been a more acceptable reason for their own step-child status than adults' choices, since these can be seen as a betrayal. It is not surprising, then, if in some cases today's restructured families generate hostility. This hostility may well be responsible for a variety of social ills, including homelessness among teenagers who have run away from unacceptable or intolerable domestic circumstances, and abuse, particularly sexual abuse by an unrelated adult living in close domestic proximity to a sexually pubescent child.

In *Fertility and the Family*, Jonathan Glover recommends "letting the future shape of the family evolve experimentally"—taking "control of our own reproductive processes."[16] But this, I would suggest, is a dangerous doctrine. Family bonds are the cement of social existence and are not subject to construction and destruction by something as fragile and volatile as individual choice.

The process of fractionalization, then, that has led to the threefold division of parenthood is dangerous, and the conclusion to be drawn

16. J. Glover et al., *Fertility and the Family* (London: Fourth Estate, 1989): 183.

from this is, I believe, that no steps in the area of reproductive medicine should be endorsed by legal change or social acceptance until some body of limited experience has been built up as a guide to the overall social implications. In these matters, in other words, it is foolish to rush in where even angels are justified in displaying a cautious conservatism.

6

Privacy and Equal Protection as Bases for Abortion Law

Citizenship, Gender, and the Constitution

ANITA L. ALLEN

This essay links constitutional abortion rights, ideals of citizenship, and ideals of gender equality. It begins with a pair of endorsements and then proceeds to assess three popular arguments that scholars offer in support of the view that a proposed doctrine of equal protection is superior to the Supreme Court's doctrine of privacy or privacy-related liberty as the constitutional basis of abortion rights.

I endorse a claim that many influential lawyers and judges regard as a fraud: the claim that abortion rights are a precondition of full or "first-class" citizenship for women. Having previously defended the Supreme Court's doctrine that privacy rights against abortion bans flow from the Fourteenth Amendment guarantee of liberty,[1] in this essay I embrace a proposed equal protection doctrine as well.

This essay includes remarks I made on 5 March 1994, at the Federalist Society Symposium at the University of Virginia, where I participated on a panel entitled "The Constitution on Sex." It also includes my lecture at a Brown University Conference, "Equal Protection and Its Critics: The Law and Politics of First-Class Citizenship," held on 11 March 1994. An earlier and longer version of this essay was published under the title "The Proposed Equal Protection Fix for Abortion Law: Reflections on Citizenship, Gender, and the Constitution" in the *Harvard Journal of Law and Public Policy* 18, no. 2 (1994). I am indebted to Norma Schrock and Elizabeth Allen for legal research and to Professor Nancy Rosenblum for critical commentary.

A constitutional jurisprudence of abortion that expressly draws on the Fourteenth Amendment's language of "liberty" and "equal protection" would meld with many of the root concerns behind privacy arguments. In one respect privacy and equal protection concerns are quite distinct. The equal protection case for abortion presupposes gender differences and would therefore evaporate if everyone were of the same gender and a potential childbearer. By contrast, the privacy case for abortion does not necessarily evaporate in the absence of gender differences. Limited government, along with opportunities for personal expression, self-development, intimacy, and repose would be important even in a hypothetical world in which all citizens were of the same gender and could bear children.

My perspective in endorsing the equal protection argument for abortion rights is "additive."[2] It implies that the equal protection argument should be *added* to the list of plausible constitutional arguments for abortion rights. A competing perspective supporting the Equal Protection Clause argument for abortion might be dubbed "fixative." This perspective maintains that the Fourteenth Amendment's privacy-related liberty argument is seriously flawed[3] and perhaps even antagonistic to ideals of sex equality and full citizenship for women.[4] The fixative perspective contends that an Equal Protection Clause argument could salvage the constitutional case for reproductive rights; privacy jurisprudence should yield to a conceptually, jurisprudentially, and politically superior equal protection alternative.

An Equal Protection Clause "fix" is tempting in light of the actual and perceived limitations of the abortion privacy doctrine. However, I will

---

1. See Anita L. Allen, *Uneasy Access: Privacy for Women in a Free Society* (Totowa, N.J.: Rowman & Littlefield, 1988). Also see my articles, "Taking Liberties: Privacy, Private Choice, and Social Contract Theory," *University of Cincinnati Law Review* 56 (1987): 461; "Tribe's Judicious Feminism," *Stanford Law Review* 44 (1991): 179; and "Autonomy's Magic Wand," *Boston University Law Review* 72 (1992): 683.

2. Professor Nancy Rosenblum suggested the term *additive* to characterize my position on the relationship of privacy and equality arguments. She suggested another apt characterization of my perspective: *co-dependency*. Privacy and equal protection are mutually dependent, in my view, inasmuch as privacy rights can promote equality, and equal protection can promote privacy and privacy-related liberties.

3. See Cass Sunstein, "Neutrality in Constitutional Law (With Special Reference to Pornography, Abortion, and Surrogacy)," *Columbia Law Review* 92, no. 1 (1992): 29–44; and Ruth Colker, "Abortion and Dialogue: Pro-Choice and Pro-Life in American Law," *Tulane Law Review* 63 (1989): 1363.

4. See Catharine A. MacKinnon, "Reflections on Sex Equality Under the Law," *Yale Law Journal* 100 (1991): 1281, 1311.

argue that some of the most popular arguments employed to sustain claims of superiority for the Equal Protection Clause argument for abortion rights do not withstand close analysis. One specific goal for this essay is to deflate some arguments commonly used by feminists and other theorists to support the thesis that equal protection is superior to privacy as a constitutional framework for abortion law. I believe abortion rights are a precondition of full citizenship for women, and I disagree with those who believe privacy-based abortion jurisprudence is more of an impediment than an aid. Even if it were true that privacy jurisprudence has delayed women's journey toward first-class citizenship,[5] it is unclear that an equal protection doctrine would have served as a surer ticket.

WOMEN AND SECOND-CLASS CITIZENSHIP

A general principle of formal equality—a principle that just institutions treat like cases alike—is arguably the core meaning of the Equal Protection Clause of the Fourteenth Amendment.[6] Blacks and whites should be treated alike because they share a common humanity; similarly, men and women should be treated alike because they too share a common humanity. Of course, neither the races nor the sexes are alike in every regard. Respect for the principle of formal equality presumably permits disparate treatment of men and women to the extent of relevant gender-specific biological differences.

For several decades abortion policy has been a focus of legal debates over regulating human reproduction. The right to privacy dominates discussions of constitutional abortion law, but connections between abortion rights and ideals of sex equality have not gone unnoticed. Though shared to an extent by men, the burdens of sexuality, pregnancy, and child rearing are overwhelmingly women's burdens. Laws restricting access to abortion make it more difficult for women to avoid these burdens. Women's legally enforced disadvantages suggest "second-class"

5. James E. Fleming, "Constructing the Substantive Constitution," *Texas Law Review* 72 (1993): 211, 277, where he suggests that Cass Sunstein's and Catharine MacKinnon's preference for an equal protection argument may be based on the idea that constitutional privacy is actually a hindrance to, rather than a precondition of, equal citizenship.

6. I disagree with views that argue that although appeals to equality are supplanting appeals to rights, equality is a purely formal, superfluous concept that should be banished from moral and legal discourse as an explanatory norm. For an example, see Peter Westen, "The Empty Idea of Equality," *Harvard Law Review* 95 (1982): 537, 542.

citizenship and unequal protection of law. Accordingly, permissive abortion laws would seem to be required by the Equal Protection Clause.

But what does it mean to be a full, first-class citizen? According to Judith Shklar, American citizenship entails "the equality of political rights" and "the dignity of work and of personal achievement."[7] Linda Hirshman embraces a similar view, extolling "a citizenship of politics and work."[8] Groups consigned to subordinate social and economic roles by virtue of race, sex, or another "immutable characteristic"[9] fall short of the ideal of citizenship Shklar and Hirshman describe. Women with unwanted children to care for, with low incomes, and with undignifying work prospects are unlikely to vote, to assume elected office, or to boast extraordinary levels of personal achievement.

By comparison, men in the United States enjoy an enhanced level of citizenship—first-class citizenship. In addition to the slate of political rights they now formally share with women, men also have social and economic power. Most relevantly, they have the ability to enjoy sex, family life, school, and careers free of certain basic, direct concerns about unwanted pregnancy and child care. Kenneth Karst partly attributes men's superior political and economic standing to differing social roles tied to their inability to bear children.[10] Many individual women arguably have achieved first-class citizenship despite childbearing capacities. But the situation for women as a group is different. Despite significant legal gains, women as a group do not yet have the control over their lives that men as a group do, especially affluent white men. For the ordinary woman to be a first-class citizen, she must, as Karst argues, gain control over her sexuality and maternity, control that includes abortion rights as an important component.

The claim that women need abortion rights as a condition of first-class citizenship is usually understood in a certain way, namely as the claim that abortion rights are necessary, but not sufficient, conditions for gender equality. The responsibilities of unwanted pregnancy and child care can relegate women to second-class citizen status when compared to men; but women who do not face unwanted pregnancy due to

7. Judith N. Shklar, *American Citizenship: The Quest for Inclusion* (Cambridge: Harvard University Press, 1991), 1.

8. See Linda R. Hirshman, "Nobody in Here but Us Chickens: Legal Education and the Virtues of the Ruler," *Stanford Law Review* 45 (1993): 1905, 1936.

9. *Frontiero v. Richardson*, 411 U.S. 677, 686–87 (1973) describes immutable characteristics as "determined solely by the accident of birth" and as an inappropriate basis for assessing "ability to perform or contribute to society."

10. Kenneth L. Karst, "The Supreme Court, 1976 Term—Forward: Equal Citizenship Under the Fourteenth Amendment," *Harvard Law Review* 91, no. 1 (1977): 53–59.

sterility, infertility, or menopause are not, ipso facto, first-class citizens. First, many women who do not care for their own children assume responsibility for the children of their daughters, sisters, or others. Second, unwanted pregnancy and child care are just two of the things that make women second-class citizens. All women have certain social and economic disadvantages. All women are "kept down" by cultural stereotypes and reproductive policies that dictate domestic, maternal roles while tracking young working women into low-paying jobs.

I am sympathetic to positions such as those of Reva Siegel that argue that abortion policy implicates both women's privacy and equality. Astutely noting that "antiabortion laws . . . like antimiscegenation laws, have moorings in both privacy and equal protection," Siegel concludes that restrictions on abortion offend constitutional guarantees of equal protection because they inflict status-based injuries on women, such as compromising their opportunities for education and employment, and because of the status-based attitudes about women that they reflect.[11]

I claim a link between first-class citizenship and abortion rights in earnest. But skeptics view such claims as hyperbole. Skeptics concede that homeless women or prostitutes in lonely jail cells may be second-class citizens, but they doubt that, in one of the richest nations on earth, women who have led lives surrounded by loving families are second-class anythings. Despite exposure to poignant accounts of women's lives, committed skeptics continue to doubt that women without liberal abortion rights are less than first-class citizens. Surely, conservatives on the abortion issue say, whether or not a person is politically free and equal does not depend on access to a medical procedure designed to end pregnancy. The implication is that it would trivialize the democratic constitutional vision to include abortion rights as essential citizenship guarantees; that the linkage claimed between first-class citizenship and abortion rights is wrong and fraudulent—just so much glib polemics, inflated rhetoric. For the conservative, the reality is that abstinence and birth control—or when they fail, adoption and moderate sacrifice—can assure that women's lives are a good as any man's.

The debate in the Supreme Court over whether access to abortion should be deemed a fundamental right can be usefully recast as a debate about whether women's citizenship status is diminished by unwanted pregnancy. Byron White's dissent in *Thornburgh v. American College of*

11. See Reva Siegel, "Reasoning from the Body: A Historical Perspective on Abortion Regulation and Questions of Equal Protection," *Stanford Law Review* 44 (1992): 261, 263, 265, 377–79.

Obstetricians and Gynecologists,[12] condemned Harry Blackmun's characterization of abortion rights as "fundamental." Applying historical and political criteria called for by the Constitution, White argued that abortion rights are neither "deeply rooted in the nation's history and tradition" nor implicit in the concept of "ordered liberty."

If constitutional liberty does not include reproductive control, then a national citizenship of persons free to engage in political participation and work continues to mean something disturbingly different for male than for female citizens. Women would be assured an inferior status since abstinence, birth control, adoption, and sacrifice are not realistic options for all women. The United States is only one of many nations whose political leaders, lawyers, and jurists fail to see the link between abortion rights and citizenship. It appears that the leaders of most Western liberal democracies view the matter as American abortion conservatives do: liberal abortion rights are not essential to equal citizenship and liberty for women. Few countries in the world have enacted abortion laws that give women the control and economic subsidy they would need to determine their reproductive capacities.

Germany, which is still undergoing a complex process of nation rebuilding, amply illustrates that Western liberal leaders do not view reproductive options as a core requirement of citizenship or "ordered" liberty. The hope of a better life for male and female citizens of East and West Germany rose from the dust of the felled Berlin Wall. German reunification required a reconciliation of the liberal abortion policies of the East with the more restrictive policies of the West.[13] In function but not rhetoric, the model of privacy governed the East and the model of permission governed the West. Reunification made abortion law as controversial in Germany as it has been in the United States.

A compromise East/West German abortion statute was enacted into law on June 27, 1992.[14] This compromise law, which moved the enlarged nation of Germany toward the model of privacy, was not liberal enough for many former East Germans. The law removed criminal penalties for

12. *Thornburgh v. American College of Obstetricians and Gynecologists,* 476 U.S. 747, 785 (1986). Blackmun authored the opinion of the Court, in which Brennan, Marshall, Powell, and Stevens joined. Stevens also wrote a concurring opinion. Burger filed a dissenting opinion, White wrote a dissenting opinion joined by Rehnquist, and O'Connor filed a dissent in which Rehnquist joined.

13. See "Key Dates in History of Germany Abortion Law," *Reuters,* 28 May 1993; and Stephen Kinzer, "German Court Restricts Abortion, Angering Feminists and the East," *New York Times,* 29 May 1993, A1.

14. Ferdinand Protzman, "Broader Abortion Law Leaves Germans Somber," *New York Times,* 27 June 1992, A3.

medical abortions prior to the twelfth week if preceded by physician counseling, thereby placing the decision for early abortion in the hands of the individual women. However, the requirement of counseling compelled women to justify and explain themselves to the authoritative designees of the state. Moreover, the captioning preamble to the law did not suggest any policy concern for women. It referred only to "the protection of prenatal/nascent life," the "promotion of a society suitable for children," and, vaguely, to "conflicts involving pregnancy, and the regulation of the termination of pregnancy."[15] The German statute of 1992 was similar to the Pennsylvania law partly upheld by the Supreme Court in the 1992 *Planned Parenthood v. Casey*[16] decision. Women must endure waiting periods and other elaborate "informed consent" rituals that the state hopes will discourage abortion.

On May 28, 1993, Germany's highest court ruled the 1992 compromise statute unconstitutional. The Court invalidated the law on the ground that it was in conflict with a constitutional provision it construed to require the state to protect *all* human life. Perhaps wary of seeming to flout post-Nazi commitments to preserving human life, the German Court found it impossible to endorse the modestly permissive scheme set forth in the 1992 law. Yet the German High Court pronounced that abortion may be obtained under its ruling if the life or health of the mother is at stake, the pregnancy results from rape, or the child would be born severely handicapped. The exceptions that the Court recognized and its failure to mandate enforcement of criminal sanctions against those who illegally abort means that there will be many abortions in Germany, and many will not meet the Court's official ideal. Germany seems trapped in the same quagmire of rules, exceptions, and hypocrisy that mars abortion policy in the United States.

I have previously suggested that the patterns of abortion law around the world suggest four "models" of express regulation: (1) prohibition, (2) permission, (3) prescription, and (4) privacy.[17] *Prohibition* is the model in nations like Ireland that punish most abortions as criminal offenses. The model of *permission* is in effect in countries like France, where laws permit abortions that meet more or less stringent criteria established by government. The model of *prescription* allows government officials to penalize unauthorized pregnancy and childbirth, as in the People's

15. Section 217 StGB (1992) (based on language of an unofficial translation of the compromise statute).

16. 505 U.S. 833 (1992).

17. Anita L. Allen, "Legal Aspects of Abortion," in *Encyclopedia of Bioethics*, 2d ed. (New York: Macmillan, 1994).

Republic of China. Finally, where the model of *privacy* obtains, government may not enact legislation that criminalizes or prohibitively restricts abortion. This was the model that prevailed in the United States immediately after the Supreme Court decriminalized abortion in 1973. None of these prevalent models, I believe, recognizes any strong connection between abortion rights and equal citizenship for women.

The U.S. and German experiences reveal that democratic nations are not yet prepared to accept the proposition that citizenship implies legally guaranteed reproductive options for women. In Japan abortion is readily available and more highly regarded by the medical establishment than oral contraceptives. But even there, abortion rights are not viewed as prerequisites of citizenship. Western democratic liberalism is not prepared to see abortion choice as a *right*—no less than the right to travel, to practice one's faith, or to be free of arbitrary arrest. For now, for our leaders, first-class citizenship does not mean reproductive control.

EQUAL PROTECTION AS A REPLACEMENT FOR PRIVACY

Many scholars now believe that gender equality and equal citizenship require reproductive freedom and that the Equal Protection Clause should be marshaled against state and federal abortion restrictions.[18] Although "laws restricting abortion plainly oppress women," explains Sylvia Law, the right to abortion was "not presented to the courts as a clear issue of sex equality."[19]

In *Planned Parenthood v. Casey*, the Supreme Court reaffirmed much of *Roe*'s traditional privacy jurisprudence. However, Justice O'Connor's opinion for the Court expressly linked abortion rights to equality as well as privacy. Without their "unique" reproductive liberty, women are unable "to participate equally in the economic and social life of the Nation," she wrote.[20] Even before *Casey*, one could detect increasing awareness that the abortion debate has a "gender dimension." In Justice Blackmun's passionate dissent in *Webster v. Reproductive Health Services*, he said he feared for the liberty *and* the equality of women.[21]

18. See Ruth Bader Ginsburg, "Some Thoughts on Autonomy and Equality in Relation to Roe v. Wade," *North Carolina Law Review* 63 (1985): 375.
19. See Sylvia Law, "Rethinking Sex and the Constitution," *University of Pennsylvania Law Review* 132 (1984)· 973, 1020.
20. *Planned Parenthood v. Casey*, 856.
21. *Webster v. Reproductive Health Services*, 492 U.S. 490, 556 (1989).

Blackmun's majority opinion in *Thornburgh v. American College of Obstetricians and Gynecologists* referred to the "promise that a certain private sphere of individual liberty will be kept largely beyond the reach of government" and asserted that this "promise extends to women as well as to men."[22]

A year after the *Casey* decision, Justice Ruth Bader Ginsburg joined the Court. Ginsburg has advanced a strong equality-based perspective on abortion rights. Her view is that sex inequality is perpetuated by abortion restrictions and that the Equal Protection Clause of the Fourteenth Amendment is a strong basis for claiming abortion rights under the Constitution. It is so strong that Roe was weakened by "concentration on a medically approved autonomy idea, to the exclusion of a constitutionally-based sex-equality idea."[23]

The growing affinity among justices of the Supreme Court for an equality jurisprudence of reproductive rights is consistent with a mounting consensus in the scholarly community that equality arguments are not only available, but better than liberty arguments with respect to abortion. A number of the feminist legal theorists who advocate strong abortion rights favor constitutional alternatives to the doctrine of privacy-related liberty. They view privacy law as distorting the truths of women's lives and actually impeding women's equal citizenship.

For instance, Catharine MacKinnon has broadly assaulted privacy jurisprudence in abortion law,[24] arguing that "the doctrine of privacy-related liberty has become the triumph of the state's abdication of women in the name of freedom and self-determination."[25] Privacy doctrine works only if women are equals within the private sphere. MacKinnon argues that privacy law and other "legal attempts to advance women" are based on false assumptions about the status quo, "as if women were citizens—as if the doctrine was not gendered to women's disadvantage, as if the legal system had no sex, as if women were gender-neutral persons temporarily trapped by law in female bodies."[26]

Joan Williams also critiques privacy jurisprudence and bases her ambivalence about arguments premised on "choice," "liberty," and "privacy" on the observation that women seeking abortion do not feel

22. *Thornburgh v. American College of Obstetricians and Gynecologists*, 476 U.S. 747, 772 (1986).

23. Ruth Bader Ginsburg, "Some Thoughts on Autonomy and Equality in Relation to *Roe v. Wade*," *North Carolina Law Review* 63 (1985): 386.

24. Catharine A. MacKinnon, *Feminism Unmodified: Discourses on Life and Law* (Cambridge: Harvard University Press, 1987), 93–110.

25. Catharine A. MacKinnon, "Reflections on Sex Equality Under the Law," 1311.

26. Ibid., 1286.

especially free.[27] The language of privacy implies that women are choosers against a background of a number of realistic, attractive alternatives. Pregnant women who consider abortion are not so situated. The concepts of privacy, liberty, and choice are at odds with the sense of "choicelessness" that women seeking abortion actually feel. In general, "choice rhetoric is not appropriate where patterns of individual behavior follow largely unacknowledged gender norms that operate to disempower women."[28]

For theorists who believe the privacy doctrine should be abandoned, equal protection doctrine promises to "fix," not just supplement, the constitutional case against abortion restrictions. They believe it is a superior constitutional framework. Are equality arguments better than privacy or liberty arguments with respect to abortion generally? I think the case has yet to be made that they are.

ABORTION AS A "PRIVACY" CONCERN

Cass Sunstein bases his thesis that equality arguments are superior to privacy arguments on a number of claims, including this one: Abortion rights relate to equality and liberty but have little to do with "conventional privacy."[29] On this point, Sunstein is wrong. "Conventional" privacy has much to do with abortion and with reproductive rights generally. Sunstein and others have missed the evident connection between conventional privacy and reproductive rights because they overlook the respect in which the traditional roles of homemaker, wife, and mother are inconsistent with ideals of individual forms of personal privacy. For many women home life is anything but a haven for the experience and enjoyment of personal privacy. Meaningful opportunities for personal privacy consist of quality time and space for one's self. Caretakers often cannot seclude themselves, since they have to be highly accessible and responsive to the wants and needs of their dependents. These responsibilities, in turn, adversely impinge on women's entry into the public realm as equal participants and contributors. All of this suggests that for the sake of conventional privacy in the senses of seclusion and solitude,

27. Joan Williams, "Gender Wars: Selfless Women in the Republic of Choice," *New York University Law Review* 66 (1991): 1559, 1584.

28. Ibid., 1633.

29. Cass Sunstein, "Neutrality in Constitutional Law (With Special Reference to Pornography, Abortion, and Surrogacy)," *Columbia Law Review* 92, no. 1 (1992): 31.

women ought to take special care when deciding whether or not to have children.

Procreative privacy rights are tools women can use, and are already using, to create opportunities for meaningful privacy in private life. This is why feminists are mistaken to dismiss "privacy" rights as mere conservative male ideology. For some feminists, "privacy" and "private sphere" connote problematic conditions of female seclusion and subordination in the home and in domestic caretaking roles. American women have had ample experience with privacy and the private sphere in this unhappy sense. Women have had too much of the wrong kinds of privacy: they have had home-centered, caretaker's lives, when they have often needed and wanted forms of privacy inside and outside the home that foster personal development, making them more prepared for participation in social life.[30]

Traditional caretaking roles have kept women's lives centered in the privacy of the nuclear family home. Conventions of female chastity and modesty have shielded women in a mantle of privacy at a high cost to sexual choice and self-expression. Expectations of emotional intimacy have fostered beneficial personal ties. At the same time, women's prescribed roles have limited their opportunities for individual forms of privacy and independently chosen personal association. Maternal and social roles have kept in the private sphere women who might otherwise have distinguished themselves in the public sphere as businesswomen, scholars, artists, and government leaders.

Women who seek out and utilize opportunities for privacy, enabling them to rejuvenate or to cultivate talents, are women with something qualitatively better to offer others. A degree of privacy in our lives can help to make us more prepared for social participation. It can help us to contribute up to the level of our capacities. It can make us better, more equal citizens. Procreative rights promote privacy by helping women preserve and create opportunities for privacy in the context of responsible lives.

Controversial or not, using "privacy" to denote a domain outside of legitimate social concern is now an entrenched practice in the United States. It may be significant that women in the United States now believe that their privacy, as well as their liberty and equality, is compromised by harsh abortion restrictions. If they did not always feel that way, feminists and liberals have taught two entire generations of women to describe the wrong they feel when denied reproductive

---

30. See Anita Allen, *Uneasy Access: Privacy for Women in a Free Society.*

options as invasions of their privacy. Whatever "privacy" may have once meant, it now also means freedom from abortion restrictions. This linguistic development undercuts some of the power of critics wedded exclusively to the "conventional" or paradigmatic understanding of privacy. Large segments of the male and female public now view excluding others from "personal" decision making as enjoying privacy.

The political concept of a limited, tolerant government is elaborated by John Locke and Thomas Jefferson as a requirement of natural rights, and by John Stuart Mill and Adam Smith as a requirement of utility. Both of these objectives require a nongovernmental, private sphere of autonomous individuals, families, and voluntary associations. Though liberals sometimes speak of public and private as if they were fixed natural categories, feminist privacy theorists often emphasize that the public and the private are not metaphysical realities but contingent understandings of how, as a matter of policy, we believe power ought to be allocated among individuals, various social units, and government. Liberals often explain privacy rights as negative liberties of freedom from government involvement; but feminists often give privacy an affirmative twist, arguing that privacy rights can mandate government involvement in situations where, without it, material needs render privacy rights ineffective.

Yet in the *Thornburgh* case, Blackmun stipulated that the "privacy" of the Fourteenth Amendment abortion cases is the claim to be free from forms of government interference with decisions affecting sex, reproduction, marriage, and family life.[31] At the same time, Blackmun expressly recognized that, in the context of abortion, conventional forms of privacy, namely anonymity and confidentiality in health-care record keeping and reporting, are key ancillaries for safeguarding decisional privacy. After *Thornburgh*, abortion law cases reviewing the constitutionality of spousal and parental notification and consent requirements have raised anonymity, secrecy, confidentiality, and other information access concerns without appearing to confuse or conflate conventional with decisional privacy concerns.[32] Indeed, the body of constitutional abortion law as a whole reflects a solid understanding of the semantics of "privacy." It acknowledges decisional and nondecisional uses of privacy and appreciates that confidentiality and anonymity are needed to protect independent abortion decision and action.

31 *Thornburgh v. American College of Obstetricians and Gynecologists*, 476 U.S. 747, 765–67 (1986).

32. See, for example, *Planned Parenthood v. Casey*, 505 U.S. 833, 875–76 (1992); *Rust v. Sullivan*, 500 U.S. 173 (1991); and *Hodgson v. Minnesota*, 497 U.S. 417 (1990).

These several considerations—the practical link between reproductive rights and paradigmatic forms of privacy such as solitude at home; the Supreme Court's eventually careful distinctions among decisional, physical, and informational privacy; the etymology of *res privatae*; and patterns of popular use of the word *private*—strongly mandate rejecting Sunstein's claim that abortion rights have little to do with conventional privacy. If an equality jurisprudence for abortion is superior to a privacy jurisprudence, it is not because the practice and regulation of abortion lack conceptual ties to privacy.

Cass Sunstein claims a second advantage for equality and equal protection arguments over privacy or liberty arguments:

> Moreover these [equality] . . . arguments have a large advantage in that unlike privacy or liberty arguments, they do not devalue the legitimate interest in protecting the fetus, and indeed make it unnecessary to take any position on the moral and political status of unborn life. Even if the fetus has all of the status of human life, the bodies of women cannot be conscripted in order to protect it.[33]

In claiming this advantage, too, Sunstein is mistaken. As I will argue, privacy arguments do not, in principle, devalue the legitimate interests in protecting the fetus any more than equality arguments; nor do they, in principle, make it any more or less necessary to take a position on the moral and political status of unborn life. Privacy is blamed for the vehemence of the conflicts even though there is little reason to think pro-life activism would have been less committed or hostile had women's equality rather than their privacy been held out as a justification for permissive abortion laws. The pro-choice position seems shrill and unreasonable to those who do not share it because it places a range of concerns, including women's privacy, equal protection, personal satisfaction, bodily integrity, and economic well-being above the protection of the beginnings of innocent human life.

Sunstein's claim that privacy needlessly devalues the unborn was doubtless prompted by *Roe v. Wade*'s stance, maddening to some, that the state lacks an interest in the unborn at the start of pregnancy. But *Casey* modified this feature of *Roe v. Wade*, holding that the state has an interest in the unborn sufficient to warrant protective regulation on behalf of the unborn at all stages of pregnancy so long as the regulation does not "unduly burden" the woman's right to privacy.[34] By affirming

---

33. Cass Sunstein, "Neutrality in Constitutional Law," 39–40.
34. *Casey v. Pennsylvania*, 505 U.S. 833, 875–76 (1992).

the basic privacy right of access to early abortion while asserting a governmental interest in the unborn at every stage of pregnancy, *Casey* enacts the analytic possibility of asserting governmental interest in the unborn while conferring strong privacy rights for women seeking early abortion. *Casey* may be an uneasy compromise, but it establishes that valuing the unborn and advocating a significant degree of decisional privacy for women are not utterly incompatible.

The privacy argument associated with *Roe v. Wade* and defended by philosophers who deny fetal personhood does not "devalue" the concept of fetal protection by government in the strong sense needed to give Sunstein's claim weight. That is, it does not ridicule the very idea of fetal humanity or community interest in the fate of the unborn. The serious privacy argument that advocates typically make simply disagrees, rightly or wrongly, that the government has certain grounds for categorically prohibiting the interruption of pregnancy.

Moreover, far from denying fetal personhood or humanity, some versions of the privacy-related liberty argument advanced by pro-choice theorists expressly concede it. Some versions of the privacy argument admit or avoid taking a position on the moral and legal status of the unborn. The privacy argument is no more wedded to the claim that the government lacks an interest in the unborn than is the equality argument.

It is implausible to suppose that privacy rhetoric inflames the pro-choice and pro-life debates in a way that equality rhetoric would not have, had it been the choice of the Court in *Roe v. Wade*. As Joan Williams points out, "Claims for women's equality, particularly in contexts involving sexuality, trigger fears of chaos, filth, and defilement."[35] Surely it is the common bottom line of permissive abortion policy that provokes the virulence of pro-choice and pro-life politics. Those who blame privacy jurisprudence for the intractability of abortion politics imply that pro-life Americans would quietly accept the deaths of the unborn if they were premised on women's right to equal treatment rather than on women's right to make their own decisions about their bodies.

In sum, neither the privacy nor the equality arguments for reproductive control, in principle, condemn unborn life as worthless. Neither assumes that claims of state interest in the unborn are spurious. Both conclude that government may not assume the absolute power to decide the fate of the unborn, given what is at stake for women. Disagreements

---

35. Joan Williams, "Gender Wars," 1586.

about bottom lines, about the extent to which abortion is permitted or restricted, are what divides Americans.

PINNING THE BLAME FOR THE FUNDING DECISIONS

Critics blame privacy jurisprudence for the Court's refusal to grant poor women the right to state and federal assistance for elective or "non-therapeutic" abortions.[36] The usual argument is that conceptually privatizing abortion, as in *Roe,* rules out public assistance.[37] Critics say the right to privacy means limited government involvement; it would be reasoning against the grain of privacy jurisprudence to find, in the idea of a governmental duty to leave people alone, the idea of a governmental duty to assist the poor in seeking abortions.

This criticism of the *Roe* decision is problematic for a number of reasons. First, it implies that liberal values in principle rule out all public programs. Although extreme libertarians have taken this view, more moderate and nuanced liberal political theories that value limited government do not proscribe all forms of public assistance. Relevantly, the "liberal" Western nations have sought, in practice, to balance independence from government interference with reliance on government aid needed to make meaningful independence possible. A number of feminists, including Rachel Pine and Sylvia Law, have suggested that American constitutionalism could accommodate affirmative understandings of privacy-related liberty that are broad enough to support abortion funding. For example, responding critically to the abortion funding cases, Pine and Law countered with a "feminist concept of reproductive

36. See, for example, *Harris v. McCrae,* 448 U.S. 297 (1980) and *Maher v. Roe,* 432 U.S. 464 (1977), which hold that neither state nor federal government must pay for a poor woman's abortion. See also *Rust v. Sullivan,* 500 U.S. 173 (holding, under Title X of the Public Health Act, that the government has no affirmative duty to commit any resources to facilitating abortions); *Webster v. Reproductive Health Services,* 492 U.S. 490 (1989) (holding that a state may restrict the use of public funds and facilities for the performance or assistance of nontherapeutic abortions); and *Beal v. Doe,* 432 U.S. 438 (1977) (holding that Title XIX of the Social Security Act does not require a state to fund nontherapeutic abortions as a condition of participation in the Medicaid program established by that Act).

37. See Ruth Colker, "Abortion and Dialogue," n. 15; and Catharine A. MacKinnon, "Reflections on Sex Equality Under the Law," n. 11. But there is disagreement on this issue. Laurence Tribe concludes that under privacy jurisprudence "it becomes difficult indeed to justify the government's decision not to fund an impecunious woman's choice of abortion" ("The Abortion Funding Conundrum: Inalienable Rights, Affirmative Duties, and the Dilemma of Dependence," *Harvard Law Review* 99 [1985]: 330, 338).

freedom" based on "affirmative liberty" and the idea that "government has the obligation to insure that people can make reproductive decisions freely."[38] Dorothy Roberts, in reaction to *Rust v. Sullivan*,[39] describes a "liberation theory" version of constitutional liberty that would "recognize the importance of information for self-determination" and therefore "place an affirmative obligation on the government to provide [abortion] information to people who are dependent on government funds."[40]

Blaming privacy jurisprudence for the funding decisions is problematic for a second reason. It implies that these decisions would have stood a chance of coming out differently had *Roe* been decided on equal protection grounds. It is highly implausible to suppose that the funding cases would have come out differently if *Roe* had been expressly defended under equal protection principles. The logic of equal protection in American constitutional law has not always demanded that the poor be given the resources needed to make them the substantive equals of other citizens. Equality is open in our jurisprudence to quite thin "equal opportunity" rather than "equality of results" interpretations. The Court could have acknowledged the goal of abolishing discriminatory abortion laws, while ruling that the Constitution's Equal Protection Clause does not require government abortion subsidies.

Roe v. Wade was a Burger Court decision. It is especially unlikely that this particular Supreme Court would have made the short leap from abortion equality to abortion subsidies. The Burger Court was notable for an expansive Due Process Clause jurisprudence, but a narrow reading of Equal Protection.[41] The Burger Court constricted the fundamental rights strand of equal protection that had enjoyed expansion during the Warren Court era. In deciding equal protection cases, the justices of the Burger Court "were more comfortable forbidding state regulation of certain spheres than requiring government equalization . . . of fundamental interests such as education, food, shelter, and medical care."[42] For the Burger Court, the "reconceptualization of equal protection as an entitlement to affirmative government assistance" was "unpalatable."[43] And

38. Rachel Pine and Sylvia Law, "Envisioning a Future for Reproductive Liberty: Strategies for Making the Rights Real," *Harvard Civil Rights–Civil Liberties Law Review* 27 (1992): 421 and nn. 53 and 54.

39. 500 U.S. 173 (1991).

40. Dorothy E. Roberts, "Rust v. Sullivan and the Control of Knowledge," *George Washington Law Review* 61 (1993): 587, 640.

41. See Michael Klarman, "An Interpretive History of Modern Equal Protection," *Michigan Law Review* 90 (1991): 213, 289–90.

42. Ibid., 289.

43. Ibid., 289–90.

because it was, the Court could have reasoned that prohibiting states from criminalizing abortion was a requirement of gender equality, but that compelling state and federal government to pay for poor women's abortions was not.

It is often assumed that concerns for women's equality argue, without question, for abortion subsidies. Yet many in the United States are mindful of the history of slavery and medical abuses of women and people of color. As a consequence, state and federal legislators supportive of gender equality can cite egalitarian reasons for caution about sponsoring nontherapeutic abortions for poor women on welfare, many of whom are Latinos, recent immigrants, and African Americans. Such sponsorship could lead to the appearance or reality of compulsory abortion. Although I favor public abortion subsidies, I do so circumspectly.

The future of meaningful health care reform in the United States is uncertain. However, the intense debates in 1993 and 1994 over abortion benefits under President William Jefferson Clinton's proposed Health Security Act are instructive on the question of whether privacy jurisprudence is to blame for the adverse outcome in the abortion funding cases. In the context of congressional legislation, as in the context of judicial adjudication, accepting the right to abortion has not entailed accepting the concept of public funding. Here too, it is unlikely that a *Roe v. Wade* premised on equal protection would have made a difference in the outcome of the debates about publicly subsidized health insurance.

Some members of Congress and their constituents oppose the idea of forcing taxpayers to subsidize acts they find heinous on moral and religious grounds. The real foe of subsidized medical abortion is not the supposed conceptual implications of privacy jurisprudence. Rather, it is widespread moral and religious substantive opposition to killing the unborn,[44] combined with pervasive political opposition to government-compelled complicity with felt moral and religious wrongs.

The rhetoric of privacy may fuel the abortion debates, but something else is driving them—plain opposition to abortion. Some people are pro-life and do not want to pay for abortions through their taxes. Indeed, some people who are pro-choice and pro-gender equality do not think it is clearly proper to ask those who are pro-life to subsidize abortions. Were the current Supreme Court miraculously to adopt the equal protection framework for abortion law tomorrow, and the next day hear a constitutional challenge to a comprehensive national health insurance

---

44. See Robin Toner, "Political Memo: Abortion and the Health Plan: Hard Questions in Both Camps," *New York Times*, 22 October 1993, A20; and Anna Quindlen, "Public and Private: Trading Card," *New York Times*, 2 December 1993, A27.

law that excluded mandatory abortion coverage, it is an open question how the Court would decide the contest. It seems probable that the Court would find the law constitutional.

CONCLUSION

Privacy jurisprudence is criticized as too flimsy to serve as a stable base for abortion rights.[45] Some critics of *Roe* embrace an equal protection alternative not yet expressly tested in the Supreme Court. Opponents of *Roe* on the Court have not said they would change their votes if the grounds of abortion were presented in equal protection terms. Nor have the pro-life activists parading in front of clinics and vying for the attention of the media promised to throw down their placards in retreat if the Court adopts an equal protection analysis of abortion law. I think there is good reason to believe that many of those who would like to eradicate legal protection of abortion rights would like to do so because they oppose the practice of abortion, not because they find "right to privacy" jurisprudence problematic.

In identifying factors that galvanized the anti-abortion movement, Justice Ginsburg does not cite privacy jurisprudence itself; rather she cites the "sweep and detail" of the opinion in *Roe v. Wade*.[46] The Court all at once swept away most of the nation's criminal abortion statutes and handed the states a trimester-based guideline for regulation aimed at protecting women's health and the state's interest in potential life. Among those who oppose "heavy-handed" judicial intervention in whatever guise are those who blame privacy jurisprudence for the unpopularity of permissive abortion laws. Yet an equal-protection-based abortion jurisprudence of similar sweep and detail—striking down all criminal abortion statutes that categorically outlawed early abortion and dividing pregnancy into trimesters of permissible and impermissible forms of regulation—might have inspired similar reactions. Equal protection can look "better" today to some people only because it has not yet been tousled in the fray.

45. See David M. Smolin, "The Jurisprudence of Privacy in a Splintered Supreme Court," *Marquette Law Review* 75 (1992): 975, 985 n. 51 (citing numerous works critical of *Roe v. Wade*'s adoption of privacy jurisprudence).

46. Ruth Bader Ginsburg, "Some Thoughts on Autonomy and Equality in Relation to *Roe v. Wade*," 381 n. 73.

7

Circumscribed Autonomy

Children, Care, and Custody

HUGH LAFOLLETTE

A child as he grows older finds responsibilities thrust upon him. This is surely not because freedom of the will has suddenly been inserted into him, but because his assumption of them is a necessary factor in his future growth and movement.
—John Dewey

For many people the idea that children are autonomous agents whose autonomy the parents should respect and the state should protect is laughable. For them such an idea is the offspring of idle academics who never had, or at least never seriously interacted with, children. Autonomy is the province of full-fledged rational adults, not immature children. It is easy to see why many people embrace this view. Very young children do not have the experience or knowledge to make informed decisions about matters of momentous significance. However, from this fact many people infer (or talk as if they infer) that all

I wish to thank members of the philosophy department at East Tennessee State University, members of the philosophy and religion department at the University of Northern Iowa, members of the audience at the 1997 meeting of the Political Studies Association (U.K.), the editors of this volume, and especially David Archard, John Hardwig, and Eva LaFollette for insightful comments on earlier drafts of this paper.

children are helpless moppets, wholly incapable of making *any* informed decisions.

This is a mistake. Even fairly young children are capable of making some decisions. More important, treating them as if they were devoid of autonomy hampers their becoming fully autonomous adults. As toddlers become preteens and then adolescents, they become increasingly able to assume responsibility and to make decisions about their own lives. We must nourish these abilities if children are to become responsible, autonomous adults. This requires that we treat them as if they were already *partially* autonomous. Of course we cannot treat children, especially young children, as if they were *fully* autonomous. Rather, we must find ways to accommodate children's volitional and experiential deficiencies while respecting and cultivating their burgeoning autonomy. This is easier said than done. The difficulty of accommodating both is vividly illustrated in the current debate about whether children should have the authority to decide where and with whom they live.

DECIDING WHERE AND WITH WHOM TO LIVE

Should children ever be able to divorce their oppressive or uncaring parents? Or, when parents divorce, should children be able to decide with which parent they will live? Those who think children are not autonomous will find these questions wrongheaded, silly, or devilish. On the other hand, those who think children are sufficiently autonomous so that they have rights roughly equivalent to the rights of normal adults will likewise find these questions foolish.[1]

However, many of us find ourselves in the proverbial middle. We want to say what both sides are prone to see as the height of evasiveness: "It all depends." That is, we want to say that children should undoubtedly be able to free themselves from abusive or uncaring parents—however that can be achieved. We also think that although older children should not singularly determine who their primary caregiver should be, their preferences should have substantial weight. Thus, we want to say children have some, but not complete, autonomy, and that older children should have considerable say in custody disputes. However, the middle ground is always difficult to defend: the position is vulnerable to attack from both sides. So we must explain why we should give children *some*

---

1. Howard Cohen, *Equal Rights for Children* (Totowa, N.J.: Littlefield, Adams, 1980).

say while denying them complete say. We must also explain just how much say we think they should have.

This current debate is important in its own right. It also provides an opportunity to think more generally about the nature and scope of children's autonomy. To answer these practical concerns as well as the underlying general issues, we should distinguish three questions: (1) Do children have the rational and experiential wherewithal to make informed decisions about their futures? (2) Should parents (or guardians) permit children to make decisions about their futures? (3) Should the state legally protect children's prerogative to make decisions about their futures? The first question concerns *descriptive autonomy*, empirical questions about the intellectual and volitional abilities of children. The second and third questions concern *normative autonomy*, questions about how parents and legal authorities should relate to children.

Historically, we have conflated these questions in our discussions about how to treat children and even in our discussions about how to treat adults. We assumed that adults, but not children, were descriptively autonomous. We then inferred that adults, but not children, should be normatively autonomous. In short, we construed both descriptive and normative autonomy as all or nothing. We assumed that an individual either is or is not descriptively autonomous, and that if she is, then she should have complete normative autonomy, complete say over her self-regarding choices. We correspondingly assumed that if someone is not descriptively autonomous, then we should not give them *any* normative autonomy. This view puts excessive moral weight on questionable empirical claims and blurry conceptual distinctions. Thus, we confine children to practical purgatory where they have no socially recognized autonomy until, upon reaching the magical age of seventeen, eighteen, or twenty-one (depending on where they live), they suddenly become infused with it. As Dewey attests, this is surely a mistake.

What we need to do is grant children, even young children, *circumscribed (normative) autonomy*. Although there are good reasons why we should not grant children (especially very young children) complete normative autonomy, we should not deny them a say in important matters. We must train children to become autonomous, and that requires, among other things, that we treat them in some respects as if they were already descriptively autonomous.

This is not merely the old view in a different guise. I am not simply saying that children should not have to live in oppressive environments in which their physical and psychological needs are ignored or thwarted. Virtually everyone—even those emphatically opposed to granting children normative autonomy—acknowledges that. On the standard view, children should be free of oppressive environments because *that is in their best interests*, not because that is their choice. That is, governmental officials, serving *in loco parentis*, decide for children based on their judgment of what is in the children's best interests. Children should have no direct say in these important matters, although at least occasionally—especially when they are older—we might ask them for their views, perceptions, and preferences. Nonetheless, we would treat the children's perspective as one additional bit of information, not as an authoritative statement by someone with normative autonomy.

WHY CHILDREN SHOULD NOT BE (NORMATIVELY) AUTONOMOUS

Those who are uncomfortable with giving a child any substantial choice over her life typically rely on one of two grounds. First, they may argue that the child is not descriptively autonomous, that she is not even capable of making a decision, let alone making a *reasonable* decision. That is, the child cannot comprehend the scope of the decision or appreciate its significance; the child may not even care about what is significant. Second, someone may claim that even if some child were descriptively autonomous, giving her the authority to decide where and with whom she lives will create an environment that will be antithetical to her or other children's best interests. Laura Purdy combines both objections to explain why children should not generally have such authority:

> Children are not just miniature adults; they need time to mature and develop the traits that make it possible for adults to live good lives. These morally relevant differences undermine the attempt to show that it is unjust to deny children the same rights as adults; they also suggest that the consequences of equal rights would be harmful to children and society as a whole.[2]

Children's Lack of Descriptive Autonomy

Clearly there is more than a mite of truth in Purdy's claim. Much, however, depends on what she means by "a child." Is Purdy referring to a

---

2. Laura Purdy, "Divorce, 90's Style," *The World and I* (September 1994), 369.

two-year-old who is not yet potty trained? Or is she referring to a fifteen-year-old who is watching her parents' marriage fall apart or a twelve-year-old who has been systematically ignored by her parents? If it is the former, then *of course* the child cannot understand the options, let alone make an informed choice. Consequently, it would not merely be misguided to let the child have a choice, it would not make sense. If, however, we are thinking of either of the latter children, then I want to say *of course* they probably have a considerable ability to make informed choices and, indeed, ought to have a defeasible say in controlling their future. I would not suggest that the children's say can never be legitimately overridden by a court exercising its role of *in loco parentis*. However, that judicial role should be exercised infrequently and then only when there is compelling evidence that these children's decisions are not only unreasonable but demonstrably imprudent. For without such compelling evidence, we have no reason to think they cannot make a decision that is reasonable enough, or that they should not be permitted to decide.

Those defending this standard position would respond that this ignores the profound intellectual and volitional deficiencies of children. These theorists claim that we are not justified in making basic decisions for (most) adults since their cognitive and volitional abilities are sufficiently well developed so that their decisions are rational, even when unreasonable. That is, since adults *can* make reasonable decisions (are descriptively autonomous), we are not justified in denying them normative autonomy, even when a particular decision is unquestioningly unreasonable. Children, however, do not just make bad decisions, they lack descriptive autonomy: they are incapable of making informed choices.

Deficiencies That Undermine Descriptive Autonomy

To evaluate this argument, we should isolate five different types of deficiencies that can constrain descriptive autonomy: (1) an intellectual deficit: an inability to mentally process information; (2) ignorance of relevant factors; (3) insufficient understanding of the implications of one's actions for the future; (4) emotional instability; and (5) temporary incapacity.

For present purposes we can ignore the first, since we are concerned about how to treat intellectually normal children. We can all agree that a severely retarded child or adult cannot be given the same autonomy as an intellectually normal adult. Therefore, we can limit discussion to the latter four deficiencies.

Ignorance straightforwardly undermines a person's ability to make a reasonable decision. If I do not know the relevant facts, then I cannot weigh those facts. If I do not weigh those facts, then my decision cannot be based on the evidence. Hence, my desires cannot be reasonable. I might stumble on the proper decision; however, that would be luck, not wisdom. Young children are often ignorant of relevant facts, so they are less likely than adults to make wise decisions. For instance, a child who does not know that arsenic is dangerous will not be able to rationally decide whether to take arsenic. A child who does not understand what alcoholism is will be unable to rationally decide to live with her alcoholic father.

It is not enough that someone knows the relevant factors, she must also understand and appreciate the consequences of her choices. For example, many young children fail to appreciate the consequences of smoking, of unprotected sex, of a failure to study in school, or of living with their clinically depressed mother. Or, even if they abstractly understand these consequences—they can recite what someone else told them the consequences would be—they fail to appreciate their *likelihood* or *seriousness*. That is why parents are disinclined to let children decide whether to smoke or study. Instead, they require their children to study and forbid them from smoking. It also explains why the courts might ignore a child's wishes to live with her depressive mother.

Additionally, even if the child knows the facts and appreciates their significance, she may make an irrational choice if she lacks emotional strength, perseverance, or personal confidence. Even if these emotional deficiencies do not bar her from making a good choice, they may bar her from executing that choice. Someone who lacks self-confidence or is emotionally fragile may be swayed at the last minute by irrelevant factors, while someone who procrastinates or gives up quickly may fail to do what she thinks she ought to do.

Finally, if a child is temporarily incapacitated—if she is extremely angry, ill, exhausted, inebriated, or depressed—then, as in the previous case, she will be both less likely to judge what is reasonable, and less likely to do what she judges to be reasonable.

No doubt these are obstacles to wholly rational choices. Moreover, these four deficiencies are more prevalent in most children than in most adults. That is why we have reason to generally think children are less descriptively autonomous than adults.

The Unreasonable and the Irrational

Nonetheless, even if children are *less* descriptively autonomous than adults, we should not conclude that adults should never or only rarely be treated paternalistically, whereas children should routinely be so treated. We can justify treating children and adults differently only if we can draw a clear empirical and conceptual line between unreasonable choices and irrational choices. Everyone acknowledges that adults sometimes make stupid choices. Children also make stupid choices. Why should we force children, but not adults, to act in their self-interests, against their express (but admittedly stupid) wishes? Presumably because the adults' choices are rational even if unreasonable, while children's decisions are irrational, full stop.[3]

Those who draw this distinction claim that unreasonable choices, although not in the agent's best interest, are nonetheless chosen by that agent and are therefore that agent's decisions to make—even when others are convinced that the decision is imprudent. Adults are presumably capable of rationally weighing and processing relevant information. Thus their choices, even when unreasonable, are nonetheless rational. Children, on the other hand, are incapable of weighing or appropriately evaluating relevant features of the available options. Hence, their choices are not fully voluntary. That is why, on this view, children should not be able to make important decisions about their lives, including decisions about where and with whom they will live. These decisions are best left to adults.

However, this distinction between irrational and unreasonable choices cannot carry this moral load. Although we can make a rough distinction between the two terms, we should not conclude that unreasonableness is qualitatively distinct from irrationality. Irrationality is nothing more than the disposition to act unreasonably. This is apparent once we try to distinguish (a) an irrational person from (b) one who always makes unreasonable choices, but is nonetheless rational. How could we distinguish between them? The latter person might display a knowledge of logic; she might cite presumed reasons for her behavior. However, if she routinely makes unreasonable choices, we cannot conclude that she is really rational.

This point can be made clearer by examining cases where children are supposedly more volitionally limited that adults. We generally assume that children, especially young children, are more ignorant than adults. This is a safe assumption. Nonetheless, children are not *invariably* more ignorant than adults. Some children are highly knowledgeable, and some adults are astoundingly ignorant. Or consider Feinberg's example of the person who cannot understand the implications of her actions. He

---

3. Hugh LaFollette, *Personal Relationships: Love, Identity, and Morality* (Oxford: Basil Blackwell, 1996).

claims that children's cognitive disabilities are "not only inabilities to make correct inferences, but also failures of attention and memory, failures to understand communications, and even failures to *care* about a belief's grounding and implications, leading in turn to a failure to grasp its full import, or adequately to appreciate its full significance."[4] Thus, he claims that a fifteen-year-old is incapable of having a "full visceral appreciation of the significance of an irrevocable transaction for his future interests over the course of a lifetime." That is why we should not let her decide where and with whom she should live.[5]

This sounds convincing enough. Surely we do not want children to suffer long-term damage because of their inability to grasp the significance of their decisions—and deciding where and with whom they live are very significant decisions. Yet any way we specify this third disability of children will either (a) fail to justify our decisions to *systematically* deny children a say in these matters, or (b) justify us in determining living arrangements for adults in far more instances than we would countenance.

For although it is doubtless true that the run-of-the-mill fifteen-year-old will fail to have a "full visceral application of the significance of an irrevocable transaction for his future interests over the course of a lifetime," those among us who have such an appreciation should throw the first paternalistic stone. Adults—like children—often fail to appreciate the long-term effects of our choices. To the extent that they *can* appreciate them, it is because they have learned by trial and error. It is not through a clear application of the principles of reason that adults see clearly and children see only darkly. Consequently, even if a diluted version of the claim were true—as it most certainly is—for example, that the fifteen-year-old fails to *largely* appreciate the significance of a *difficult-to-revoke* transaction for her future interests over many years, that is equally true of the forty-year-old chain smoker and the twenty-nine-year-old helmetless cyclist. On the other hand, if we weaken the criteria of reasonableness so that most adults are properly deemed reasonable, then we can no longer plausibly claim that many children—certainly most older children—have substantially impaired capacities.

Forcing Children to Become Adults: Worries About Normative Autonomy

Of course most people recognize that children are not wholly incapable of making rational choices. Nonetheless, they may contend that parents

---

4. Joel Feinberg, *Harm to Self* (Oxford: Oxford University Press, 1986), 317–18.
5. Ibid., 325.

and especially the state should not grant children normative autonomy. These objectors fear that in granting children some normative autonomy, we will grant them too much, that we will force them to make significant personal decisions that they are ill-prepared to make.

This is a sensible concern if we are talking about a five-year-old making a complex decision with important consequences for the remainder of her life. What, though, about older children? The previous arguments give us some reason to think that even late preteens are, in relevant cognitive and volitional respects, already mature enough and reasonable enough to decide. They are already more like adults than infants. Most children past infancy are more capable of judging and acting on their own than we typically grant. They are less capable than many adults, no doubt, but they are capable nonetheless.

However, let's consider a child who is admittedly less rational than most adults. Suppose Sue is an emotionally limited twelve-year-old living in an abusive home. Should she be given the right to divorce her parents? Some people might claim that we already have social mechanisms in place to rescue such children. This is highly dubious. Social service agencies are unaware of many cases of abuse and neglect. Moreover, many abused children will be reluctant to approach those agencies for help as long as they think the agency is likely to simply return them to their abusive parents. Often the child's only realistic hope is to divorce her parents the old-fashioned way: to run away. If we permitted children to legally divorce their parents, then Sue would have another option.

Should we deny her the authority to "divorce" her abusive parents simply because she is incapacitated? No! The reason that she is incapable of making an informed choice is almost certainly that her parents, who are, *ex hypothesi,* abusive, have not prepared her to make them. Consequently, we cannot justifiably deny her the authority to divorce her parents *on the grounds that* giving her that choice will not prepare her for life as an adult. That assumes she would be so prepared were she left in the current environment. We know otherwise. The best chance to prepare *her* for life as an adult is for her to escape from her parents, by whatever means, before it is too late.

The real fear here is that establishing legal and social institutions giving Sue the right to divorce her abusive parents will necessarily give the same right to all children. Yet giving *all* children the authority to decide where and with whom to live will damage many children's (children other than Sue) chances of being well prepared for life as adults. That is, children in nonabusive homes—children who would, in the current conditions, be well prepared for life as adults—will be harmed by prematurely giving them normative autonomy.

Those defending this tack would note that a law that benefits some individuals may be inappropriate for others. However, we should be morally queasy about denying abused children the right to free themselves from detrimental environments so that luckier children do not have to face decisions they might be ill prepared to make. Nonetheless, if the dangers to other children are substantial, perhaps we must sacrifice children like Sue to protect these other, already luckier, children.

Before we do so, however, we must ascertain the nature of the dangers children will face if we give them normative autonomy. Some fear that many children will abuse the power given them: perhaps hordes of them will be scrambling to divorce their parents because their parents did not give them an adequate allowance or forced them to eat their spinach. I see no reason, however, for thinking that more than a minuscule number of children would even consider this option, and even less reason to think courts would permit many of these children to act on their preferences.

I think this objection is more plausible if interpreted as a worry about the indirect costs of giving children normative autonomy. To give children autonomy is to grant them certain rights. However, if children and their parents get mired in squabbles about which rights the children have, it will create an atmosphere detrimental to children. Some two decades ago, Francis Schrag argued that giving children rights, even limited rights, was detrimental to them and to society. He claimed that the clamor for children's rights would mean that the relationships between parents and children would be:

> defined increasingly by mutual rights and obligations and that the natural affection and sympathy most parents feel for their children would be undermined. Parents would focus more and more on meeting their obligations or if not on meeting them, at least appearing to meet them in the eyes of the law. Parents would begin to practice "defensive parenting," i.e., the art of meeting the letter of the law to forestall the threat of a future suit.... Parents ... would tend to see themselves more and more as sub-contractors to the state performing a definite service in exchange for pay.... The present relationship of a competent nurse to a psychiatric patient would be the paradigm for the new relationship.[6]

6. Francis Schrag, "Children: Their Rights and Needs," in *Whose Child: Children's Rights, Parental Authority, and State Power,* ed. W. Aiken and H. LaFollette (Totowa, N.J.: Rowman & Allenheld, 1980), 246–47.

These are legitimate worries. Injecting rights talk into an intimate relationship can seriously damage it. That is true not only of relationships between parents and children, but also of relationships between partners. The proper response, though, is not to deny that each party to such relationships is autonomous. Rather, we should find new ways to describe and understand these relationships. We should understand that both parties have the ability and the authority to make choices about matters that profoundly affect them even though they need not (regularly) resort to the language of rights. Intimates should care for and respect one another. Parents should likewise love and respect their children. To fully respect another means we must sometimes let them choose for themselves, even when we may think their decisions are misguided.[7]

Furthermore, although Schrag raises legitimate worries, these are wholly irrelevant when discussing the fate of a child—especially an older child—whose parents are divorcing. Here the child finds herself in circumstances that *demand* that she make a choice. Perhaps she is not as well equipped to make as wise a decision as she will be able to make later in life (let us hope not). Perhaps it is unfortunate that she must make such a choice. In a different world, political, legal, and social institutions might make it easier for children to maintain regular contact with *both* parents. Nonetheless, in our world circumstances often demand that a decision be made, and it is difficult to know why the child—whose welfare is directly and substantially affected by this decision—should not have a say.

Some people might claim that we can accommodate these cases simply by requiring appropriate judicial and administrative authorities to seek the child's view. However, I fail to see why this is a better solution. If giving children the (defeasible) choice of where and with whom to live is unduly onerous, then merely asking them what they want to do is likely to be as onerous. It may be more problematic if the children know that their opinion will simply be one opinion among many and far from determinative. Then they might say what they think these officials want them to say, rather than what they really believe.

Finally, although Schrag's worries are not wholly unfounded, I fail to see that they justify completely denying children normative autonomy, especially if there is a better option.

---

7. Hugh LaFollette, "Two Forms of Paternalism," in *Law, Justice, Rights, and the State*, ed. A. Peczenik and M. Karlsson (Stuttgart: Franz Steiner Verlag, 1995), 188–94.

CIRCUMSCRIBED AUTONOMY

The preceding analysis supports my earlier contention that our difficulties in thinking about children and autonomy arise because we construe autonomy as all or nothing. We assume an individual is either
descriptively autonomous—in which case she should have *complete* say
over her self-regarding choices—or else that she is not descriptively
autonomous—in which cases, she has *no say at all*. We can better understand what is wrong with this standard view once we identify a sixth
factor that undermines autonomy: the lack of practice making decisions.
John Stuart Mill notes what at some level everyone recognizes: that the
ability to make informed choices does not descend on a person, as from
heaven. It is acquired by effort and practice:

> The human faculties of perception, judgment, discriminative feel-
> ing, mental activity, and even moral preference, are exercised only
> in making a choice. . . . The mental and moral, like the muscular
> powers, are improved only by being used. The faculties are called
> into no exercise by doing a thing merely because others do it, no
> more than by believing a thing only because others believe it.[8]

The lack of volitional exercise not only directly diminishes autonomy
but also intensifies the other deficiencies, especially the second and
third. If someone has never had to live with the consequences of her
decisions, then she is more likely to be ignorant of factors relevant to her
decisions. After all, we want to know the relevant facts only if we real-
ize that we need to know them. Likewise, someone who has not made
significant decisions on her own cannot adequately appreciate the significance of her decisions. How could she? Simply hearing someone say
that our decisions matter is different from discovering that they matter.
If someone is always intervening to save us from our bad choices, then
we will neither see nor appreciate the need to make wise choices. That is
why, as Dewey puts it, taking on responsibilities and making decisions
are "necessary factor[s] in our *future* growth and movement."

In summary, the standard view of children's autonomy errs in two
ways: first, it assumes children are less capable of making informed
decisions than they are; and second, it ignores the crucial fact that the
only way children can learn to become fully autonomous is by first
being permitted to act on their growing descriptive autonomy.

To avoid these errors, we should stop thinking about autonomy as all

8. John Stuart Mill, *On Liberty* (1865; reprint, Indianapolis: Hackett, 1978).

or nothing. We should begin to think of children as having circumscribed normative autonomy, albeit in three different stages: (1) administered autonomy, (2) monitored autonomy, and (3) minimally constrained autonomy.

(1) *Administered autonomy.* When children are very young, they have little ability to decide. However, they must learn, and they must start to learn at an early age. Yet parents and the state must be careful to protect children from serious repercussions (for themselves or others) of children's unwise decisions. So although parents should give children some prerogatives, autonomy should be carefully administered, much in the same way as one might administer a medication. The parent tries to let the children acquire a sense of making choices and of taking responsibility in small matters. Nonetheless, the choices here are a bit more apparent than real since the parent is always ready to step in.

One related option is to give the child certain responsibilities and then expect the child to fulfill them: for instance, expecting the child to carry out the garbage, and then expecting that they will do just that. This will help the child to see that success or failure matters. However, although this may help the child learn to assume responsibility, unless the child also has some autonomy, even if limited, she is unlikely to learn how to make wise choices on her own rather than simply fulfilling the demands of others.

(2) *Monitored autonomy.* When children are still quite young, but after they have coped with the minimal doses of administered autonomy, the parent should give them greater choice and greater responsibility. Here parents do not parcel out autonomy in a precise regimen that gives children little latitude. Instead, the parents let the children make choices and assume responsibilities and, to some degree, let the child cope with the consequences of her decisions. Nonetheless, the parents will loosely monitor their child's choices. That is, the parents let the child act in ways that hurt her a bit; but they are prepared to intervene if it appears the decision is dangerous or highly detrimental. Nonetheless, they will not intervene as quickly or often as they would in the previous stage.

(3) *Minimally constrained autonomy.* As a child becomes still older and has developed the increasing intellectual means and emotional stability to generally make wise choices, parents must give her increasing autonomy. The parent may still intervene from time to time, but only infrequently, and even then not with a heavy hand. The parents will knowingly let the child make more serious errors than they would have at earlier stages, although they might still intervene in ways they might

not intervene in the life of another adult. Moreover, if the parents have taken the children through the first two stages, then typically they can intervene best by simply talking with the child.

THE PARENT AND THE STATE

The previous discussion explains why the parents rather than the state play the pivotal role in giving children normative autonomy. The child's metamorphosis from the irrational through the partly rational to the mostly rational must be overseen by a caring and proximate parent, not by a distant judge. Judges may be required to intervene, however, if relationships between children and parents fail. In the ideal world, though, astute parents will give imperceptibly increasing normative autonomy to their increasingly descriptively autonomous children. There are no clear rules that tell them how much autonomy to grant or when to grant increasing prerogatives to their children. Parents must be attentive to the ways in which their children have behaved in the past and be ever alert to what they can do to enable their children to make better decisions. Often the best way is by letting them make decisions for themselves and then expecting them to cope with the consequences.

Still, the state does play an important role. Skeptics will not want the state to play more than a minimal role. They will defend the current view of the legal status of children by saying that although some children are descriptively autonomous much of the time, many are not. The state, however, must "draw the line" somewhere: they must distinguish those people to whom we should grant *normative* autonomy from those to whom we should not. Of course, there is no way to draw the line that always leads to the correct result. Anywhere we draw the line we will give normative autonomy to some adults who are not descriptively autonomous, while denying normative autonomy to some children who are descriptively autonomous. What the state cannot do, they say, is decide on a case-by-case basis how much scope to give children; that could have even worse consequences. Therefore, we should deny all legal rights to children until they reach the age of majority.

There is, of course, a morsel of truth to this view. As I argued earlier, there are dangers of granting children too much normative autonomy. However, there are still greater dangers to children, and ultimately to society, if we cannot find some model of autonomy that allows that children are descriptively and normatively autonomous *in different degrees.*

More important, this model must recognize that the only way children will ever become descriptively autonomous is by granting them increasing normative autonomy. Even if the legal system does not get into the business of deciding how every parent should treat every child, legal pronouncements can set appropriate expectations that would make it more likely that children are given increasing normative autonomy.

We see a move in this direction within both the U.S. and U.K. legal systems. U.S. federal courts have ruled, in various cases, that we cannot categorically deprive all children of normative autonomy, since many older children are, in fact, descriptively autonomous—at least as autonomous as many adults. For instance, the courts have acknowledged that high school students should have some freedom of speech, even in the public schools.[9] Likewise, the British Children Act of 1989 specifies that in cases where children must be placed, the courts must "give due consideration (having regard to his age and understanding) to such wishes of the child as they have been able to ascertain" (section 20). These decisions will not only benefit children who should be given more normative autonomy, but they also send a message to parents—a legal sermon from the legislative and judicial pulpits—encouraging them to grant their children increasing normative autonomy.

Of course neither the courts, nor the legislatures, nor parents can find a consistent way to resolve all these questions: one law or decision appears to permit what another denies. I think we should see these confusions and difficulties, however, not as signs of sloppy judicial, legislative, or parental thinking, but as a faithful rendering of the confusing psychological facts and fuzzy moral boundary between the unreasonable and the irrational. If my earlier arguments are correct, then we should expect fuzzy rulings, laws, and decisions—after all, when it comes to children, there are no clear "objective" standards on which we can always rely. Instead, parents, the state, and judges must ascertain the salient facts and attend to relevant considerations. Deciding how much normative autonomy children should have will be difficult. Deciding whether we should honor the wishes of a seven-year-old child in the midst of a heated custody dispute will not always be evident. However, that in no way implies that we should condemn children to abusive homes from which they cannot escape, or to letting others, no matter how well-meaning, make all profound decisions about the future of their lives.

9. *Tinker v. Des Moines Independent School District*, 393 U.S. 503, 111.

8

Boundaries of Authority

Should Children Be Able to Divorce Their Parents?

LAURA M. PURDY

In 1992 twelve-year-old Gregory K. did something outrageous: he hired a lawyer to terminate his legal relationship with his mother.[1] The country was in an uproar. Children, the press suggested, aren't supposed to make those kinds of decisions—and the next thing we know, they'd be dragging their parents through divorce court at the drop of a hat. No longer would parents be able to make children abstain from sex or drugs, do their homework, or even take out the garbage.[2]

Although children are not forever wedded to their biological parents, it is others who have had the legal right to decide when a family should be broken up. Of course, some children have always taken matters into their own hands by running away, but that is a desperate measure that often ends badly for them. Otherwise, although in some cases children, especially older children, may be consulted about their preferences, nobody had been prepared to leave the final decision to them. Until recently.

The Gregory K. case raised the burning question: When, if ever, is it justifiable for children to "divorce" their parents? This question raises a

An earlier version of this chapter was published in *The World War I* (September 1994).

1. See Lewis Pitts, "Family Values?" *The Nation,* 21 September 1992, 268.
2. See Kenneth Jost, "Children's Legal Rights," *CQ Researcher* 3, no. 15 (1993): 339.

fascinating array of fundamental questions about the boundaries of authority between child, parent, and the state, and so about children's nature and about the kind of society we want to live in.

CHILDREN, PARENTS, AND THE STATE

Let us start by considering the relationship between child, parent, and the state. An extreme parent-oriented view would say that parents should have the ultimate say about how much freedom children will have. This position is compatible with a child's leaving home, but only with a parent's permission. Yet it also holds that very restrictive parents are within their rights and that neither child nor state have any business interfering. Although relatively few people probably hold the most extreme version of this position—one that would assert life-and-death power over children—quite a few seem content with a more moderate one. This position is often grounded in the view that a biological relationship confers special authority over children.

At the other extreme are those who champion children's liberation, arguing that there are no morally relevant differences between children and adults; consequently, customs and laws that distinguish between them are unjust. And since adults are permitted to decide how and where they shall live, the same right should be recognized on behalf of children. This position is usually based on the view that children are as competent as adults at achieving their goals, and that provides sufficient grounds for counting them as equals. It also tends to be associated with contractarian moral outlooks that base all human relationships on consent.[3] Again, although there are few full-fledged proponents of children's liberation, many people are attracted to some parts of its program.

Finally, some believe that the state, not parent or child, should have the last word about children's lives. That view is more characteristic of totalitarian governments that seek to subordinate individual liberty to what they see as the overall welfare. In the United States most people probably believe that when families are unable to care adequately for their children some agency of the state is the best source of help.

The Gregory K. case is a good place to begin investigating the question of whether children should be able to divorce their parents. Gregory's

---

3. See, for example, Howard Cohen, *Equal Rights for Children* (Totowa, N.J.: Littlefield, Adams, 1980).

parents separated when he and his two brothers were very young. After Rachel K. took over Gregory's care, she had a difficult time and repeatedly had to park him with relatives or in foster care. By the time he was twelve, he had lived with her only seven months. George R., a visiting attorney, noticed Gregory when he was living at the Lake County Boy's ranch. George and his wife took him in as a foster child and agreed to adopt him if the lawyer they helped him hire succeeded in terminating his legal relationship with his mother.[4]

This case seems tailor-made to support the claims of proponents of children's liberation who believe that we should recognize children as equals who are, like adults, free to choose where they live. Since his mother and father weren't caring for him adequately, and he had fallen through the cracks in the state-run backup system, he should obviously have been permitted to join another family if he could find one. However, by examining this case as well as other kinds of cases, I will argue that children should be allowed to terminate the relationship with their parents only when there is no other good means of protecting their interests.

This position is not extremely parent-oriented, since parents would not always have the ultimate say regarding whether a child leaves home. It does not endorse full-fledged children's liberation, since it would not recognize a child's right to terminate parental rights on trivial grounds. Nor would it always allow the state to have authority over children's lives. Instead, my position asserts that parents' and children's interests would be best served by a flexible approach that can accommodate the variety of cases in which parents and children actually find themselves. Furthermore, to the degree that we as a society claim to endorse "family values" that take the parent-child relationship seriously, we should set up a variety of institutional mechanisms that nurture the parent-child relationship, protecting the long-term interests of both parents and children, and seeking to prevent "divorce."

THE EXTENT OF CHILDREN'S RIGHTS

Children should not have the full-fledged right to terminate the relationship with their parents for just any reason. Why wouldn't we want

4. Pat Wingert and Eloise Salholz, "Irreconcilable Differences," *Newsweek*, 21 September 1992, 85.

to recognize children's right to divorce their parents in this way? If the right to do so is linked with the full liberationist program, there are a variety of good reasons for rejecting it.[5] There is space here to do no more than briefly indicate a few of the objections to equal rights for children. That view is based on the false assumption that there are no morally relevant differences between children and adults. Children are not just miniature adults; they need time to mature and to develop the traits that make it possible for adults to live good lives. These morally relevant differences undermine the attempt to show that it is unjust to deny children the same rights as adults; they also suggest that the consequences of equal rights would undermine justifiable parental authority, make schooling optional, and thrust many vulnerable children into the world of work. Most likely, it would increase still more the growing gap between rich and poor. Children's liberation is also based on an unsatisfactory libertarian moral theory that fails to recognize humans' fundamental interdependence.

Although leaving children no recourse to staying with their parents is a bad idea in certain cases, this does not require us to be full-fledged proponents of children's right to determine where they live. What would be wrong with recognizing the children's right to make their own living arrangements where that is conceived of as a more limited right within a generally protectionist framework? The fact of the matter is that children are not necessarily good judges of their own interests. Some children live in harmful situations; conversely, some children are fed up with their parents. Unfortunately, the fed-up children are not necessarily the ones who are at risk of harm. Although we as a society need to rethink how to deal with children who may be at risk of harm, that problem is beyond our scope here.

What sort of complaints bring children to the point of seriously considering other living arrangements? Most people would probably agree that children who are beaten to the point of physical injury or who are being sexually abused at home have a good case for leaving. In such cases, children should be permitted or even encouraged to terminate relationships with their parents. Other situations would be much more controversial, however. What, for instance, are we to do about gay children of actively homophobic parents? Many such children now run away from home or are thrown out, but what about those who feel trapped in a situation where they are made to feel like the scum of the earth? Or what about children who feel the weight of their parents'

5. For a fuller explanation of these issues, see my *In Their Best Interest? The Case Against Equal Rights for Children* (Ithaca, N.Y.: Cornell University Press, 1992).

sexist stereotypes especially strongly? What if a parent undermines a girl's attempt to be strong and independent? Or repeatedly punishes a boy for crying or for allegedly sissy interests? More generally, what about the many fundamental conflicts that may arise in matters of religion or politics?

Once again, the social disagreement about the rights and wrongs of these kinds of situations would make it difficult to reach a consensus about how they might best be resolved by children's agencies. However, help may be urgently needed. Not only may children suffer serious harm if they stay in some of these situations, but, as they get older, they may commit suicide, run away, or try to find another home. Suicide is tragic, and running away is a recipe for disaster because many runaways wind up living on the streets, caught up in the drug culture and/or prostitution. Seeking shelter with friends or relatives may work, but there may be no appropriate alternative of this sort available.

One solution will not serve the interests of all children and parents. When children desire, or could benefit from, other living arrangements, their complaints range from the silly to the compelling. Despite the obviousness of this point, a good deal of the press coverage of both the Gregory K. case and of Hillary Clinton's alleged extremism on children's rights reduced the issues to their lowest common denominator: we were invited to consider the prospect of children divorcing their parents to avoid doing their chores. This turn of events was as significant for the issues it avoided as for the ones it raised, because the opportunity to have a badly needed public dialogue on family life was lost.

One can be sympathetic with Gregory K.'s plight without endorsing equal rights for children. There is no doubt that his case is heartbreaking. Parents need to be able to provide children with some continuity of care and a measure of emotional warmth, as well as the basics like food, shelter, and so forth. Although Gregory K.'s mother had taken responsibility for him, she had not been able to meet these standards. As an unskilled worker, she was in continual financial trouble, at times attempting to maintain three children on $2.15 an hour. Yet, as she noted, the state was willing to pay $1200 a month for foster care for her children.[6] If the state had supplemented her income by $1200 a month, she might well have been able to meet her children's needs. At a time when many parents are raising children in poverty, this is a pressing issue. And although not all parents' difficulties in meeting their children's needs can be traced to their financial straits, anybody who has

---

6. Wingert and Salholz, "Irreconcilable Differences."

raised children on a tight budget knows how money problems permeate daily life. Income support programs would reduce the number of children tempted to follow in Gregory K.'s footsteps.

Of course, doing an adequate job of child rearing isn't just a matter of money, even if poverty usually makes it difficult to meet children's needs. Some people—possibly including Gregory's mother—might not know how to care for children, or may be unable to meet their needs for other reasons. However, Gregory K.'s case is different from cases in which parental rights are revoked because the children are abused or abandoned. In Gregory's case, however unintentional the cause, he was deprived of a chance to have a stable and permanent "family life." In such cases, the state may need to be more active in establishing and sustaining permanent parent-child bonds, for without such bonds the child may suffer serious emotional harm. If the state were more alert to this problem, children would not need a right, however tenuous, to divorce parents, since the state would do so on their behalf. For now, the best short-term solution may be to allow children the right to petition for a "divorce" from their parent when a more stable familial relationship is available.

SOCIAL POLICIES TO PROTECT CHILDREN'S BEST INTEREST

Deciding how to deal with these situations raises fundamental questions about our priorities as a society. The central question here is what price we are willing to pay to keep families together. If keeping families together is a serious value, then it seems clear that society must institute more effective measures intended to address parents' problems. More extensive and better funded social work programs would probably help prevent many difficulties. In some cases mandatory counseling and parenting classes might be needed. This preventive approach might be quite expensive, although it is not clear whether it would cost more than the inadequate programs now in place. It could also be quite intrusive, but again, it is not clear whether it would be more intrusive than existing programs. In any case, it is hard to see viable alternatives that value both families and children's welfare.

Proponents of children's liberation argue that more extensive social programs are just refurbished versions of the hopelessly inadequate policies now in place. After all, if Gregory K. hadn't been able to take matters into his own hands, he would still be languishing at the boys' ranch. Better programs could certainly reduce the number of such cases. However, it might be important, as a sort of insurance policy, for children to have the more limited right to hire lawyers to get their views heard in court, not necessarily a right to determine where they live. In any case, neither right would, by itself, solve children's problems. Having legal standing to hire a lawyer would help only the most enterprising young people, those who are able to enlist the help of other adults.

There are, however, many reasons why children should not have the sole authority to terminate the legal relationship with their parents at will. Confusion about appropriate parental authority is a major problem in our society. Many parents are reluctant to assert anything like the authority necessary for helping children to mature, and many children are unwilling to accept the guidance inherent in this process. Both tend to conflate the parent-child relationship with the kind of voluntary contractual relationships that dominate market-oriented societies like ours. So parents may feel insecure about putting pressure on children to take school seriously, to help around the house, and to stay away from drugs or sex. Children whose parents do assert this type of authority may tell their parents to "butt out" of their lives, and some parents just give in. Although that may lead to domestic peace in the short run, nobody's interests are served by such capitulation. Other parents persevere, confident that they are doing what is best for their children, even if their policies lead to a temporarily stormy relationship.

Sometimes, though, things really get out of hand, and a family is flung into a state very much resembling war. What is needed in such cases is a free and confidential forum where children can go to discuss their problems, and which would be empowered to offer both advice and practical help. So when children in warring families show up at children's agencies asking for a divorce from their parents because of this kind of conflict, what should be done?

Given the pluralism in American society about parental authority, it would be tempting for children's agencies to leave battling families to sort out these problems as best they can. But that approach would be seriously mistaken. On the one hand, the situation in such households can become quite destructive to its members. On the other, the objections to equal rights for children, and even to a more limited right on their part to decide where to live, suggest that staying out of these affairs, and thus perhaps leaving disgruntled children to strike out on their own would not be in their best interest. On the contrary, these situations are ones in which the state may be a good source of help.

Before the state can provide such help, however, we as a society need to articulate a set of reasonable expectations about freedom and responsibility for growing children. Only then will thoughtful liberal-leaning parents have the self-confidence to exercise appropriate parental authority instead of, as is often now the case, being torn by doubts about when it constitutes oppression. Such dialogue would also help clarify the reasonable limits of authority, helping all parents develop guidelines about which kinds of restrictions are justifiable and which are not.

Doing this would show that children are not necessarily oppressed by protections and limits that would be inappropriate for adults. On the contrary, some such limits increase the likelihood that they will develop desirable character traits like prudence and morality. Of course, these are very general conclusions; applying them to specific situations needs an issue-by-issue investigation. The evidence so far suggests that an optimum environment includes relatively strict limits and demands on young children, followed by a carefully graduated expansion of both freedom and responsibility as they grow older. This approach increases the burden of proof on limits to liberty as children grow older, but it also increases the degree to which children are held accountable for their behavior. It recommends that majority be attained by steps, as children mature. To some extent this approach would reduce the arbitrariness of an all-or-nothing legal marker of adulthood. We already take this approach with driving, and expanding it would make the system fairer at the same time as it emphasizes the link between freedom and responsibility. Children who approach a children's agency with the relevant sorts of complaints about parental restrictions need to hear these principles, although the family in question may also benefit from counseling about constructive ways to apply them.

Now, of course, most children—even those who are not content at home—do not really want to leave their parents. And most of those who have considered the possibility would probably prefer to have help in resolving their problems rather than dissolving their family ties. So the children's agency's first job would be to see whether a given relationship can be saved. It is plausible that some problematic situations could be improved by counseling and other such measures. Unfortunately, even in those cases where parents ought to change their behavior, the potential for change may be quite limited.

What then? One way to rescue children from these kinds of situations would be to create group living arrangements that they, perhaps after a certain age, could choose to join if the children's agency is unsuccessful in its reconciliation attempts. Such a children's house could not be a haven from legitimate demands, however: it would have to provide the same close personal relationships, supervision, and rules as a good family. Concurrently, society might develop new kinds of legal relationships between child and parent, with differing levels of liberty for children. Some such relationships could be reversible, just as divorce is preceded by reversible separation agreements in some states.

Such carefully controlled partial separation might be a constructive solution both for obviously abused children and for those experiencing other kinds of serious conflict at home. And though remedies of this sort would be intended primarily as an escape hatch for children, they might also benefit parents whose children are driving them crazy. For although it is most often children who need protection from parents, there are also cases where children need to be reminded that parents have rights too. A period of separation might help families avoid more harmful alternatives like reform school or foster care.

A well-run home of this sort would be expensive, for to work well it would have to be much more than a minimally provisioned warehouse for unhappy children. Therefore, no such proposal could be realized without outside support. Parents could be asked to contribute, although, since that might foreclose this option for some children, other sources of support would be necessary. Children themselves could provide some of it in the form of the labor necessary to maintain the house. If, as might be desirable, older children were required to engage in some minimal amount of paid work, they could also be expected to pay in a percentage of their wage. However, tax subsidies would probably still be necessary; and for this reason, a plan of this kind might be rejected as utopian. However, it still seems to me a more feasible way of coping with family trouble than current approaches.

Are there serious objections to this approach to family conflict? One might argue that the existence of children's houses might cause some otherwise contented children to contemplate leaving their parents. Another problem might arise in families where the behavior of one parent causes a child to leave home, creating a serious rift with the other parent. A plausible response to the first objection is that it would probably be hard to find a child who has not occasionally considered leaving home. It is true that the existence of a decent alternative might precipitate an otherwise unlikely departure. However, it is far from clear that a stint away from home is always a bad thing. On the contrary, as I suggested earlier, no doubt many children would return with a salutary new appreciation for their parents. Having the choice available, even if children do not avail themselves of it, or do so for only a short time, would create a desirable sense that the choice to tough out a difficult situation is a commitment rather that a trap. The second problem is more difficult; however, it is hard to see any better resolution of such painful situations. Staying behind to satisfy one parent may be costly, and leaving may precipitate marital divorce or some other change, which could be either good or bad in the long run. Incidentally, the existence of children's houses might help defuse struggles between divorced parents and their children by providing a neutral base for children to retreat to, away from the manipulation and bribery to which hostile ex-spouses sometimes resort.

What might happen to children who join a children's house? Immature children who are trying to get away from their parents' legitimate rules might quickly come to see that such rules are widely accepted as appropriate and perhaps might even recognize their necessity. Many would be ready to go home after a relatively short stay, having realized that their parents are imposing rules on them because they love them, not because they are ogres. Some children would undoubtedly choose to stay. Among them would be those who left home because of abuse or deep incompatibility with their parents. Among the others might be children who simply enjoy the more communal environment of the children's house.

Would that last outcome be a failure? I think we should not see it as such. Adolescence in developed countries has become very long, and it is to be expected that teens' desire for independence will come into conflict with family life. At present few good alternatives exist, and there is a great need for more workable arrangements that recognize the difficulties inherent in this stage of family life. After all, even voluntarily chosen relationships have quite a high rate of collapse. It should hardly be surprising that nonvoluntary ones can be so difficult. People may choose to have children but not the particular children they get. Children—as they never tire of reminding us—didn't choose to be born, nor did they choose their particular parents. Ideally, children and parents can learn to get along well together, and they should be encouraged and helped to do so. Where those efforts are unsuccessful, a good society must create alternatives to the desperate measures to which people now resort.

In conclusion, it seems clear that children should not have the full-fledged right to divorce their parents. However, society also needs to provide more help in preventing the kinds of problems that lead children to want to divorce their parents, as well as to recognize that some problems cannot be prevented or resolved by already existing measures. To deal with all the problems that may arise, innovative social arrangements are needed to provide new kinds of relationships between children and parents.

9

Regulating Sexuality

Gender Identity Disorder, Children's Rights, and the State

ELLEN K. FEDER

In this paper I describe the problematic ways that the behavior of children and their parents—in particular their mothers—is monitored and regulated via the psychiatric diagnosis of Gender Identity Disorder (GID). I contend that GID is not a clinical disorder in any acceptable normative usage of the term. Rather, the diagnosis has flourished because the behavior of the "affected children" violates social stereotypes of masculine and feminine behavior. Moreover, the diagnosis most frequently applies to young children, raising serious questions about the rights and interests of children. It is worth noting also that although the diagnosis of GID applies most frequently to children, teenagers who identify as gay or lesbian are often diagnosed with GID. I want to suggest, in short, that there is a continuity between the "psychiatric treatment" of children for GID and the "medical treatment" of gay and lesbian youth, a phenomenon that I also address. After showing why the

This essay is a substantially revised version of a paper that appeared in *Philosophical Studies* 85, nos. 2–3 (1997): 195–211, as "Disciplining the Family: The Case of Gender Identity Disorder." I am grateful to Uma Narayan for her guiding hand and tireless encouragement in preparing the current version. I also thank Laura Cherry, Jennifer Di Toro, Barbara Gault, and Sharon Meagher for their suggestions.

subjection of children and adolescents to treatment on these grounds is troubling, I consider the way the structural interaction of the institutions of family, medicine, school, and law makes these children and youth especially vulnerable.

THE BIRTH OF A DIAGNOSIS: GENDER IDENTITY DISORDER, ITS SYMPTOMS AND ITS CURE

In 1977 George A. Rekers, a pioneer in the field of Gender Identity Disorder, together with James W. Varni, presented a case study of one of the first subjects identified as suffering from GID—Nathan, an "extremely effeminate" four-year-old diagnosed with "confused gender identity and moderate cross-dress behavior disturbance." The case study describes Nathan's symptoms as follows:

> [Nathan] frequently verbalized his wish to be a girl, and identified himself predominantly with female roles, occasionally displaying pronounced feminine voice inflections. Even though both boys' and girls' dress-up were available at pre-school, Nathan dressed exclusively in girls' clothing. His stereotypic feminine gender-role behaviors elicited comments from other children, such as "You can't be a little girl." This concerned Nathan's teacher and parents and ultimately led to referral for treatment.[1]

It is striking that Nathan's referral for treatment is apparently prompted by the other four-year-old children's negative judgments of Nathan's desire to play "like a girl." A definitive sign of pathology for Rekers and his colleague, teasing and name-calling by peers constitutes "one of the manifest symptoms of child gender disturbance."[2] Four-year-olds' intolerance of deviant gender expression is, in the case of Nathan, given the power to activate a whole machinery of interlocking interventions—by his teacher, his parents, and ultimately by a whole team of psychologists,

1. George A. Rekers and James Varni, "Self-Regulation of Gender-Role Behaviors: A Case Study," *Journal of Behavior Therapy and Experimental Psychiatry* 8 (1977), 428. For some of the details of the therapy, I draw also from a similar case study published the same year by Rekers and Varni, "Self-Monitoring and Self-Reinforcement Processes in a Pre-Transsexual Boy," *Journal of Behavior Therapy and Experimental Psychiatry* 15 (1977).

2. George A. Rekers et al., "Child Gender Disturbances: A Clinical Rationale for Intervention," *Psychotherapy: Theory, Research, and Practice* 14, no. 1 (1977): 3.

assistants, and technicians. This machinery is put to work to "cure" Nathan of a "disorder" from whose "symptoms" Nathan "suffers" only because his behavior violates generally accepted gender-norms although his behavior does not otherwise result in any harm to either himself or others. That this behavior does not otherwise result in any harm distinguishes GID from other physical or mental illnesses that intrinsically threaten a child's well-being or capacities to function, and it does not constitute "illness" merely because it violates traditional gender norms. The "treatment" for GID consisted of surveillance and behavior modification to make him behave according to prevailing gender norms.

Nathan's treatment began in a playroom where he was presented with two tables, one displaying "affect toys" and the other displaying "dress-up" toys. Affect toys consisted of "girls' toys" or "toys associated with 'maternal nurturing' (e.g., baby dolls with accessories)" and "boy's toys" or those "associated with 'masculine assertion' (e.g., a set of cowboy and Indian figures)." Initially, Nathan was instructed to play alone while observers behind a two-way mirror logged "masculine" and "feminine" behaviors. The second phase of treatment entailed the training of Nathan's mother to "reinforce the boy's masculine play." Equipped with a "bug-in-the-ear receiving device," she was prompted to encourage Nathan's play with boys' toys with smiles and compliments and to discourage his play with girls' toys by ignoring him and "picking up a magazine to read."[3] A period of "self-regulation" followed, where Nathan was initially prompted to press a wrist-counter when playing with boys' toys and eventually told to give himself points for playing with boys' toys—for instance, for choosing pirate costumes over playing "Mommy"—points whose accumulation meant he could reward himself with candy. Twelve months after the completion of the "treatment," Nathan was evaluated and confirmed to have a "male gender identity and no emotional disturbance."[4] Just as the "disorder" consisted of Nathan's deviation from prevailing gender norms, the "cure" consisted of therapeutically forcing Nathan to accept and conform to these norms.[5]

3. Rekers and Varni, "Self-Regulation of Gender-Role Behaviors," 428–29; Rekers and Varni, "Self-Regulation and Self-Reinforcement Processes," 179.

4. Rekers and Varni, "Self-Regulation of Gender-Role Behaviors," 430–31.

5. In light of the success of Nathan's treatment, it is notable that the possibility is never entertained that the children's intolerance of gender nonconformity should warrant intervention. Indeed, children's intolerance remains a central rationale for treatment of GID. See the most recent and comprehensive overview of treatments and rationales in Kenneth J. Zucker and Susan J. Bradley, *Gender Identity Disorder and Psychosexual Problems in Children and Adolescents* (New York: Guilford Press, 1995).

THE PROLIFERATION OF GID AND ITS TREATMENT

Since the introduction of the diagnosis, psychiatric interventions as a result of GID diagnoses have extended in two important directions. First, the disorder has been redefined in ways that encourage and promote diagnoses of GID. Second, psychiatric interventions have come to focus more on the mothers of GID children. I will discuss each of these in turn.

Gender Identity Disorder was first introduced as a diagnosis in the third edition of the *Diagnostic and Statistical Manual of Mental Disorders* (DSM-III) in 1980, the first DSM that did not include an entry for homosexuality. As Eve Sedgwick has noted, GID in its earliest version was nominally gender-neutral but was:

> actually highly differential between boys and girls; a girl gets this pathologizing label only in the rare case of asserting that she actually is anatomically male (e.g., that she has or will grow, a penis); while a boy can be treated ... if he merely asserts "that it would be better not to have a penis"—or alternatively, if he displays a "preoccupation with female stereotypical activities as manifested by a preference for cross-dressing or simulating female attire, or by a compelling desire to participate in the games and pastimes of girls."[6]

Later definitions of GID (DSM-III-R 1987; DSM-IV 1994) mitigate this gender disparity by specifying the "features" of GID in girls—including persistent marked aversion to feminine clothing, insistence on wearing stereotypically masculine clothing, or "repudiation of female anatomic characteristics." A girl's avid interest in sports and rough-and-tumble play begin to figure in discussions of the disorder even though not counted among the diagnostic criteria with respect to girls. There is a conspicuous proliferation of detail about GID symptoms in later definitions, allowing an increasing range of behaviors to count as indicia of GID. For instance, while GID in boys was initially described in general terms as a preference for cross-dressing and playing with dolls (DSM-III), the most recent description mentions the simulation of long hair using towels, aprons, and scarves; playing house; drawing pictures of beautiful girls; and watching television shows or videos of favorite female characters (DSM-IV).[7] Similarly, GID in girls assumes its own increasingly

---

6. Eve Kosofsky Sedgwick, "How to Bring Your Kids Up Gay," *Social Text* 29 (1991): 20.

7. Also notable in the lengthy formulation of the GID in DSM-IV (the first that does not include separate entries for GID in children, adolescents, and adults) is the section enumerating "Associated Features and Disorders." The juxtaposition of the different manifestations of the

detailed description. In addition to a preference for boys' clothing, it comes to include a preference for short hair, having powerful male figures such as Superman as fantasy heroes, asking to be called by a boy's name, or being misidentified as boys by strangers. Most important, perhaps, by 1994 the diagnostic criteria for GID no longer require that cross-gender behavior be accompanied by a "stated desire to be, or insistence that he or she is, the other sex." This revision reflects a notable shift in emphasis upon nonstereotypical behavior and marks an effective transformation of the standard articulated in previous formulations. The removal of this requirement opened the possibility that greater numbers of children could be located within the spectrum of disorder. While Rekers initially concluded in 1977 that GID is extremely rare and "might appear only once in every 100,000 children,"[8] by 1990 psychiatrists were concluding that "GIDC [Gender Identity Disorder in Children] or its subclinical variants may occur in two percent to five percent of children in the general population"[9]—an estimated prevalence that is at least two thousand times greater than the original.

Along with the increasing numbers of diagnoses, there has been an expansion of psychiatric scrutiny of the mothers of GID children. During the course of Nathan's treatment for GID, although his mother could be understood to have been trained to offer gender-appropriate responses to Nathan's play, she herself underwent only minimal examination. In more recent work on GID, however, there is increasing attention to the mother of the gender dysphoric child. A representative statement that attributes etiological significance to the mother's behavior asserts:

> A consistent empirical and clinical observation is that parents are prone either to tolerate or to encourage the emerging cross-gender behavior, which ultimately appears to contribute to the consolidation of a cross-gender identity in a child. The reasons for such

---

disorders seems calculated to identify peer teasing of children, among the first of the related disorders mentioned, with the assertion that "[s]ome males . . . resort to self-treatment with hormones and may very rarely perform their own castration or penectomy. Especially in urban centers, some males . . . may engage in prostitution, which places them at high risk for human immunodeficiency virum (HIV) infection"; in addition, "suicide attempts and Substance-Related Disorders" are common. The description then returns to related disorders in children and adolescents, thereby framing the lurid description of the lives of "some males" with the enumeration of problems commonly associated with children, such as "isolation and ostracism" at the beginning, and "Separation Anxiety" at the end (DSM-IV 1994, 535).

8. Rekers, "Child Gender Disturbances," 4–5.

9. Susan J. Bradley and Kenneth J. Zucker, "Gender Identity Disorder and Psychosexual Problems in Adolescents," *Canadian Journal of Psychiatry* 35 (1990): 478.

tolerance or encouragement seem to vary. In some instances it appears related to an intense desire of the parent's [sic] particularly the mother's to have a child of the opposite sex.[10]

Other examples suggest an increasing focus on the role of mothers in producing gender dysphoric boys. In a frequently cited study of "twenty-five extremely feminine boys," Coates and Person suggest that these boys exceed normal children in separation anxiety and suggest a correlation between their separation anxiety and intensely close but disturbed relationships with their mothers,[11] who themselves suffer from depression and personality psychopathology.[12] By 1990, Coates has identified the disorder of the mothers of GID boys as a "maternal psychopathology" attributable to her "fear, anger, and devaluation of men" and to the mother's own "gender role difficulties."[13] In contrast to the early case of Nathan, whose mother was not overtly psychologically evaluated, interventions in later GID cases resulted in mothers' assessments "using the Rorschach, Beck Depression Inventory, and the Gunderson Diagnostic Interview for Borderlines. In addition they received a structured interview that focused on their relationship with their own parents, on their relationship to their child during the first 3 years of life, and on their own psychological states during the child's first 3 years of life."[14]

In the face of proliferating diagnoses of GID and an increasing number of tests and evaluations to which the mothers of children diagnosed with GID are subject, it is worth reminding ourselves that the underlying "problem" that provokes these tests is not harmful or antisocial behavior by the sons of these mothers, but behavior that would be deemed perfectly normal, and perhaps even praiseworthy, if the very same conduct was engaged in by these boys' sisters. It appears that one has to look a

10. Kenneth J. Zucker et al., "Delayed Naming of a Newborn Boy: Relationship to the Mother's Wish for a Girl and Subsequent Cross-Gender Identity in the Child by the Age of Two," *Journal of Psychology and Human Sexuality* 6, no. 1 (1993): 58.

11. Susan Coates and Ethel Spector Person, "Extreme Boyhood Femininity: Isolated Behavior or Pervasive Disorder?" *Annual Progress in Child Psychiatry and Child Development 1986* (New York: Brunner/Mazel, 1987), 210.

12. Bradley and Zucker, "Gender Identity Disorder," 481. See also Sonia Marantz, "Mothers of Extremely Feminine Boys: Child Rearing Practices and Psychopathology" (Ph.D. diss., New York University, 1984).

13. Susan Coates, "Ontogenesis of Boyhood Gender Identity Disorder," *Journal of American Academy of Psychoanalysis* 18, no. 3 (1990): 423, 429. See also the excellent literature review of "Maternal Psychosexual Development" in Zucker and Bradley, *Gender Identity Disorder,* 230–39.

14. Coates and Person, "Extreme Boyhood Femininity," 203–4.

little deeper to understand why such arguably innocuous behavior by children like Nathan elicits this degree of anxiety, surveillance, intrusion, and interference.

GID AND THE SLIPPERY SLOPE TO HOMOSEXUALITY

When Rekers wrote in 1977 that "evidence indicates that gender identity problems in childhood are strongly predictive of sexual orientation disturbance in adulthood,"[15] it is as if it went without saying that such an outcome would be reason enough to warrant psychiatric intervention. Despite the fact that four years earlier homosexuality was removed from the *Diagnostic and Statistical Manual of Mental Disorders* (1973) as an official diagnostic category, Rekers vehemently takes issue with the conception of psychotherapy as a means of helping an individual to "adjust to his homosexual orientation and behavior," and argues that failure to intervene "seriously reduces the possibility of choice for the individual and actually unjustly narrows the person's options."[16]

Those who have since taken up the mantle of GID, perhaps most prominently among them Susan Bradley and Kenneth Zucker of Toronto's prestigious Clarke Institute of Child and Adolescent Gender Identity Clinic and Child and Family Studies Center, describe, in terms not so very different from Rekers's of a decade before, the two short-term goals

---

15. Rekers et al., "Child Gender Disturbances," 7.

16. Ibid., 9. In the abstract of the paper in which this claim is made, Rekers et al. raise the question of the "nature of informed consent in children for such intervention" (2). In the body of the paper this issue is not addressed, implying perhaps that the consequences that would so limit a person's choices would indubitably constitute an overriding duty to act on behalf of a child afflicted with GID. In addition, the authors assert that "[o]nce parents and professionals have concluded that a boy has a gender disturbance, a therapist cannot ethically refuse to treat a child. The therapist cannot impose his values against those of child's parent" (9). Richard Green more frankly admits the priority of parental authority cast as the "rights of parents to oversee the development of their children [a]s a long established principle. Who is to dictate that parents may not try to raise their children in a manner that maximizes the possibility of a heterosexual outcome? If that prerogative is denied, should parents also be denied the right to raise their children as atheists?" (*The "Sissy-boy Syndrome" and the Development of Homosexuality* [New Haven: Yale University Press 1987], 260). Kenneth Zucker, cautioning against this line of argument, remarks that "a treatment rationale based on 'the rights of parents to oversee the development of children' would equally well justify a couple's efforts to obtain the assistance of a professional therapist in raising one or more of their children as homosexual" ("Treatment of Gender Identity Disorders in Children" in *Clinical Management of Gender Identity Disorders in Children and Adults*, ed. Blanchard and Steiner [Washington, D.C.: American Psychiatric Press, 1990], 29), presumably a position that Zucker would not support.

of GID as "[t]he reduction or elimination of social ostracism and conflict, and the alleviation of underlying or associated psychopathology. Longer term goals have focused on the prevention of transsexualism and/or homosexuality."[17] Bradley and Zucker's research is perhaps particularly illustrative of what appears to be a collective effort to yoke the officially recognized pathology of GID to homosexuality.[18]

Psychiatric interventions into homosexuality have not, then, come to an end or been completely displaced by attention to GID.[19] Recent articles appearing in both straight and gay publications report the continuation of disturbing abuse of lesbian and gay youth in mental hospitals and residential treatment centers. "Setting Them Straight," Bruce Mirken's exposé of the therapeutic treatment of gay teenagers recounts the story of Paul Komiotis, who was sent to Rivendell of Utah, one of a national chain of psychiatric hospitals. Much of Komiotis's treatment

> involved a device called a plethysmograph that uses electronic sensors attached to the genitals to measure the subject's sexual arousal. But in Komiotis's case, the procedure went a step further. "They'd put electrodes on our private parts," he explains, "and show us pictures of men and women. When you got attracted to people of the same sex you got a little electric shock to your penis, strong enough to sting."[20]

Mirken reports that Komiotis was also subject to regular sessions with Mormon church representatives who would "tell us that homosexuality was wrong and could be changed through God." The experiences of Komiotis and others suggest that what Sedgwick calls the "war on

---

17. Bradley and Zucker, "Gender Identity Disorder," 482.

18. See articles appearing in the special issue of *Developmental Psychology* 31, no. 1 (1995) on "Sexual Orientation and Human Development," e.g., Blanchard et al., "Birth Order and Sibling Sex Ratio in Homosexual Male Adolescents and Probably Prehomosexual Feminine Boys"; and Bailey and Zucker, "Childhood Sex-Typed Behavior and Sexual Orientation: A Conceptual Analysis and Quantitative Review."

19. It is not a matter of coincidence that the proliferation of discourse concerning GID occurred at the precise historical moment when "Gay Liberation," the first wave of gay rights activism in the early 1970s, gave rise to concerted demands by gay men and lesbians to remove homosexuality from the DSM. See Ronald Bayer's *Homosexuality and American Psychiatry: The Politics of Diagnosis* (Princeton: Princeton University Press, 1981). The earlier pathologization of homosexuality and the subsequent diagnosis of GID show that the authority that psychiatry assumes is in no small measure contained in its power to regulate gender, that is, to generate and enforce the standards that make gender make sense. In the face of lesbian and gay resistance intended to question and disrupt the assumed naturalized "congruence," as Rekers puts it, of sex with gender and gender with sexual desire, the new generation of specialists in GID reassert psychiatry's authority to regulate gender.

20. Bruce Mirken, "Setting Them Straight," *10 Percent*, June 1994, 55.

effeminate boys" is currently being waged on the defiant bodies of gay teenagers.

While the treatment of GID in children is relatively noncorporal and noncarceral, gay and lesbian teenagers are clearly seen to need harsher forms of intervention. From a "therapeutic group home" in the Midwest, sixteen-year-old Phil writes:

> I'm sorry I didn't write sooner. I tried to write you a letter by hand, but it was too frustrating. It's the drugs. I get Melleril shots, PRN, Haldol, Clozapine, and a pink hormone pill. I try to move and it is really hard because it makes me all stiff and that's why I couldn't write. They know I am gay, but they don't say that is the reason that I am here. They say it is depression, but I didn't feel depressed until I got locked up here.[21]

Shock treatment, drugs, isolation, and "covert desensitization"—the process by which a patient is conditioned to associate "undesirable" behaviors (in this case homosexuality) with negative or repulsive images and "desirable" behaviors (heterosexuality) with positive or pleasant images—are all among the "therapies" to which gay and lesbian teenagers have been subject. Lynn Duff, a young lesbian who escaped from Rivendell and whose court battle prevented her mother from returning her, reports having been sedated, hypnotized, placed in physical restraint, and administered "hold therapy"—where she was held down while staff members screamed at her to admit she was hurting her family by being lesbian.[22]

Either by behaving in ways that belie normative gender expectations or by "acting out," lesbian, gay, and transgender youth have been entered in treatment as a result of an incongruous array of "problem behaviors" that are indicative, or thought to be indicative, of a developing homosexual orientation. A result of participating in an ACT-UP (AIDS Coalition to Unleash Power) demonstration or attempting suicide, being sexually active or withdrawing socially, coming out to a teacher or hanging out with "those kinds of kids"— even seeking assistance for peer harassment[23]—is that teenagers have found themselves delivered to treatment centers, sometimes for years at a time.[24]

21. Ibid., 57.

22. Ibid., 56.

23. Conversation with Shannon Minter, Staff Attorney and Youth Project Coordinator at the National Center for Lesbian Rights, 1994.

24. See, for example, Daphne Scholinski's story in *The Last Time I Wore a Dress*, written with Jane Meredith Adams (New York: Riverhead Books, 1997).

REGULATING PSYCHIATRY AND PROTECTING CHILDREN

Gay and lesbian youth are subject to harsher and more punitive forms of the psychiatric intrusions than children diagnosed as suffering from GID. While different in degree, they are not different in kind, since the examples suggest that the behavior that elicits treatment in both cases is often perfectly harmless except for the fact that it violates dominant social norms with regard to gender identity and sexual identity. The behavior of the teenagers described above is not violent; yet because it deviates from dominant norms with regard to gender and sexual identity, it calls for dramatic efforts to restrain it. These sentiments, reflected in norms such as the idea that certain toys and forms of play are appropriate for little girls and not for little boys, are arguably no more than social prejudices and presuppositions about what boys and girls are "essentially like." The "disorders" imputed to gay and lesbian youth and to children diagnosed with GID may be seen as problems embedded in the "social gaze" that is directed at them and finds them disordered only because they fail to comport with its unjustified presuppositions about gender and sexual identity.

In a society that had less rigid notions of masculine and feminine behavior in children and less narrowly heterosexist ideas about teenagers' sexual desire, GID children and gay and lesbian youth would not be perceived to be suffering from psychiatric disorders. In such a society, four-year-olds might have broader conceptions of what constituted appropriate behavior and would be less likely to denounce peers who wished to play Mommy. Parents of gay and lesbian youth or of children like Nathan would not react to negative responses from their children's peers by concluding that their children were suffering from "disorders" that needed clinical and psychiatric intervention. Perhaps most important, the legitimizing gaze of the psychiatric establishment would not so eagerly concur with the negative judgments directed at such youth and children, using its authority to officially constitute them as disordered and in need of therapeutic intervention.

If, as I am arguing, these children and youth suffer from nothing except the effects of social prejudice that results in negative perceptions of their conduct, then subjecting them to medical and psychiatric intrusion and intervention arguably amounts to subjecting them to unjustified harm. Even in the least intrusive cases, such as the "treatment" of Nathan, children are not merely being subject to needless manipulation and surveillance, but are unjustifiably given the message that there is something wrong with their inclinations and dispositions. In addition to subjecting youth and children to violation and manipulation, the arbitrary psychiatric labeling of their conduct as "disordered" works to further subject parents generally, and mothers in particular, to expensive and time-consuming therapeutic intervention. Finally, such arbitrary psychiatric classification serves to reinforce, reinscribe, and legitimize problematic social norms with regard to masculinity and femininity.

Any state that is seriously committed to the prevention of harm and the protection of rights has an obligation to intervene when the rights and welfare of its young citizens are threatened. In what manner should the state intervene? One way is through its ongoing and well-established legal obligation to ensure that the practices of various branches of the medical profession do not operate to adversely affect the well-being of citizens. For example, states and the federal government routinely monitor the safety and side-effects of various drugs and therapies, requiring scientific standards of proof for the efficacy of drugs, and attempt, through licensing standards, to regulate the quality of medical care.

In the context of psychiatric intervention, the state has a corresponding obligation to ensure that diagnostic categories with respect to mental and behavioral disorders are not simply legitimizations of social prejudices. The former classification of homosexuality as a psychiatric disorder was clearly nothing more substantive than a legitimization of homophobic social prejudice, and there is reason to believe that GID is another example of the same. The state must make efforts to prohibit the psychiatric construction of disorders where the behavior that is at issue is not intrinsically harmful and does not diminish the individual's capacities to function. Neither adults nor children should be subject to treatment merely on the grounds that their behavior is unpopular with other individuals. If psychiatric intervention has any legitimate role to play in such cases, it is to provide these children and youth with the skills and strength to negotiate the prejudiced judgments of their peers and families. The state must also ensure that children and youth are not subject to psychiatric intervention on the bases of diagnoses that are no longer officially recognized to constitute illnesses and disorders.[25] It makes little sense that, following the removal of homosexuality from the DSM, gay and lesbian youth can forcibly be sent for treatment to institutions under federally subsidized programs to be "cured" of their

---

25. In an admirable treatment of the subject of homosexuality and adolescence, Bradley and Zucker address this very problem in their recent overview, "Homosexuality in Adolescence" (in *Gender Identity Disorder,* 339–53). However, homosexuality continues to be figured as a "risk factor" for children diagnosed with GID.

homosexuality. It makes even less sense that the state does not intervene to protect the interests of children in these cases.[26]

That is not to say that the state would have an easy time of it. Evidence suggests that lesbian and gay youth who have been institutionalized have been "officially" diagnosed with other disorders.[27] In order to play its regulatory role, the state must be responsive to the evidence of mistreatment of children and adolescents brought to light by journalists, civil rights organizations, and victims themselves. State regulation of psychiatric practice along these lines alone will clearly not suffice to ensure that children who manifest the "symptoms" of GID or gay and lesbian adolescents will face no harassment from their peers who are disturbed by their lack of conformity to prevailing social norms. Nor does it ensure that these children and youth will not be subject to lack of acceptance, manipulation, and anxiety by their parents and families.

While the generation of GID as a clinical disorder may at first appear to be wholly in the hands of psychiatry, maintenance of the disorder is in fact dispersed. In the early case of Nathan, as we have seen, it was not Nathan's behavior but his peers' teasing that alarmed his teacher and parents. This suggests that parents and teachers threatened by a child's nonconformity to prevalent gender norms or made anxious by the fact that a child is teased by his peers would also benefit from a state-supported program of education that could encourage parents and

26. The Bush administration's repudiation and subsequent suppression of Paul Gibson's analysis of "Gay Male and Lesbian Youth Suicide" in the nationally commissioned Report of the Secretary's Task Force on Youth Suicide seems especially pernicious when we consider Gibson's finding that among the risk factors of gay and lesbian youth suicide is the reception of "professional help" from mental health and social work services. See Marcia R. Feinleib, ed., *Report of the Secretary's Task Force on Youth Suicide* (1989), vol. 3. For additional considerations of gay and lesbian suicide rates—estimated to be two to three times more frequent than the rates for other young people—see, for example, Gary Remafedi, ed., *Death by Denial: Studies of Suicide in Gay and Lesbian Teenagers* (Boston: Alyson Publications, 1994).

27. See Ann Heron, ed., *One Teenager in Ten: Writings by Gay and Lesbian Youth* (Boston: Alyson Publications, 1983), and Mirken, "Setting Them Straight." There is, in addition, mounting evidence of the growing numbers of lesbian and gay youth in residential care, as well as the disproportionate representation of gay youth in treatment: e.g., Curtis McMillan, "Sexual Identity Issues Related to Homosexuality in the Residential Treatment of Adolescents," *Residential Treatment for Children and Youth* 9, no. 2 (1991); Gary Mallon, "Gay and No Place to Go: Assessing the Needs of Gay and Lesbian Adolescents in Out-of-Home Settings," *Child Welfare* 71, no. 6 (1992); James B. Teague, "Issues Relating to the Treatment of Adolescent Lesbians and Homosexuals," *Journal of Mental Health Counseling* 14, no. 4 (1992); Louise Armstrong, *And They Call It Help: The Psychiatric Policing of America's Children* (Reading, Mass.: Addison-Wesley, 1993); Margie, "Notes from the Inside," *Sassy*, June 1994; Mirken, "Setting Them Straight"; Carole Rafferty, "Mistaken Identities," *San Jose Mercury News*, 18 July 1995; Scholinski and Adams, *The Last Time I Wore a Dress*.

teachers to respond differently to children's gender nonconformity. Such a program of education would make it less likely that concerned parents would willingly subject their children (and themselves) to institutional scrutiny, surveillance, and attributions of pathology.

Education may play an especially important role in light of the vested interests of the mental health industry in the treatment of adolescents. Between 1980 and 1984 (the last time statistics were available), adolescent admission rates to psychiatric units of private hospitals "jumped dramatically, increasing four-fold."[28] Lois Weithorn has argued that such figures are attributable in part to a series of legal reforms enacted during the 1970s that considerably checked the authority of courts and mental health professionals to commit adults against their will, establishing "procedural protections and substantive standards ... [which] did not extend to juvenile hospitalization procedures."[29] These reforms left a considerable gap in the mental health industry, one that it was able to fill in the wake of the decriminalization of status offenses (e.g., truancy, running away), which had previously placed juvenile offenders under the authority of the justice system.[30] At the same time, laws affording great latitude to parents to oversee their children, such as the 1979 Supreme Court decision *Parham v. J. R.*, endorsed "unbridled discretion for parents ... and admitting staffs in decisions concerning juvenile admissions to [psychiatric] facilities."[31] Education, directed not only at parents but also at health care workers, could circumvent the substantial legal barriers to interventions on behalf of lesbian and gay youth.

Children and adolescents are a socially and politically powerless group, often vulnerable to harm and manipulation by authority figures such as parents and doctors, who often may sincerely act out of their own sense of what is in the child's best interests. And while a liberal state must respect parental authority to bring up their children in the ways they see fit, it must also actively intervene when the exercise of parental prerogatives threatens the child's well-being. Just as the state acts to protect the rights and interests of seriously ill children whose parents refuse them medical treatment on religious grounds, the state

28. Lois Weithorn, "Mental Hospitalization of Troublesome Youth: An Analysis of Skyrocketing Admission Rates," *Stanford Law Review* 40 (1988): 773; see also Nina Darnton, "Committed Youth," *Newsweek,* 31 July 1989.

29. Weithorn, "Mental Hospitalization of Troublesome Youth," 779–80.

30. Ira M. Schwartz et al., "The 'Hidden' System of Juvenile Control," *Crime and Delinquency* 30, no. 3 (1984).

31. Weithorn, "Mental Hospitalization of Troublesome Youth," 809.

must also act to protect children in cases where their parents wish to subject them to medical and psychiatric treatment simply for nonconformity with parental norms of sexuality and gender. The cases of GID and the psychiatric "treatment" of gay and lesbian youth that I have discussed vividly bring home the need for the state to accord children and youth these forms of protection.

10

Protecting Faith Versus Protecting Futures

Religious Freedom and Parental Rights in Medical Decision Making for Children

LYNN PASQUERELLA

With few notable exceptions, current policy presumes that minors, defined in most states as children under the age of eighteen, are incompetent to make decisions about their health care. However, recent highly publicized cases, including the case of a fifteen-year-old Florida boy who engaged in a legal battle over the right to refuse treatment following a liver transplant and the case of a Massachusetts teenager who fled across the country in order to avoid chemotherapy for Hodgkin's disease, have resulted in renewed calls for policy review concerning the rights of children to assent to medical care.

The debate is both multifaceted and complex. It encompasses such diverse issues as whether parents should be allowed to enroll their HIV–positive children in clinical trials when there is no obvious benefit to the individual (though there may be a benefit to other children), whether dying children should be given the right to possess living wills, whether parents should be allowed to give consent to organ donation from one of their children for the sake of a sibling, and whether children whose parents have requested institutionalization should be allowed hearings to refuse psychiatric care. Yet, nowhere is the debate over medical care for children more contentious than when discussing the justified societal limits and legal sanctions that may be placed on religiously motivated parents who make medical decisions affecting their children. As a result of adherence to their religious convictions, such parents either fail to provide necessary medical care for their children or impose medically futile treatment, sacrificing a child's health, well-being, and at times, the child's life itself.

The polemic surrounding this particular issue has been intensified by the introduction in the U.S. Congress of a parental rights bill sponsored by conservative politicians and religious leaders who are seeking broader protections for parents against intrusions by the state in the realm of education and public health. The proposed "Parental Rights and Responsibilities Act" is accompanied by amendments to the constitutions of twenty-eight states that follow model language asserting that "the right of parents to direct the upbringing and education of their children shall not be infringed."[1] Although the major impact of this bill would likely be felt in the area of education, children's rights advocates, including members of the American College of Pediatrics, have expressed concern over the potential ramifications for children's health. They, along with other critics of the proposal, argue that parental rights must be balanced against a legitimate governmental interest in the protection of children, that allowing individual states to place legislative obstacles in the way of government's duties under the principle of *parens patriae* will only jeopardize the health and welfare of children.[2] Furthermore, such legislation is likely to obfuscate the already muddled case law surrounding what limits may be placed on parental decision making when a child's life is at stake.

In what follows, I will consider the extent to which we are justified in restricting religiously motivated parents from refusing medical treatment for their children.[3] This, in turn, will involve an investigation into how influential the values of religious tolerance and pluralism should be in shaping policies that involve not only determining and protecting the

1. Peter Applebome, "Array of Opponents Battle over 'Parental Rights' Bills," *New York Times*, 29 April 1996, A1.

2. Ibid., B7.

3. Although my focus here will be on instances where parents are withholding traditional medical care out of religious conviction, equally compelling are those cases in which religiously motivated parents demand medically futile treatment on the grounds that they have a "right to expect a miracle." Such cases include parents who, on religious grounds, refuse to accept brain death as equal to death and thereby demand futile treatment to sustain biological function, along with circumstances under which parents refuse removal from a ventilator that serves no benefit other than prolonging biological life and at the same time imposes substantial burdens by prolonging suffering.

child's interests, but also determining who has the right to make such decisions. I will further consider the basis on which these decisions should be made and how conflicts should be resolved when a child's interest in health, well-being, and future self-determination is at odds with the parents' interest in freedom of religious belief and practice. I argue that strict limits ought to be placed on parents' rights in the context of medical decision making and that these limits should take two forms: (1) the repeal of exemption clauses in child abuse and neglect statutes that pertain to religiously motivated denial of necessary medical care, and (2) the inclusion of legal standards that give a voice to children in the courts, allowing them to participate in medical decision making.

A BRIEF HISTORY OF PARENTAL RIGHTS IN RELATION TO MEDICAL DECISION MAKING

Throughout its legislative history, the U. S. Supreme Court has never directly addressed the question of what limits the government may impose on parents making medical decisions for their children. Still, a number of important cases related to parental rights and state intervention have had a significant impact on decisions in this area. In these cases, the courts were involved in assessing the appropriate limits of the state's infringement on parental autonomy. During the first half of this century, three cases were paramount in setting the stage for determining limits on state intervention. First, in 1923 the U.S. Supreme Court, in *Meyer v. Nebraska,* invalidated a state law enacted during World War I that banned the teaching of foreign languages prior to the eighth grade. In deciding this case, the justices cited, among the liberties falling under the provisions of the Fourteenth Amendment, the "right to marry and [the] right to establish a home and bring up children."[4] The Court further ruled that these rights "may not be interfered [with], under the guise of protecting the public interest, by legislative action which is arbitrary or without reasonable relation to some purpose within the competency of the State to effect."[5] A second case, *Pierce v. Society of Sisters,* struck down Oregon's compulsory public school attendance law in 1925, allowing parents to "direct the upbringing of their children as they see fit."[6] Both rulings are considered decisive in establishing the family as a

4. *Meyer v. Nebraska,* 262 U.S. 390 (1923).
5. Ibid.
6. *Pierce v. Society of Sisters,* 268 U.S. 510 (1925).

private realm that the state cannot enter without a compelling interest. In addition, in the case of *Pierce*, the Court recognized for the first time parental authority to waive the positive claim rights of children—in this case to be provided with a public education. Notably, like its predecessor *Meyer*, the *Pierce* decision was based on parental claims to due process under the Fourteenth Amendment.

Whereas the two previous cases reinforce parental authority with respect to child rearing, including the right to control that child's religious development, limits to this authority were outlined in a now-famous 1944 ruling, *Prince v. Massachusetts*. The *Prince* case involved the question of whether appeal to rights under religious freedom could exempt a Jehovah's Witness defendant from prosecution under child labor laws for having a nine-year-old niece in her custody distribute religious reading material in the evenings. Despite the fact that this case did not involve consenting to medical care, its repercussions for the rights of parents to refuse medical treatment on behalf of their children has been quite extensive. In setting limits on the activities one can permissibly impose on children, the court made clear that "the right to practice religion freely does not include liberty to expose ... the ... child to ill health or death."[7] The justices maintained that "the state has a wide range of power for limiting parental freedom and authority in things affecting the child's welfare."[8] Furthermore, in a passage most often cited against parents seeking religious exemption from prosecution for refusing necessary medical treatment for their imperiled children, the Court asserted, "Parents may be free to become martyrs themselves. But it does not follow they are free, in identical circumstances, to make martyrs of their children before they have reached the age of full and legal discretion when they can make the choice for themselves."[9]

In spite of the ruling in *Prince*, however, the position favoring parental authority that began with *Meyer* and *Pierce*, culminated in 1972 with the Supreme Court's decision in *Wisconsin v. Yoder*, which has been the only Supreme Court decision upholding a parental free exercise claim. In *Yoder*, Amish parents argued that compulsory education laws for their children through the age of sixteen violated their rights under the Free Exercise Clause of the First Amendment. Being forced to educate their children outside the Amish community past the eighth grade would expose their children, they argued, to "higher learning which tends to develop values the Amish reject as influences that alienate man from

---

7. *Prince v. Massachusetts*, 321 U.S. 158 (1944).
8. Ibid.
9. Ibid. at 170.

God."[10] In balancing the rights and interests of the parents against the interests and duties of the state, the Court noted that, "the Wisconsin law affirmatively compels them, under the threat of criminal sanction, to perform acts undeniably at odds with fundamental tenets of their religious beliefs."[11] The state's interests in this case were framed in terms of a societal interest in preparing children to "meet the duties of citizenship"[12] and "not become burdens on society because of educational shortcomings."[13] The Court ruled that the state failed to justify overriding the religious rights of parents in this instance, citing the self-sufficiency of the Amish community and the absence of the Amish from dependency on welfare and embroilment with the criminal justice system.

While the *Yoder* decision rendered by the Court was framed solely in relation to the members of this particular religious community, whose existence was deemed threatened by state compulsion to expose their children at a vulnerable age to the influences of the outside world, the decision has been widely used by the courts to expand parental rights. Since this landmark decision, states have gone well beyond the intended scope of this case to accommodate the religious beliefs of parents, denying subgroups of children protection under child welfare and education laws.

Indeed, despite the fact that *Yoder* subjects parental duties and rights to limitations "if it appears that parental decisions will jeopardize the health or safety of the child, or have potential for significant social burdens,"[14] beginning in 1974 Congress invited a flurry of legislation in the form of statutes designed to protect religiously motivated parents from neglect and endangerment charges for choosing spiritual treatment or care over traditional medical care for their children. The statutes were encouraged by the Child Abuse Prevention and Treatment Act and regulated by the Department of Health, Education, and Welfare (HEW), which required states receiving federal financial assistance to include a religious exemption in their definitions of "harm or threatened harm to a child's health or welfare." As a result of this religious exemption, accommodations were made such that "a parent or guardian legitimately practicing his or her religious beliefs who thereby does not provide specified medical treatment for a child, *for that reason alone shall not be considered a negligent parent or guardian.*"[15]

10. *Wisconsin v. Yoder,* 460 U.S. 205 at 212.
11. Ibid. at 218.
12. Ibid. at 227.
13. Ibid. at 224.
14. Ibid.
15. 45 C.F.R. s 1340.1–2 (b) (1) 1975.

In 1983, after the Department of Health and Human Resources had taken over for HEW, the Secretary of Health and Human Services concluded that there was no legal support for this sort of religious exemption. Therefore, the regulations related to the Child Abuse and Prevention Act were expanded to include parental "failure to provide adequate medical care." However, this expansion was ineffective given that most states had by this time drafted independent statutes allowing for religious accommodation in instances of misdemeanor neglect. In fact, even though the religious exemption clauses have been dropped from the guidelines issued by the Department of Health and Human Services, most states have adopted and retained statutes that restrict definitions of child abuse and neglect from applying to religiously motivated actors. In the absence of a federal mandate, there remains a good deal of state and local flexibility regarding the scope and interpretation of such exemptions.

SETTING STATE'S LIMITS ON PARENTAL DECISION MAKING

Those who have sought to shield religiously motivated parents from prosecution under child abuse and neglect laws believe that the exemptions are justified by appeal to the Free Exercise clause of the First Amendment. Thus, along with the liberty interests under the Fourteenth Amendment to raise children as one sees fit and to engage in religious indoctrination, the respect for tolerance and pluralism implied by the First Amendment is seen as justifying the exclusion of this particular group of parents from having neglect statutes applied to them. Are such exemptions truly justified, or do they go beyond the scope of permissible accommodation?

As we have seen, the *Prince* case, while upholding parental free exercise rights that include training and indoctrination of children on religious matters, did not extend the scope of protected conduct to practices seriously endangering a child's physical health or safety. Parents have the right under free exercise of religion to control the minds and behavior of their children, but their rights are limited with respect to religious practices that risk the lives of children under their care. *Prince* makes it clear that the state's interest in protecting the welfare of children and in promoting certain social values must be balanced against parental free exercise rights and may, in many cases, override them. I believe that in elevating the religious interests of parents over state concerns for the lives and welfare of children, these exemption statutes violate the principle made explicit in *Prince* that parents do not have the right to make martyrs of their children who have not yet reached the age of full legal discretion.[16]

I will set out four arguments that provide additional support for *Prince's* restriction of parental religious rights in contexts where significant interests related to children's health and well-being are at risk. The first is a moral and political argument that appeals to the state's role in ensuring "open futures" for children. The second argument appeals to children's rights to equal protection from the state. The third argument draws out the implications of equal protection for laws that punitively affect children as a result of their parent's conduct. The fourth and final argument will make the case that such parental exemptions violate the Establishment Clause of the First Amendment.

Childhood is in many ways a stage when children are understandably dependent upon their parents not only for the provision of basic material needs but also for the socialization and education that provides them with values and worldviews as well as the skills that will enable them to function independently of their parents in the future. Though childhood is an inevitable condition of dependency, it is also a temporary condition. It normally leads to adulthood, when children not only function independently of their parents but also may choose paths in life that are not wholly congruent with the worldviews and values of their parents. While parents may predictably raise their children in accordance with their values and worldviews, the recognition that their children must choose their own paths in life when they reach adulthood entails that parents have a responsibility to refrain from decisions that close off significant future opportunities for their children.

This point has been emphasized by Joel Feinberg, who additionally connects these considerations to the role of the state. Feinberg argues that increased intervention on the part of the state is deemed justified if one adopts the view that the state plays a role as an equalizer, assuring that children from vastly different social, economic, and cultural backgrounds all receive a decent minimum level of health care and education, thereby allowing for what Feinberg terms an "open future." I would argue that for those children whose parents are exempted from providing standard medical treatment and immunizations against crippling and life-threatening diseases, the risks are even greater of being denied Feinberg's "open future." In fact, such laws place the child at risk of having no future at all.

16. *Prince* at 170.

In addition to the state function that Feinberg mentions, we need to keep in mind another important state function, that of protecting the rights and interests of all its members. The state regulations from which religiously motivated parents are exempt are intended to serve as protections for children against parental abuse, neglect, and ignorance. Denying this statutory protection to a group of children simply because their parents happen to hold particular religious views violates constitutional provisions for equal protection. Legal scholar James Dwyer points out that an equal protection approach to challenging exemption statutes for religiously motivated parents has the advantage of viewing children as constitutional rights bearers instead of merely the property of their parents.[17] Dwyer contends that when the parents' free exercise claims seem to be the only constitutional rights in the picture, it may seem that the state ought to deny protection to the child. However, an equal protection challenge to this view emphasizes that the child has competing constitutional rights to equal protection in his or her own right, and that the state has a constitutional obligation to protect the child.

Following Dwyer, I would argue that provisions offering religious exemptions for parents allow parental rights to completely subsume the rights and interests of children and fail to acknowledge children as legal individuals who deserve state protection. Since child abuse and neglect laws exist precisely to protect children from the harmful conduct of others, including their parents, these exemptions make no sense unless we have some reason to think that religiously motivated parents would not act in ways that adversely affect the rights and interests of their children. However, we do not have any good reason to make this assumption. Religiously motivated parents may differ from many other abusive or neglectful parents in that they may believe their decision not to provide medical treatment for their sick child is in the best interest of the child. However, where such beliefs are arguably false, and where parents acting on such beliefs endanger the child's life and well-being, the state fails in its duty to provide equal protection to children if it permits parental good intentions to justify child neglect and abuse.

A third and related argument against religious exemption appeals to the idea that it is unfair for children to suffer punitive consequences as a result of their parents' conduct. As the Supreme Court decisions in *Gomez v. Perez*,[18] striking down laws exempting fathers of illegitimate

17. James Dwyer, "The Children We Abandon: Religious Exemptions to Child Welfare and Education Laws as Denials of Equal Protection to Children of Religious Objectors," *North Carolina Law Review* 74 (June 1996): 4.
18. *Gomez v. Perez* 409 U.S. 535 (1973).

children from paying child support, and *Plyler v. Doe*,[19] which invalidated attempts by Texas to deny education to undocumented children of illegal aliens, made clear, it is judicially unacceptable to punish children "on the basis of a legal characteristic over which children can have little control" given that "children can affect neither their parents' conduct nor their own status."[20] Thus, the Court held that imposing a burden on children because of their parents "does not comport with fundamental conceptions of justice."[21] Exemptions for religious objectors likewise impose a substantial burden on children whereby they are allowed to suffer punitive consequences because of their parents' conduct. In this case, the punitive burden is imposed on those children who are excluded from the protections offered by child abuse and neglect statutes.

Our long tradition of respect for parental autonomy and our commitment to the values of tolerance, pluralism, and cultural diversity lessen neither the children's rights claims nor the state's responsibilities to protect children from abuse. Here, the state affirms that the same acts in one case are sufficient to constitute abuse but that in exactly similar circumstances accommodation of the religious beliefs of the parents eliminates the acts from the category of abuse and neglect. By their very nature, then, such exemptions undercut the purpose of protecting the health and welfare of children.

A fourth and final reason for opposing exceptions for religiously motivated parents rests on the argument that such exemptions reflect an endorsement of religion contrary to the Establishment Clause of the First Amendment. According to Justice Sandra Day O'Connor, "Endorsement [of religion] sends a message to nonadherents that they are outsiders, not full members of the political community, and an accompanying message to adherents that they are insiders, favored members of the political community."[22] An analysis of whether the prohibition against endorsement has been violated requires administering a two-pronged test asking: (1) Is the actual purpose of the government to endorse or disapprove of religion? (2) Irrespective of the government's actual purpose, is the effect of the practice to convey a message of endorsement or disapproval? An affirmative answer to either question is sufficient to render the challenged practice invalid. Thus, in the case of *Employment Division Services of Oregon v. Smith,* concerning whether the state could deny unemployment benefits to two Native Americans who were fired

19. *Plyler v. Doe* 457 U.S. 202 (1982).
20. Ibid.
21. Ibid.
22. *Corporation of Presiding Bishop v. Amos,* 483 U.S. 327 (1987) at 348.

for engaging in the ceremonial use of peyote as part of a religious practice, Justice Antonin Scalia contended that the First Amendment should
not be construed to permit governments to enact legislation "solicitous
of religious belief."[23]

While the *Smith* decision is regarded as problematic by many, it raises
considerations pertinent to the issue of exemptions for religiously motivated parents at the center of this essay. Allowing the state to uphold the
religious-freedom rights of the parents at the expense of their children's
rights to protection from abuse and neglect arguably sends a message
of state endorsement to an "objective observer." Both the negative rights
of children to be free from harm and the positive rights to protection
from the state are sacrificed in favor of preserving the rights of religiously motivated parents to exercise their religion as they see fit. Since
exemption laws impermissibly provide increased protection from prosecution simply in virtue of parents' religious beliefs, supporting this type
of legislation has the unconstitutional effect of benefiting religious over
nonreligious individuals. *Smith* upheld the view that there was no constitutional basis requiring governments to enact legislation "solicitous
of religious belief" in a case where the only harms suffered as a consequence of religious belief were those suffered by adults who adhered to
those beliefs and where the harms arguably did not amount to serious
risks to their health or life. I contend that it is far more objectionable to
enact legislation solicitous of religious beliefs where the central harms
that occur as a result of the beliefs are suffered by the children of those
who adhere to these beliefs and where the harms amount to serious risks
to the lives and well-being of children.

LISTENING TO CHILDREN'S VOICES

While the most direct approach to redressing unjust laws involving religious exemption statutes is to repeal the statutes themselves, children's
rights advocates have argued that this approach must be accompanied
by judicial reform that provides children with a voice that, until now,
has been denied them in the courts. Thus, Wendy Anton Fitzgerald has
urged that just as critical race theorists and feminists have asserted that
the law's definition of personhood must expand to include racial, gender,
cultural, and other differences, the law should respect and appreciate

---

23. *Employment Division v. Smith*, 494 U.S. 872 (1990).

children's perspectives and provide a mechanism for the inclusion of children's voices.[24]

Traditionally, the exclusion of children's voices from the courtroom has been based on findings such as those in *Thompson v. Oklahoma*, where the court stated that "the difference that separates children from adults for most purposes of the law is children's immature, undeveloped ability to reason in an adultlike manner."[25] This incapacity theory of childhood, supporting much of the current constitutional law about children's rights, typically denies children any decision-making role in their own medical treatment. However, proponents of including children's voices in the courts point to research indicating that children are often capable of making important life decisions in a rational manner, including decisions about medical and psychological treatment. In addition, apart from the quality of their decisions, studies suggest that "children as young as six can be astute in perceiving procedural injustice."[26] Allowing children to participate in decision making regarding their own health is likely to enhance children's perceptions that they have been treated fairly. In turn, children's involvement in the process has potential therapeutic benefits as well. Thus, even if children's voices merely echo the voices of their parents, who have succeeded in religious indoctrination, this approach may improve the well-being of the child and encourage the establishment of the child as a person independent from the family.

This leads to a second reason traditionally offered for not giving a voice to children in the courts—namely, that it is unnecessary since parental interests *are* the family interests. I believe such arguments not only mistakenly equate parental interests with family interests but assume idealistically that parents, in consultation with the clinician, will make treatment decisions based on the child's best interest. These assumptions have been made even when the child has suffered demonstrable harm as a result of the parental decision. Consider, for instance, the 1912 case of Tony Tuttendario, which set the standard for upholding parental autonomy unless there is a clear "life-threatening exception." Tuttendario was seven years old when doctors sought to perform corrective surgery to repair his legs, misshapen from the effects of rickets. Without the surgery, his parents were informed, Tony "would likely be

---

24. Wendy Anton Fitzgerald, "Maturity, Difference, and Mystery: Children's Perspectives and the Law," *Arizona Law Review* 36 (1994): 5.

25. *Thompson v. Oklahoma*, 487 U.S. 815 (1988) at 835.

26. Laura J. Gold et al., "Children's Perceptions of Procedural Justice," *Child Development* 55 (1984): 1752.

a cripple all his life and unable to provide for himself." Upon the refusal of his parents to consent to the surgery, school authorities notified the Society for the Prevention of Cruelty to Children, who subsequently sought temporary custody in order to have the surgery performed.[27]

Focusing on the fact that Tuttendario's parents were not motivated by cruelty and that the refusal of surgery was not in itself life-threatening, the court remarked:

> We see no warrant in the statutes for granting this request. We have not yet adopted as a public policy the Spartan rule that children belong, not to their parents but to the state. . . . Even if the law had advanced so far as to consider defective judgment of parents in a critical case a good reason to deprive them of their guardianship, we would not be prepared to say that a clear case of defective judgment has been here made out. The science of medicine and surgery, notwithstanding its enormous advances, has not been able to insure an absolutely correct diagnosis in all cases, and still less an absolutely correct prognosis. There is always a residuum of the unknown, and it is this unknown residuum which scientists, by a necessary law for the development of science, disregard, but which parents, in their natural love for their children, regard with apprehension and terror.[28]

The Tuttendario decision served as the basis for ensuing courts holding that unless a parent were proven unfit, the state had no authority to intervene. In this regard the impact of the Tuttendario decision was far-reaching. Underlying the affirmation of parental rights in this case was the presumption that parents would act in their child's best interest out of natural love. Scientists, on the other hand, might readily sacrifice the needs of an individual child to promote their own research and the cause of scientific advancement. These assumptions, together with the uncertain efficacy of treatment protocols at the time, led the court to reject claims that Tony's parents were unfit in virtue of their decision to refuse surgery for their son. The Tuttendario decision was made despite a history beginning as early as 1860 of explicit legislation designed to protect children's lives and health. In fact, a movement to protect children from abuse was capped off by an 1893 bill enacted to permit judicial transfer of minors to charitable societies to guard against child

27. Walter Wadlington, "David C. Baum Memorial Lecture: Medical Decision Making for Children: Tensions Between Parent, State, and Child," *University of Illinois Law Review* (1994): 3.
28. In *re Tuttendario*, 21 Pa. D. at 563.

endangerment, suggesting rightly that parents do not always act in the best interests of their children.[29]

Perhaps because parents exercising their religious beliefs, like Tuttendario's parents, are not motivated by cruelty, the courts have been careful to distinguish neglect involving refusal of medical treatment on religious grounds from other kinds of abuse and neglect. Even so, since the Tuttendario decision, there has been an expansion of the "life-threatening exception" to include nonemergency procedures designed to improve a child's quality of life. Emerging in the second half of the century, this trend in policy related to child protection was evidenced in two interrelated movements—the development and advancement of child abuse reporting statutes, and the provision of guidelines for both emancipated and unemancipated minors to consent to treatment for certain medical conditions.

Of particular interest for our present discussion has been the continued development of the "mature minor" doctrine in the aftermath of the U.S. Supreme Court decision in *Planned Parenthood v. Danforth*.[30] In this decision, the Court ruled that states were prohibited from requiring parental consent for an unmarried minor's abortion. They did, however, permit a state requirement of a judicial determination that a minor is mature enough to give informed consent. Under current common law, a minor is granted the right to consent to or refuse treatment if there is clear and convincing evidence that the child is mature enough to exercise the judgment of an adult. The privacy rights cited as the basis for allowing mature minors to consent to abortions and the treatment of certain other conditions and diseases without parental approval might also be seen to justify extending the mature minor doctrine to different circumstances.

For instance, consider the cases of fifteen-year-old Benny Agrelo, who refused to take necessary medication following a liver transplant, and sixteen-year-old Billy Best, who fled from Massachusetts to California because he couldn't cope with the hair loss, nausea, and weakness from his regimen of chemotherapy.[31] Similar to the case of a young woman seeking an abortion, medical decisions involving life-sustaining treatment are irreversible and must be made within a limited amount of time. Moreover, the burdens imposed by infringements on privacy and

29. Wadlington, "David C. Baum Memorial Lecture."

30. *Planned Parenthood of Missouri v. Danforth*, 428 U.S. 476 (1976).

31. For a discussion of these cases, see Jessica A. Penkower, "The Potential Right of Chronically Ill Adolescents to Refuse Life-Saving Medical Treatment: Fatal Misuse of the Mature-Minor Doctrine," *DePaul Law Review* 45 (1996): 1165.

bodily autonomy are substantial in both contexts. Thus, while the "mature minor" standard is vague and lends itself to differing judicial determinations in individual cases, explicit expansion of the mature minor doctrine to the realm of medical consent and treatment refusal would have the benefit of promoting children's rights to self-determination based on privacy and bodily integrity. While ultimately the courts ruled in their favor, an earlier recognition of these rights could have spared Agrelo and Best untold pain and suffering.

Yet even with a statutory or common law acceptance of children's rights to self–determination in such cases, there are special challenges when dealing with children of religious objectors. This follows from the fact that pediatricians have ordinarily served as gatekeepers concerning whether a child's case should be brought to the courts. What is problematic in cases involving religiously motivated parents is that the child may never see a medical practitioner outside of the religious community. Hence, if we want to provide meaningful protection for children, efforts to include children in the decision-making process must be preceded by mandatory reporting to the state by parents who seek to deny traditional care in cases of serious illness. Disputes concerning the effectiveness of such laws in serving as either specific or general deterrents have not prevented abuse and neglect statutes from being enacted overall and should not be an overriding consideration here either. Moreover, the often-cited problem of determining the exact point at which otherwise legal behavior becomes illegal, when, for instance, the child becomes seriously ill, is not exclusive to this type of situation and has not served as sufficient justification for failure to apply the law.

CONCLUSION

Allowing exemptions from abuse and neglect statutes for religiously motivated parents who deny their children traditional medical care has provided unprecedented protection for one group at the expense of another. Even in instances where states have aggressively sought to end this injustice and prosecute parents for the deaths of their children, the existence of various statutes around the country and differing interpretations of laws protecting the rights of parents have led to successful postconviction appeals on the bases of vagueness and failure to provide adequate notice of the law, in violation of due process. By refusing to take a firm, unified stance forcing the repeal of statutes protecting religiously motivated parents and by excluding children's perspectives from the courtroom, we have denied equal protection to some of our most vulnerable citizens.

Several factors, including the notion of parents' ownership of children, the essentially private nature of families that makes it difficult to know what goes on behind closed doors, and the extreme powerlessness of children, make it necessary for the courts to establish the child as a person, independent from the family. Indeed, unless we are willing to take the obvious step of abolishing laws that overtly discriminate against children, we will continue to relegate children to the status of a legally oppressed minority.

11

Fear of God

Religious Education of Children and the Social Good

JULIA J. BARTKOWIAK

The role of religious education in the public schools in the United States of America has a varied and controversial history. In recent debates, many participants have relied on liberal principles to favor the introduction of mandatory religious education classes at the secondary, and sometimes even the elementary, level. I intend to reject this liberal view that there are good reasons for public schools to provide children with courses about the world's religions, arguing instead that the public school systems of modern liberal democratic states should *not* offer children mandatory courses in the world's religions. Critically examining common arguments for the view that the public schools in a liberal state should, or must, teach religious studies courses, I intend to show that these arguments are seriously flawed because proponents do not consider the distorted and harmful ways in which such courses are likely, in practice, to be taught. Additionally, I will argue that those proponents who believe that such courses should be *mandatory* are requesting a program of study that is inconsistent with recent Supreme Court decisions

I would like to thank Uma Narayan for her extensive comments on several drafts of this paper. Gereon Kopf and Dwayne Mulder both offered helpful comments on the final draft.

and that unjustifiably infringes on parental rights and freedom of religion. Finally, I will argue that the liberal goals envisioned by proponents can be better achieved without offering religious education in the public schools.

LIBERAL ARGUMENTS FOR RELIGIOUS EDUCATION

Discussions concerning the teaching of courses on world religions in the public schools often assume that such courses would advance liberal values. Those liberals who favor religious education rely on a few common arguments regarding the envisioned goal of such courses. The first argument suggests that exposure to a wide range of religious views is in the best interests of children.[1] Such exposure is claimed both to present children with an important range of alternative worldviews and value schemas and to prevent parents from indoctrinating their children. Proponents believe that, compared to being provided with a monolithic religious upbringing that "constricts children's future possibilities,"[2] it is in the child's interest to be offered a wider range of options from which they can choose as they mature. Religious studies courses, it is argued, help offer children an "open future." In other words, proponents of this view argue that, while parents have a right to provide training and grounding for their children in a particular religion, the liberal state may have an interest in requiring children to have exposure to a wider range of religious and moral views than those provided or endorsed by their parents.

Contemporary liberal positions that offer such "open future" rationales for supporting world religion classes in public schools often rely on J. S. Mill's views in *On Liberty*. However, it is not clear that Mill's views support these contemporary arguments. When Mill directly addresses the state's role in religious education, he claims:

> There would be nothing to hinder them [children] from being taught religion, *if their parents chose*, at the same schools where

---

1. For a detailed example of this view, see Hugh LaFollette, "Freedom of Religion and Children," in *Children's Rights Re-Visioned: Philosophical Readings*, ed. Rosalind Ekman Ladd (Belmont, Calif.: Wadsworth, 1996), 159–69. More general arguments addressing the "open future" of the child can be found in Tibor R. Machan, "Between Parents and Children," *Journal of Social Philosophy* 23, no. 3 (1992): 16–22; and Michael S. Pritchard, *Reasonable Children: Moral Education and Moral Learning* (Lawrence: University Press of Kansas, 1996), 96–97.

2. Laura Purdy, "Schooling," in *Children's Rights Re-Visioned*, 155.

they were taught other things. All attempts by the State to bias the conclusions of its citizens on disputed subjects are evil; but it may very properly offer to ascertain and certify that a person possesses the knowledge requisite to make his conclusions on any given subject worth attending to. . . . and there is no reasonable objection to examining an atheist in the evidences of Christianity, provided he is not required to profess a belief in them.[3]

Mill's position includes parental choice in children's religious education. Since this is the case, Mill's views do not offer uncontroversial support for the "best interest" arguments regarding the introduction of religious education in the public schools.

Although I would agree that narrowly defining any child's future may not be in her best interest, it does not follow that children must be able to choose from many, or all, available options. Garvey has argued that parents regularly make choices that significantly affect their children's futures, and he rejects the liberal view that it is in the child's interest to increase the number of options they have available to them as adults. He points out:

There are two problems with this theory. The first is what Joel Feinberg calls the self-determination paradox. . . . Parents may do their best to keep choices open for X, so that he can make up his own mind when he becomes an adult. But when X finally gets around to choosing, he will be guided by values, talents, and propensities that are themselves largely the result of parental influences.

The second problem is this, even if parents could promote self-determination by offering X a smorgasbord, it is not objectively clear that they should. Autonomy is an ideal just as knowledge, power, virtue, and the service of God are ideals. Each states a certain view of what people ought to be like, of how they can best live their lives. Adults do not all subscribe to the same ideal, and courts should not require children to.[4]

Garvey and Feinberg have offered reasons to question the argument that the state, acting in the child's best interest, can legitimately interfere with the parents' right to teach their children only those religious

3. J. S. Mill, *On Liberty*, ed. Elizabeth Rapaport (Indianapolis: Hackett, 1978), 106. The emphasis is mine.
4. John H. Garvey, "Freedom and Representation," in *Kindred Matters: Rethinking the Philosophy of the Family*, ed. Diana Tietjens Meyers et al. (Ithaca, N.Y.: Cornell University Press, 1993), 188.

views they deem appropriate. Thus, proponents of the "best interest" view cannot simply assume that the state has an obligation to provide children a wide range of options. It is unlikely that such options will automatically have a dramatic effect on children's choices for their future. Additionally, providing a wide range of options is not a value-free goal; it is a goal that is not shared by all citizens and would not be in the state's interest in many cases. For example, the liberal state would be under no obligation to provide children with their choice of political systems from which to choose in adulthood. Proponents of the "best interest" view concerning religious education must address these objections, and it is not clear that an adequate response can be developed.

Another argument that is often relied on in the "best interest" argument is that lack of choices about religious views results in significant harm to the child. Based on the traditional liberal view that state interference is legitimate when there is harm to others, proponents claim that mandating religious education in the public schools is within the government's authority. However, invoking this liberal principle does not help to resolve this issue. Arguments that rely on the liberal principle of preventing harm must accept that some parents, at least from their own perspectives, have good reason for denying their children access to alternative religious views. From these parents' perspective, mandatory exposure to differing religious views would significantly increase the risk of harm to their children—their children would be in danger of accepting views that would be far more dangerous for them than any physical harm. These opposing sides, both of which rely on this harm principle, seem unlikely to agree on who has correctly identified the "true" harm. Other than rejecting particular religious views as false, I see no way to resolve this disagreement. Consequently, a religiously neutral state cannot effectively use this principle to settle the matter.

Another liberal argument for religious courses in public schools appeals to both the interests of citizens and of the liberal state. Proponents suggest that a well-functioning liberal state, especially one with a diverse population, requires citizens to be respectful and tolerant of a wide range of worldviews and ways of life. Since religious differences are an important and defining aspect of the views and ways of life espoused by various groups within contemporary nations, exposing children to a wide range of religious views would be an important step toward the cultivation of religiously tolerant citizens who are respectful of diversity. Advocates of this position point out that intolerance of religious differences has been the source of serious political conflicts within and across nations in the past as well as the present, leading not only to war but also to civil unrest and the suppression and oppression of religious minorities. They believe that it is in the liberal state's interest, and the interest of its citizens, to encourage tolerance.[5] The study of the world's religions as part of a public education is seen as an effective means of satisfying the state's interest in promoting tolerance and understanding in its citizens.

However, advocates of mandatory world religion classes within the public schools have not always realized that the introduction of such classes, by itself, is unlikely to perform the envisioned role of increasing tolerance. If children are to learn tolerance, exposure to others' religious views must be positive. In other words, exposure to a variety of views, by itself, does not automatically result in tolerant children. Children can easily be taught to criticize the practices of others and become less tolerant when the exposure they have to the views of others is one that finds fault and grievous errors with such beliefs.

There are good reasons to think that, under existing conditions within many public schools, such courses would fail to promote tolerance. First, teachers can easily fail to make exposure to religions positive. If teachers have dogmatic religious views, or even views that are opposed to all religious beliefs, they may teach about religions in a derogatory manner. This kind of undermining of some or all religious views can occur even in settings that have a standardized curriculum. The teacher's intonation, gestures, presentation of material, and suggestions during class cannot be closely monitored even under such circumstances, and these methods of inducing criticism can easily undermine the purpose for which the course was intended. This is especially problematic in those public schools in which most of the children within the class and the majority of the community share the teacher's religious views. Under such conditions, a teacher who is not providing positive exposure to other religious or moral views will only reinforce the children's own prejudices, and this teacher would be unlikely to face strong sanctions from school officials or the community. A world religions course taught in a derogatory manner certainly will not increase tolerance.

Another serious concern is that teachers, *despite good intentions* to promote tolerance and understanding, will teach world religions courses poorly. Such courses will be successful only if teachers are well informed about, and familiar with, the religious traditions of the world. In practice,

5. For an example of this view, see Laura Purdy, "Schooling," 149–58; or Stephen Macedo, "Multiculturalism for the Religious Right? Defending Liberal Civic Education," *Journal of Philosophy of Education* 29, no. 2 (1995): 223–38.

teachers who do not have this knowledge could present unfamiliar traditions poorly, and inadvertently make the views sound bizarre and contemptible rather than positive. Ignorance of the religions of the world could also cause the teacher to explain more thoroughly the views of the familiar/dominant religions and answer students' questions about those religions more skillfully than those about less familiar religious traditions. The overall effect then would be that students in such a class might be left with the sense that the views of the unfamiliar religions were strange, arbitrary, or immoral compared to those of the more familiar religious traditions. If the person teaching the course is not able to provide students with an understanding of why different people hold the beliefs they do (and also allay the fears of students and parents who have been taught that even discussing such issues can be immoral), the class will not achieve its goal; it will not encourage tolerance of others.

In fact, many teachers in the United States are currently not well prepared to teach these classes. Thus, a policy of instituting mandatory world religions courses would require a method to ensure that the persons teaching the course would be competent. Presently, a few states do have a certification for teaching about religion, but these certifications are typically for a teaching minor.[6] Because of this lack of training, teachers in most public schools are not proficient enough to teach a world religions course, and we can safely assume that many secondary school teachers did not receive an education in world religions as part of their own schooling. Consequently, in practice, the teachers assigned to a world religions course would often be poorly prepared for teaching such a class. If religious education is mandated in the public schools, a school district will be required to implement such a course even when it does not have teachers who are adequately prepared to teach it.

These practical concerns suggest that the liberal goals envisioned by proponents of religious education in the public schools are unlikely to be achieved. Before implementing mandatory religious education in the public schools, there must be clear evidence that this area of state interference is a legitimate one, that the goals are desirable, and that the goals can be accomplished by the suggested means. Liberals who favor these courses have not provided this evidence, and I have provided reasons for thinking it unlikely that such a requirement would, in practice, promote the envisioned goals.

6. Charles R. Kniker, *Teaching About Religion in the Public Schools* (Bloomington, Ind.: Phi Delta Kappa Educational Foundation, Fastback 224, 1985), 15.

"TEACHING *ABOUT*" VERSUS "TEACHING *OF*" RELIGION

Many of the current conflicts over the role of religion in U.S. public schools raise issues of how a liberal state is to balance its constitutional commitment to freedom of religion with its constitutional commitment to a separation of church and state. In 1963, with the *Schempp/Murray* decisions, the Supreme Court declared it unconstitutional for public schools to conduct morning prayers. This decision followed the 1948 *McCollum* ruling that banned religious education classes that promoted particular religious views (in reality this primarily meant Christian views) within a public school education. However, neither of these rulings prohibited the discussion of religion within public schools. In fact, the majority and concurring opinions in *Schempp/Murray* distinguished between teaching *about* religion and the teaching *of* religion.[7] They deemed only the latter unacceptable and encouraged the former. These rulings were intended to place restrictions on *how* religious views can be taught. They required that religion be taught comparatively or historically rather than with a view to promoting one religion as the universal truth. The justices declared that while the U.S. constitutional right to freedom of religion does not allow religious practices to be forced on children who attend public schools, courses that presented the religious practices of various people in a historical and comparative manner were essential to being well educated and were constitutionally permissible.

Liberal proponents of a world religion course in the public schools rely heavily on the Supreme Court's distinction between "teaching *about* religion" and the "teaching *of* religion." Although the distinction is believed to be a clear one, with teaching *about* religion involving a historical and comparative approach and teaching *of* religion involving a dogmatic indoctrination of children, this distinction is unclear at best, and is unable, in practice, to provide an adequate means of determining which courses would be acceptable and which would not. Whether a teacher teaches *of* religion or teaches *about* religion depends on how religious views are taught, not how many religions are addressed. There are a number of ways, including those previously mentioned, in which a teacher could, deliberately or inadvertently, teach comparative and historical material on religions in a manner that amounts to the teaching *of* a particular religion. Since teachers can present materials in ways that endorse one set of religious views and communicate disdain or contempt for others, teaching *about* religion does not result from insisting that the

---

7. I would like to thank Gereon Kopf for pointing out that this distinction is sometimes referred to as the "study in religion" vs. the "study of religion."

course syllabus or the materials presented are comparative and historical. The liberal state cannot (and should not), in practice, engage in adequate surveillance and monitoring of teachers and classrooms where such courses are taught. Consequently, the liberal state that mandates world religion courses must rely on the goodwill and competence of teachers in ensuring that the teaching *of* religion is not engaged in under the guise of teaching *about* religion.

There is little doubt, however, that some teachers would use such courses to proselytize about their own religious views. For those teachers who adhere to a religion that believes there is only one correct set of religious beliefs, there is little incentive to accept the validity of alternative beliefs or to present them as alternatives that deserve tolerance and respect. Such teachers might also believe that acceptance of alternative views can only result in a decrease in moral behavior and grave spiritual harm. They might well believe that tolerance of competing views would have negative consequences not only for individual children but also for the entire society. Consequently, such teachers would have little reason to attempt to provide students with the type of world religions course envisioned by its proponents. Instead, these teachers would have an incentive to use such courses as a method to teach *of* religion. Additionally, since such teachers would typically view the consequences as eternal ones, this incentive is significantly stronger than in other subject areas.

Since 1963, public schools have dealt with recent Supreme Court rulings in a variety of ways. Religious education and practices in some schools provide evidence that, contrary to the Court rulings, particular religious views are regularly taught. Federal courts have dealt with a number of legal challenges to public school practices that concern the separation of church and state, and some of these cases demonstrate that schools have gone so far as to ignore the prohibition on the teaching *of* religion. In those schools that have abided by the Supreme Court decisions, the religious studies courses have not accomplished the liberal vision. Instead, a pattern has emerged. As Kniker points out:

> Surveys of religion studies in the public schools since 1963 show that they tend to fall into three areas. The most popular is the "Bible as Literature" course followed by "Comparative Religions" or "Religions of the World." The third most common course or unit deals with the broad area of religion in American history. All these courses are at the secondary level; much less has been done at the elementary level.[8]

8. Kniker, *Teaching About Religion in the Public Schools*, 14.

In two of the three types of courses—the Bible as literature, and religion in American history—it is especially easy for teachers to promote a particular religious view, most likely the dominant Christian view.[9] Thus, given the significant risk that in a great number, if not the majority, of such courses, teachers may end up engaged in the teaching *of* religion, the state's interest in ensuring that public education does not promote particular religious views, I believe, would be better served by not mandating world religion courses in public schools.

IMPLEMENTING RELIGIOUS EDUCATION IN PUBLIC SCHOOLS

Schools that offer religious education courses in their curriculum have three options for implementing such courses: providing them as mandatory courses, as required courses that provide parents an opportunity to exclude their children, or as elective courses. Typically, liberal proponents of religious education in the public schools have argued that these courses should be a part of a mandatory curriculum,[10] and I have rejected this position for practical reasons. However, mandatory religious education raises another important set of concerns. First, it seems clear that offering these courses as a mandatory part of the curriculum is unconstitutional. Previous federal court decisions have rejected mandatory courses, including sex education courses, which parents have claimed interfere with their ability to teach their children particular religious views. Offering mandatory world religion classes clearly violates these rulings.

In their eagerness to provide children with "open futures" and encourage tolerance, proponents of mandatory world religion courses have often overlooked the fact that such courses might seriously infringe upon parental rights to determine their children's upbringing and religious training. Such parental rights may justifiably be infringed upon when

9. In fact, a case from the Fifth Circuit Court of Appeals provides one example of such a class: "In *Hall v. Board of School Commissioners of Conecuh City* (1982), the circuit court ruled that a high school Bible in Literature course violated the First Amendment because its intent, effect, and practice was to teach religion rather than study about religion. The textbook for the course was *The Bible for Youthful Patriots,* which the court found to be fundamentalist and evangelical in nature and tended to promote Protestantism over all other types of religion. The court ruled that for the course to meet constitutional guidelines, it must be taught in an objective fashion that complied with a secular purpose." Quoted from Eugene T. Connors, *Religion and the Schools: Significant Court Decisions in the 1980s* (Bloomington, Ind.: Phi Delta Kappa Educational Foundation, Fastback 272), 30.

10. See LaFollette, "Freedom of Religion and Children"; and Macedo, "Multiculturalism for the Religious Right?"

there are serious risks to the health and well-being of children, as in cases of parents who refuse, for religious reasons, to provide medical treatment for their seriously ill children. However, it is not clear that there are serious enough competing rights or interests at stake to justify the imposition of mandatory education concerning world religions when parents are opposed to their children's attending such courses. Any competing interests, such as allowing children to have an "open future" or a liberal society's need for tolerant citizens, do not seem to clearly outweigh parental rights to religiously educate their children and are made less compelling by the fact that these courses could be taught in a manner that promotes dogmatism.

Brenda Almond rejects religious education in public schools. She argues that the liberal state should not be engaged in encouraging or discouraging particular religious views, claiming that:

> the principle that should guide a Government which sets a high priority on liberty is that of leaving the ultimate determination of any child's individual experience to the maximum possible extent in the hands of the child's own family. Within schools, the aim should be to recognize and develop diverse talents and interests, rather than to attempt to produce a uniform product.[11]

Almond, following the Universal Declaration of Human Rights, argues for the primacy of the parents to determine what their children learn regarding religious views. She believes that religious freedom in a liberal state requires that people be allowed "to bring up their children according to their own beliefs, even if to others, perhaps even to the great majority, these beliefs seem in many ways irrational or misguided."[12] It is interesting to note that Almond supports the same liberal ideals that have motivated many of the arguments in favor of mandatory world religion classes. Based on these very different interpretations of the connection between the liberal state and the religious instruction of children, invoking the liberal tradition and what it requires of us will not resolve this debate.

However, previous federal court decisions have been "surprisingly consistent" in ruling that the constitutional guarantee of freedom of religion is not violated when public school courses are required but offer some type of exemption for religious reasons.[13] The options of providing

---

11. Brenda Almond, "Education and Liberty: Public Provision and Private Choice," in *Children's Rights Re-Visioned*, 148.

12. Ibid., 145.

13. Connors, *Religion and the Schools*, 31–36.

religious education in the public schools either as a required course that provides parents an opportunity to exclude their children or as an elective part of the school curriculum both allow parents to deny permission for their child to take a world religions class. In a liberal democratic state, these two options are the only acceptable ones. Unlike mandatory classes, these options provide parents with an opportunity to determine that such a course is not acceptable for their child. Undoubtedly, some people would still be opposed to world religions courses even if their children were not required to participate in them. However, this opposition can reasonably be assumed to be less adamant than would be encountered if parents were not able to deny participation in such a course to their own children.

Parents may wish to exclude their children from religious education courses for two kinds of reasons. They many regard such courses as harmful to the spiritual well-being of the child. But as my previous discussion shows, parents may also have qualms about such courses being poorly or dogmatically taught. Parents who desire their children to be tolerant of others' religious views have good reason to withdraw their children from a world religions course in which the teacher is unprepared or dogmatic. Not only will such courses fail to meet the educational objective envisioned for them, but they will also do little to encourage tolerance or provide children with an "open future." In fact, a course taught by a dogmatic teacher would promote the very indoctrination that the proponents of mandatory religious education courses are opposed to, and even these proponents would object to their children's attendance in such a course.

Finally, a rejection of mandatory attendance in religion classes typically would not result in a lack of exposure to other religious views for those children who do not attend. In many areas of the United States today, children who are old enough to attend public schools will acquire some acquaintance with different religious views and traditions outside the classroom. This contact is even available to Amish children who, at least, have seen that other people do not live the same style of life that is lived within their religious community. In addition, children who attend a school in which a world religions course either allows for exemptions or is optional are likely to hear some discussion of this subject outside of the classroom. Lunchroom conversations, talk in the hall, and discussions after school are likely to include some mention of what the students have learned within the world religions course. Thus, many children in a public school may be exposed to alternative religious views even if they do not take these courses. Those children who still lack this exposure to other religious views are unlikely to remain ignorant of all other religious views during their adult lives. Additionally, it is not obvious that exposure to other religious views is essential for children's religious choices when they are adults or for creating tolerant individuals.

Religious education as it is legally allowed within the public schools is also not an effective means of achieving liberal goals. If parents have the ability to exclude their children from these courses, then parents whose own religious views promote intolerance would be most likely to exercise the option of keeping their children out of such courses. Children whose parental upbringing makes them most in need of acquiring tolerance and understanding of other religions also are likely not to elect such courses on their own. Thus, those children who have the kind of dogmatic upbringing that is claimed to deny them an "open future" are precisely those who will not have the benefits of an education in the world's religions. Those parents who desire such a course for their children are precisely the ones whose own efforts at raising their children are already likely to involve strong encouragement of tolerance and acceptance of diversity. Their children would already be raised in the manner claimed to provide them with "open futures." Offering religion courses as either dependent on parental consent or optional, as they legally must be, guarantees that those children most likely to benefit will not take the class, and those children who do take the class will be least in need of these envisioned benefits. Thus while the options of either having religious education as a mandatory course that allows for denial of parental consent or as an elective are preferable to mandatory courses, it is not clear how much good they will achieve in practice even if well taught. Given the previous reasons for thinking that many of these courses will not be well taught, I believe the social good is better served by not implementing religious education in the public schools.

INCREASING TOLERANCE WITHIN THE LIBERAL STATE

Liberal polities have an understandable concern about intolerance and violence that results from strong disagreements between people holding differing religious views. One need only look at the violence within the world at the present time to recognize that numerous political conflicts are connected to religious disagreements. However, allowing individuals to freely practice the religious beliefs of their choice is critically important because religious beliefs are a fundamental part of who we are as individuals. Our religious beliefs provide us with a way of interpreting the world. Thus, restrictions placed on our religious beliefs can also be viewed as restrictions that limit who we are. Behind the separation of church and state lies an awareness that a society that determines what religious beliefs will be allowed simultaneously places restrictions on individuals that set limits on what those citizens, and that society, can attain.[14]

At the same time, freedom of religion *will* result in some intolerance. In spite of the relatively common religious prohibition on killing or harming other human beings (or all living creatures), religious views have historically been used to justify violent behaviors ranging from verbal attacks to torturing someone to death—all in the name of God or Gods. One need only look around the world today to find that religion is part of some of the most aggressive actions of human beings. Why does this happen? I agree with those liberals who suggest that increased violence is more likely to occur when individuals hold religious views claiming that anyone who does not accept those views is completely wrong—especially if those views claim that the nonbelievers are immoral or evil. When this attitude is prevalent, it is not difficult to create an environment in which believers become the enemies of nonbelievers. Consequently, although many religions claim that they are interested in promoting love and peace, there is a tendency for some religions, in practice, to promote intolerance and violence. Thus, not only does religious education within a family or community not always accomplish the goals of love and peace, but it often ensures that we will continue to see intolerance, hatred, and violence between individuals of diverse religious communities. However, the liberal state already has legal mechanisms that can address violence between individuals. Since the introduction of world religions classes, especially mandatory ones, clearly violates important liberal goals and does not guarantee an increase in tolerance, such courses should not become a part of public education.

How to eliminate or drastically reduce violence in a diverse society is a difficult question. Violence resulting from religious differences is so prevalent that historically there have been violent episodes between various sects even within the same faith. For example, differences between Christian sects, such as Baptists and Catholics, have often resulted in violence between them. One person is unlikely to have all the answers

14. This claim should not be taken as endorsing those religious practices that result in physical or even severe psychological harm to others.

regarding increasing tolerance in a diverse society. Instead, many people will have to work together to increase tolerance, and if these efforts are going to be effective, they must come from individuals with a variety of religious beliefs. Since very few societies exist in which a single religious group is able to maintain isolation from all others who do not accept their views, it is imperative that efforts toward encouraging tolerance become an important part of life within each community. This is especially true since individual communities can have vast differences in their composition. Some communities are still homogeneous, whereas others encompass numerous religious beliefs.

Because of these differences between communities, one solution will not work for all communities. Consequently, the government is not the best source for implementing these ideas. Any program that the government would implement would tend to be structured in a manner that would prove ineffective for some communities. In addition, any effort that is not strongly supported by those individuals within the community is doomed to fail. Harmony cannot be mandated from a source outside of the community. Instead, individuals within the community must accept this goal as their own and earnestly work toward accomplishing it. They must be determined to accomplish some gains, even if minimal, within their distinct community.

The government or private organizations could play some role, however. These agencies could provide a community with incentives for initiating programs that attempt to increase tolerance and rewards for programs that have proven effective in promoting understanding and friendship between diverse religious groups. These awards could consist of a variety of benefits, such as national and state recognition for the community, monetary awards that allow the community to implement a program designed to increase tolerance, funding for a park or community center, or funding to continue a particular project that has proven successful. I believe that this approach will better serve the liberal state's and citizens' interests than the introduction of religious education in the public schools.

CONCLUSIONS

I have argued that the goals of a liberal state are best achieved by not offering religious education in the public schools. However, I have not addressed the argument that existing world religion courses should be banned from the public school curriculum. In fact, I believe that it is unlikely that such a ban would be legally enforceable; and, ideally, such courses may decrease the "religious illiteracy"[15] that is so prevalent within the United States today. However, my position does support the view that, in those schools where such a course is already a part of the curriculum, parents, for both legal and moral reasons, must be allowed to exempt their children in much the same manner as they currently can refuse to allow their child to attend sex education classes. What I have demonstrated is that liberal arguments that claim that world religions courses either should be implemented in public schools or that these courses, if encouraged, will provide a valuable means of attaining the goals of a liberal state are seriously flawed. Religious education within the public schools is not an effective means of maintaining peace or allowing for religious freedom.

15. Gereon Kopf suggested this phrase.

List of Contributors

ANITA ALLEN is Professor of Law at the University of Pennsylvania. She is author of *Uneasy Access: Privacy for Women in a Free Society* (Rowman & Littlefield, 1988) and co-editor of *Debating Democracy's Discontent* (Oxford University Press, 1998) and *Privacy: Cases and Materials* (John Marshall Publishing Co., 1992).

BRENDA ALMOND is Professor of Moral and Social Philosophy at the University of Hull. She is the author of *Exploring Ethics: A Traveller's Tale* (Blackwell, 1998), *Exploring Philosophy* (Blackwell, 1995), *Moral Concerns* (Humanities Press, 1987), and *Education and the Individual* (Allen & Unwin, 1981). She is editor of *AIDS: A Moral Issue* (Macmillan, 1990, 1996) and *Introducing Applied Ethics* (Blackwell, 1997).

JULIA J. BARTKOWIAK is Associate Professor of Philosophy at Clarion University in Pennsylvania.

ELLEN K. FEDER teaches social and political philosophy at American University. She is co-editor of a special issue of *Hypatia* on "The Family and Feminist Theory" (1996).

SHELLEY GAVIGAN is Associate Professor of Law at Osgoode Hall Law School, York University, Toronto, Ontario, Canada. She is co-editor of *The Politics of Abortion* (Oxford University Press, 1992) and *Regulating Sex: An Anthology of Commentaries on the Badgley and Fraser Reports* (Simon Fraser University, 1986).

HUGH LaFOLLETTE is Professor of Philosophy at East Tennessee State University. He is author of *Personal Relationships: Love, Identity, and Morality* (Blackwell, 1995), co-author of *Brute Science: Dilemmas of Animal Experimentation* (Routledge, 1996), and editor of numerous anthologies including *Ethics in Practice* (Blackwell, 1996), *Blackwell Guide to Ethical Theory* (Blackwell, 1999), and the *Oxford Handbook of Practical Ethics* (Oxford, 2000).

UMA NARAYAN is Associate Professor of Philosophy at Vassar College. She is the author of *Dislocating Cultures: Identities, Traditions, and Third World*

Feminism (Routledge, 1997), which won the 1998 Victoria Schuck Award of the American Political Science Association, and co-editor of *Reconstructing Political Theory: Feminist Perspectives* (Penn State Press, 1997).

LYNN PASQUERELLA is the Chair of the Philosophy Department at the University of Rhode Island and a Fellow in the John Hazen White Sr. Center for Ethics and Public Service. She has published extensively in the areas of theoretical and applied ethics, public policy, medical ethics, and the philosophy of law. She is co-editor of *Ethical Dilemmas in Public Administration* (Praeger, 1996).

LAURA PURDY is Professor of Philosophy at the University of Toronto Joint Centre for Bioethics and Bioethicist at the Toronto Hospital. She is author of *Reproducing Persons: Issues in Feminist Bioethics* (Cornell University Press, 1996) and *In Their Best Interest? The Case Against Equal Rights for Children* (Cornell University Press, 1992). She is co-editor of *Embodying Bioethics: Recent Feminist Advances* (Rowman & Littlefield, 1998), *Violence Against Women: Philosophical Perspectives* (Cornell University Press, 1998), and *Feminist Perspectives in Medical Ethics* (Indiana University Press, 1992).

MARY LYNDON SHANLEY is Professor of Political Science on the Margaret Stiles Halleck Chair at Vassar College. She is author of *Mothers and Families: Dilemmas for Feminism and the Law* (Beacon Press, 1999) and *Feminism, Marriage, and the Law in Victorian England* (Princeton University Press, 1989). She is co-editor of *Reconstructing Political Theory: Feminist Perspectives* (Penn State Press, 1997) and *Feminist Interpretations and Political Theory* (Penn State Press, 1990).

IRIS MARION YOUNG is Professor of Public and International Affairs at the University of Pittsburgh, where she teaches ethics and political philosophy. Her most recent book is *Intersecting Voices: Dilemmas of Gender, Political Philosophy, and Policy* (Princeton University Press, 1997).

Index